THE CORPSE
IN THE CELLAR

And Further Tales of Cleveland Woe

Also by John Stark Bellamy II:

They Died Crawling
The Maniac in the Bushes

THE CORPSE IN THE CELLAR

And Further Tales of Cleveland Woe

John Stark Bellamy II

GRAY & COMPANY, PUBLISHERS
CLEVELAND

Gray & Company, Publishers
1588 E. 40th St., Cleveland, OH 44103
(216)431-2665
www.grayco.com

Library of Congress Cataloging-in-Publication Data
Bellamy, John Stark.
Corpse in the cellar / by John Stark Bellamy.
p. cm.
ISBN 1-886228-33-7
1. Crime—Ohio—Cleveland—History—Case studies. I. Title.
HV6795.C5B44 2000
364.15'23'0977132--dc21
99-6828
CIP

This book is the third volume in a series of books on
the Cleveland of yesteryear. Narrative slide shows
chronicling some of the chapters are available for a
fee and additional slideshows are under development.
For more information or bookings, contact John Stark
Bellamy II via e-mail (jstarkbII@aol.com) or by mail
via the publisher of this book.

ISBN 1-886228-19-1

Printed in the United States of America

10 9 8 7 6 5 4 3 2

To my brother,
Stephen Paul Bellamy,
and his wife,
Gail Ghetia Bellamy,
with thanks for their love,
interest, and support
throughout my adventures
in Cleveland Gothic

CONTENTS

CONTENTS, *continued*

PREFACE

It is now almost 10 years since I more or less unwittingly embarked on what has become a consuming exploration of the Forest City's dark side: Cleveland's "best" murders and disasters. Now, with *The Corpse in the Cellar*, I have completed the prose pilgrimage I began with *They Died Crawling* and continued with *The Maniac in the Bushes*. Once again, I have written about these . . . bad things . . . because I wished to read about them and could not find much to the purpose, notwithstanding the existence of the still-vintage *Cleveland Murders* (1949), and what has become a minor literary growth industry of publications on the Kingsbury Run torso murders/Eliot Ness phenomena. So, if nothing else, I have continued to keep myself well amused with the research and retelling of what now amount to 53 Cleveland-area horrors.

My criteria for selection remain arbitrarily subjective: the criminous or catastrophic subjects must have a strong human element, a frisson of fear, shock, or perversity (not in the strictly sexual sense)—and they must be intriguing to me. And, as I have probably now exhausted the supply of first-class Cleveland tragedies available, it is likely this is my last collection of Cleveland woes—although I soon intend to turn my hand to other criminal matters at greater length than has been my wont in this now-completed trilogy. Readers may continue to look in vain to these three books for the relatively recent atrocities of Cleveland history, such as the 1965 Colby-Young murder, the Beverly Jarosz butchery, Judge Robert Steele's murder-for-hire scheme, the double slaying of Dorothy and Phil Porter, the Amy Mihaljevic horror, and my most requested but still untold story, the "Dr. Love" scandal that captivated Cleveland's inquiring minds in the mid-1970s. Such unfortunate occurrences have their points of interest, as Sherlock Holmes would say, but they are too recent, in my opinion, to have acquired a vintage character in terms of the period detail their telling may display; moreover, such unpleasantnesses are still fresh enough to feature living victims: the sons, daughters, parents, and other loved ones who have endured and survived the crimes and disasters of the last 30 years. Leave them in peace for another decade or two, and I may get around to those tales.

Readers often ask me where I get my stories and which ones are my favorites. The answer to the first query is "everywhere and anywhere." Some stories, such as the Sheppard murder or the East Ohio Gas Company explosion, are part of one's patrimony as a Clevelander: shared folklore that pervades our local culture like Indians fever or Euclid Beach nostalgia. Other subjects, such as the death of Hazel Gogan or the Potter murder, are suggested to me by helpful persons with connections to the stories, sometimes even people who possess research materials and personal memories of the bloody events chronicled. And some tales just evolve out of hard work: hundreds of hours spent browsing bleary-eyed through miles and miles of newspaper microfilm in search of those magic headlines that make it all worthwhile, stories that begin with words like "Crazed Killer . . ." or "Joe Blow Goes Smirking To Death Chair . . ." As to the second question—which ones I like best—well, that's like asking a fond mother to single out her favorite children. I love all of these stories in the exact measure that they have given me pleasure, diversion, and moral profit. Anyone desiring a more graphic answer should seek out one of the dozen or so slide shows I present about Cleveland murders and disasters throughout the Cleveland area. And to those mirthless souls who fail to find anything of merit or virtue in my woeful preoccupations, I offer these words by William Roughead, the great Scots true-crime writer, in defense of my fascination for infamous deeds and satanic people: "Murder has a magic of its own, its peculiar alchemy. Touched by that crimson wand, things base and sordid, things ugly and of ill report, are transformed into matters wondrous, weird and tragical. Dull streets become fraught with mystery, commonplace dwellings assume sinister aspects, everyone concerned, howsoever plain and ordinary, is invested with a new value and importance as the red light falls upon each." I couldn't agree more.

ACKNOWLEDGMENTS

As ever, I have accumulated a host of debts and unpaid kindnesses in the creation of this book. The writings of George Condon and Peter Jedick continue to inspire me, and it is unlikely that I would have begun these chronicles without their entertaining example. Likewise, I never would have perpetrated even one, much less three Cleveland crime books without the encouragement and aid of Faith Corrigan and Doris O'Donnell. My institutional researches have been much aided by the knowledge and professionalism of these individuals: William Becker of the *Cleveland Press* Collection, Cleveland State University; the IMS staff at Cleveland State University for their tireless and expert reproduction of the images used in my slide shows and books; the staff at the Cleveland Public Library, especially those employed in the Photograph Collection and Newspaper Reference departments; Ann Sindelar and Barbara Waitkus Billings of the Western Reserve Historical Society; Anne T. Kmieck and the staff of the Cleveland Police Historical Society; Elizabeth Tidwell of the Cuyahoga County Coroner's office and the staff at Lake View Cemetery; and Elizabeth Nelson and the staff of the Medina County Public Library.

Two ex-*Cleveland Press* writers, Fred McGunagle and Tom Barensfeld, also deserve thanks for their encouragement, interest, and research tips. I owe tremendous and unpayable debts to Evelyn Theiss of the *Plain Dealer*, June Bailey of *Westlife*, and John Lanigan of WMJI-FM for their crucial aid in publicizing my endeavors over the past few years. Also deserving much gratitude for her infatigable labors on my behalf is Gray & Company's Jane Lassar, the hardest-working publicist in the world.

It is my special pleasure to thank my beautiful wife, Laura Serafin, whose love, support, and participation in this project made it not only possible, but enjoyable, and (relatively) stress free. And to thank again my mother, Jean Bellamy, who made all of this possible with her unfailing love, support, and—especially—patience over the long years of my sometimes misspent life. Thanks are also due to my fellow employees at the Cuyahoga County Public Library, who have tolerated and even encouraged my odd enthusiasms and unseemly topics of conversation for far too many years. They include: Avril McInally, David Soltesz, Mary Ann Shipman, Mary Erbs, Judy Vanke, Holly Schaefer, Catherine Monnin, John Lonsak, Madeline Brookshire, Karen Rabatin, Geli Valli, Nancy Pazelt (who assiduously nagged this book into existence), Ruth Rayle, Pam DeFino, Sarah Lindberg, Victoria "Vixen" Richards, Martha Maloney, and Mary Ryan. Their fruitless attempts to stimulate the growth of my self-modesty are herein acknowledged.

The Corpse in the Cellar is dedicated to my brother Stephen Paul Bellamy and his wife, Gail Ghetia Bellamy. I could not have produced my books on Cleveland crime without their encouragement, support, and unfailing belief, and they are as much to blame as I for what follows.

John Stark Bellamy II
June 7, 1999

THE CORPSE IN THE CELLAR

And Further Tales of Cleveland Woe

Chapter 1

"JESUS SAVE ME FROM THE CHAIR"

The Lonesome Death of Michael Hahnel

There's one in almost every sizable police station in this country. It's a case, usually prominently displayed, containing the badges of policemen killed in the line of duty. Some, such as Cleveland's, are large. Others, such as the one in the Shaker Heights police station on Lee Road at Van Aken Boulevard, are small. But the one at Shaker Heights contains the badge of Michael Hahnel, mortally wounded by robbers on the night of October 17, 1924, scant yards away from the building that enshrines his badge and memory. There were lots of policemen killed in the 1920s, and too many of them in Greater Cleveland. But the death of Michael Hahnel deserves notice; it held a special horror and featured melodramatic characters, plotting, and dialogue that would be hard to beat this side of a hard-boiled gangster movie starring James Cagney and Humphrey Bogart.

The 1920s were a bad time for Cleveland cops. During that Jazz Age decade they enjoyed a reputation as one of the most inept and corrupt forces in the country. Adding injury to insult, no fewer than 12 of them were murdered in that 10-year stretch, many of them in circumstances of chilling callousness and brutality. Which is probably why 28-year-old Michael Hahnel, just recovered from an industrial accident, decided to apply for a job as a roundsman with the village of Shaker Heights in May of 1924. Shaker Heights was still the small gentry village envisioned by the Van Sweringens at that time, and Hahnel must have looked forward to mundane and relatively peaceful duties far removed from the speakeasies, poverty, and violence of nearby Cleveland. Indeed, there was so little to do in the way of criminal work in Mayor William Van Aken's

Albert ("Red") Holt and Bruno ("Joe") Prymas.

suburb that Hahnel and the other Shaker policemen were often put to work on more practical tasks, things like sprucing up village property and keeping the traffic signage current and trim.

Which is why, as an unkind fate arranged it, Hahnel and fellow officer Frank H. Dietrich were out in the middle of the intersection of South Moreland Boulevard (now Van Aken Boulevard) and Lee Road that chilly night of October 17, 1924. Although on duty, the armed officers were wearing overalls and employed in the non-gangbusters activity of repainting the word "stop" on the pavement. They had been painting steadily for some time when a seven-passenger Peerless touring automobile suddenly roared right through the fresh paint at about 40 miles per hour, headed southbound on Lee toward the Cleveland border. A second later, Hahnel yelled "Halt!" and the Peerless came to a skidding halt about 50 yards away.

When Hahnel and Dietrich walked up to the car they noticed two men sitting in the front. One, a dark-skinned, sallow-faced man, didn't say anything, but the other, a red-haired man, began pleading with Hahnel to let them off. "I must go to work in the morning; let us go, will you?" he said. But Dietrich, who was Hahnel's senior, wasn't buying any excuses. "You'll have to take 'em to the station, Mick," he ordered Hahnel. "You're arrested for careless driving. You're going to the station." Hahnel jumped in the back seat and told them to drive to the Shaker Heights Town Hall at Lee Road and Shaker Boulevard, and the Peerless turned around and headed north toward Shaker. Dietrich rode a hundred yards on the fender before hopping off to finish up the interrupted painting job.

It was a fatal decision. Hahnel and Dietrich had no way of knowing it, but the two strangers in the front seat of the speeding and, as it happened, stolen Peerless were bad, desperate men. The red-haired driver, Albert ("Red") Holt, was a 25-year-old stickup felon with a prison record for burglary and auto theft. His darker companion was no better: Bruno ("Joe") Prymas was 24 years old and a graduate of the Mansfield Reformatory and the Cleveland work-house. Another thing Michael Hahnel and Frank Dietrich didn't know was that Holt and Prymas had robbed the Standard Oil Company gas station at Fairmount Boulevard and South Taylor Road in Cleveland Heights just minutes before. The stolen money was still in the front "shotgun" seat with Joe Prymas, and neither he nor Red Holt was anxious to talk to authorities at the Shaker Heights police station.

Michael Hahnel and map of murder scenes.

It happened about 10 feet south of the intersection of Lee and South Woodland. Holt kicked his companion in the foot, and Prymas whipped around in his seat, jammed a gun into the unsuspecting Hahnel's side, and said, "Hands up!" Hahnel's left hand started to rise, but as he simultaneously reached for his pistol, Joe Prymas shot him once in the side. The bullet pierced the stomach, liver, and intestines and came to a rest in Hahnel's spine between the seventh and eighth ribs. Bleeding heavily, he slumped to the floor of the Peerless and feigned death.

Red Holt turned the Peerless left onto Shaker Boulevard and headed west. Somewhere on Shaker, probably at Southington Road, he turned south. The car turned left onto Ashwood Road and came to a stop in a deserted stretch of road. Pulling the wounded Hahnel out of the back, Holt and Prymas stripped off his gun and badge, carried him to the side of the road, put him down, and got back in the car and sped off. "Drive like hell!" was the last thing Hahnel heard his shooter tell the red-haired driver.

Hahnel lay there in agony for perhaps 20 minutes. He managed to crawl to a sandy patch near the pavement, and there he laboriously scrawled the license number of the Peerless, "516712," in the sand. Then he began to turn his flashlight on and off, hoping to attract help. A few minutes later, Mr. and Mrs. Alex Armstrong, who were motoring on Ashwood, saw the light and heard Hahnel moaning "Help me! Help me!" They stopped, put him in their car, and took him to St. Alexis Hospital. Armstrong then returned to the scene, discovered the number in the sand, and informed the Cleveland police.

The discovery of the wounded Hahnel touched off the biggest manhunt since, well, since the dragnet for John Leonard Whitfield only a year before. Like Whitfield, Hahnel's unknown assailants had shot a policeman in their car and then dumped his body in a remote area. News of the Standard Oil station robbery arrived shortly after Hahnel's shooting, and police quickly realized, from the descriptions offered by gas station manager John Schmit and officer Dietrich, that the same men were involved in both crimes. One was described as having a thin face, a long nose, a "New York accent," and red hair; the other as a dark-skinned white man with a slight stammer. Before the night was over every red-haired man, any male with a speech impediment, and every Peerless automobile in the county was under intense scrutiny. Both the Shaker Heights and Cleveland police insisted it would be only a matter of time before the guilty men were apprehended.

As it happened, there was little prescience in such police prognostications. Red Holt and Joe Prymas were a daring and violent duo, but—as the clues they strewed in their path soon indicated—also unusually stupid criminals. Early the next morning, both Hahnel's revolver and the murder weapon—a Hopkins & Allen .38 "bulldog" type with an exploded shell in the chamber—were found wrapped in towels sewn together and thrown on a slag heap at East 88th Street and Union Avenue. Minutes later, the purloined Peerless was found abandoned at 2995 East 61st Street—out of gas. More important, the mortally wounded Hahnel was able to give police a good description of his killers before he died on Monday night, October 20. Although doctors had initially been optimistic, his condition deteriorated as peritonitis set in, triggered by fragments of his clothing driven into his wound by a rusty bullet. Two blood transfusions proved to be in vain, and the last words Michael

Hahnel said to his grieving brothers and his sister, Katherine, were about his unidentified killers: "They didn't even give me a chance."

They were not to remain unidentified for long. The sites where the abandoned Peerless and the guns were found suggested to police that the killers were familiar with the area. Authorities began to conduct house-by-house and store-by-store interrogations in the rooming-house district that stretched along Broadway Avenue east from East 55th Street. Inquiries soon turned up John Kalbac of 3414 East 66th, who vividly remembered the men who had rented his garage for their Peerless on Friday afternoon, just hours before the murder. So did the clerk of a nearby hardware store who had sold one of the suspects a padlock for Kalbac's garage door. Patrick Lynch, the manager of the Price Lodging House at 6117 Broadway, remembered a man resembling the red-haired driver who had lived there in mid-October.

These witness accounts soon became public knowledge, as did a cumulative reward of $6,000 offered for the arrest and conviction of Hahnel's killers ($4,000 from the *Plain Dealer*, $1,000 from the Cuyahoga County Commissioners, and $1,000 from Shaker Heights Village). What the police weren't yet disclosing publicly was the discovery of three critical witnesses who willingly identified the driver of the death car as Albert Holt. One of them, George J. Henkel, a soft-drink-parlor entrepreneur, went to police with a story of Holt coming into his store on Bessemer Avenue on Monday night, October 20, and telling him he was one of the men the police sought. Another was one of Holt's fellow workers at the Ohio Transfer Company, who told police that Red had begged $50 from him on Monday, whining that he had "made a bad mistake but I'm going to go straight." The third was Marie Holt, Red Holt's angry and scorned wife.

It wasn't public-spiritedness that made Marie Holt finger her own husband. Nor was it the $6,000 reward, a sum that was already generating false arrests by the dozen and causing hysterical greed throughout Northeast Ohio. No—it was that classic incubator of broken marriages and hell-hath-no-fury spite: the other woman. Red had always been a good husband, the angry Marie told police, until he got mixed up with a bad woman. First it was powder and paint that he couldn't explain on his clothes; next, it was staying away for days and murmuring the name "Margaret" repeatedly during his rare nights of sleep at home. Now he was in a real mess,

Margaret Horton.

and she was sure it had something to do with that hussy Margaret. "I still care for him, although his actions made it impossible for me to live with him," the pregnant Marie eventually told reporters on Saturday, as her children, Alberta, 5, and Rosemary, 7 months, gaped at the crowd of strangers in the house.

Marie was not entirely correct, although the police didn't care about her inaccuracies as they tightened their net around the elusive Holt. There was another woman, and she was involved with Marie's husband. But she was far from the brazen and man-stealing conniver expected by the public. Margaret Horton had been a naive 18-year-old when she married her high-school sweetheart in Maryland in 1918. A year later, she gave birth to a daughter, Leota, and when Leota ended up terribly crippled from polio as a toddler, Margaret's husband vanished. Shortly thereafter, Margaret came to Cleveland and began to eke out a meager existence for herself and her child at menial jobs. It was a cheerless, exhausting grind of a life until one day, perhaps six months before Michael Hahnel's murder, she looked up from a grimy Cleveland streetcar seat to see a smiling Red Holt looking back at her.

It was like something out of *High Sierra*, with the tough, but surprisingly vulnerable Red Holt playing the Bogart role of smitten gangster. In a few short weeks of strap-hanging courtship, Red became the man that an unsuspecting Margaret had never even dared to dream of. He was kind, he was generous, he liked to take her places, and—best of all—he doted on her crippled child. Little Leota returned the affection twofold with all the force of her love-starved nature, and the three of them dreamed of a happy future together.

It was not to be, of course. There was the little problem of Red's wife—of whom Margaret was kept in blissful ignorance—and the increasing expenses of his two-family lifestyle to bedevil the habitually impatient Red Holt. He needed money to keep the women of his dual lives happy, and he wasn't able to get it with his job as a driver for the Ohio Transfer Company. He met Joe Prymas in the late summer of 1924. Prymas, like Holt, was no stranger to stick-ups, burglary, or auto theft. They began to pull stickups at Cleveland-area gas stations, using the small towels, such as those used to wrap the two pistols found at East 88th and Union, as gags in silencing their victims. They had gone to the Standard Oil Company station at Fairmount and South Taylor on the night of October 17 to get gas and then returned to rob it as an afterthought. Locking the attendant in the lavatory, Joe Prymas came out of the office with the loot in his hands and told Red to "drive like hell." Minutes later they rolled over the paint at South Moreland and Lee on their way to a Murder One rap. Ironically enough, they probably would have gotten off with a mere traffic ticket if they had only gone peacefully to the station with Hahnel, as word of the gas station robbery had not arrived there yet.

It was one thing to identify Holt; it was another to catch him. They almost had him on Friday, October 24, when a suspicious auto with a flat tire was spotted on a hill outside Chagrin Falls. By the time the police arrived, however, it was gone—along with the tire from a nearby Ford truck. It was Holt, of course, and by the wee hours of Saturday he, Margaret, and Leota were on the highway to West Virginia in a stolen Ford coupe. The plan was to get to the home of Holt's parents in Florida and then figure out what to do next. It wasn't going to be easy: by now the police knew their identities, and the search for the trio was nationwide. Even as they drove southwest, three thousand wanted posters with Red's picture began to go up on walls and telephone poles all over the country.

The fugitives only got as far as Wheeling, West Virginia. Holt was short of funds, and after he rented a room for the three of them there, he sent Margaret and Leota to the Western Union office on Sunday morning to wire friends in Cleveland for money. That was just what the police were waiting for; when the wire was delivered to P. B. Mitchell, Holt's ex-employer at the Ohio Transfer Company at 1201 Prospect, the police detective there wired back, "Money will be here for you before noon Monday." By the time Margaret and Leota left the office a platoon of West Virginia detectives was already on her trail.

Margaret Horton may have been naive about Red Holt, but she knew when she was being followed. For several hours she led them on a weary chase as she and an increasingly fatigued Leota, who had heavy metal braces on her legs, wandered aimlessly through downtown Wheeling. Finally, Margaret led them back toward Red's lair, but she managed to "give him the high sign" before the police caught on. The next thing anyone knew, a taxicab came out of nowhere, and Margaret and Leota got in and sped off. The surprised police commandeered a passing motorist's car and chased the taxicab almost 15 miles outside the Wheeling city limits. Just as they were gaining on it, Red Holt's Ford coupe tore past them and cut off the taxicab. As the car full of police attempted to brake, Red pulled Margaret and Leota into his own car, and the chase resumed. While police held their fire for fear of hitting Margaret or Leota, Holt led them back to Wheeling. After driving around in circles for awhile, he suddenly stopped the car, leaped out, and ran off on foot. Margaret took the wheel, only to smash almost immediately into another car. Seconds after she and Leota were apprehended from the wreck, unhurt, Red was captured at gunpoint by U. S. Marshal Bert E. Phillips at 1 p.m. and taken to Cleveland by train the same day. Red refused to talk to police, except to say that he had been at the murder scene, but that it was his companion who did the shooting.

If Red Holt's capture was the stuff of high melodrama, the apprehension of Joe Prymas more closely resembled low comedy. When Joe read the newspapers on Monday, October 27, he knew the bloodhounds of justice were closing in on him. He, too, had a woman who loved him. Brassy Stella Janakas was tall, "good-looking," and 36 years old, and the two of them had been living together intermittently as "Mr. and Mrs. Joe Snyder" in a basement flat at 1892 East 59th Street. But she had left him in early October, and he suspected it was just a matter of time before someone turned him in for the $6,000 reward. That night, as midnight loomed, Joe wrote a suicide note to Stella and swallowed carbolic acid. The note read: "Goodbye all, sweetheart. I am the man that was out with Red the night of the murder. I didn't want to say anything to you, because you always believed in me . . . Don't mention anything to mother . . . Red was not a man. If he was, he would not have said the things he did about [what happened in] the car." Scrawled on the back was a postscript, "If I was man enough to kill Mick [Hahnel] I was man enough to kill myself."

Unfortunately for Prymas, he wasn't quite man enough. The amount of carbolic acid he swallowed was only about a half-teaspoonful, and he was never in danger of death. But he sure thought he was: seconds after he downed the liquid, his neighbors in the rooming house were awakened by his screaming, as he thrashed in apparent delirium, knocking down a door and smashing furniture in his agony. They called the police for an ambulance, but they refused to come and sent Dr. D. J. Bryant instead. Bryant looked at Prymas's throat, told him not to worry, and gave him something for the pain. But Prymas refused to calm down, screaming for hours that he was a dying man, so at 9 a.m., someone called the 4th District again for a police ambulance. They were too busy, so it was Patrolman Clarence May of the 9th District who came that morning to take Joe Prymas to the hospital.

Luck was not with Prymas. As they motored toward City Hospital, the chatty May said, "Well, old timer, I've seen you before somewhere, I think. Did you ever play baseball?" "Yeah," muttered Prymas. "That's where I saw you," continued May, "what's your name?" "Joe King," replied Prymas, who by now was uneasy with the turn the conversation was taking. "King?" said May. "That's a funny name for a guy living where you do." That was the last clue the suspicious May needed. Stopping the ambulance at a nearby newsstand (all three Cleveland dailies would later say it was one of theirs), he looked at the picture of Joe Prymas on the front page, looked back at Prymas, and said to the ambulance driver: "Drive like hell to Central Police Station!" Before the week was over, Clarence May was rewarded for his Tuesday morning's work with a promotion to detective rank.

There is no honor among thieves and less among murderers. The day after Joe Prymas was arrested and held in City Hospital under armed guard, County Prosecutor Edward C. Stanton had Holt and Prymas indicted on three counts of murder. These included: 1) murder in perpetration of a robbery; 2) murder of a police officer in performance of his duty; and 3) premeditated murder. Held without bail, Holt and Prymas turned on each other with the desperate ferocity of wounded animals. While they both admitted to being in the death car, they each attempted to convince everyone that it was the other who had robbed the gas station and shot Michael Hahnel. Both men were abetted in this process by their loving women, all of whose tearful words were reported in the *Press*, *Plain Dealer*, and *News*. Although initially hostile to her erring husband, especially after she saw him at the police station with Margaret Horton, Marie Holt retreated from her initial anger—"I'll fix you! I'll help to send you to the chair!"—to sympathetic, repetitive warbling about what a good husband and father Holt had been before he was misled by bad companions: "Al always was a good kid. He was always a good provider and then he began to go with the gang and went wrong. I've decided to fight for Red . . . I thought he had stopped loving me." Stella, granted the courtesy title of "Mrs. Snyder" by Cleveland's sob-sister journalists (she was actually still married to a man in Detroit), attempted to garner support for her "li'l feller Joe" with bleatings about the unfairness of it all ("If [cop-killer John Leonard] Whitfield didn't get death, why do they talk of it for my li'l feller, my Joe?") and the bombshell announcement that she was pregnant with Prymas's child.

Stanton made it clear from the outset that he intended to make an example of Holt and Prymas as a deterrent to would-be cop killers. Although Ohio law prohibited trying the two men together, Stanton scheduled the trials for the earliest possible date—November 17, exactly a month after Michael Hahnel was shot—and arranged that they be prosecuted simultaneously in the old County Court House on Public Square. To make sure no one missed the point, he announced that the third charge of premeditated murder, which was the only one of the three charges that allowed lesser verdicts of second-degree murder, manslaughter, and assault-and-battery, would be dropped. Holt and Prymas would have to gamble for either Murder One or freedom. "First degree or nothing," swore Stanton. "There'll be no weak-kneed verdicts in these cases."

Holt's trial was set for Courtroom No. 3, Judge Samuel E. Kramer presiding, James T. Cassidy and James Connell prosecuting, and Louis D. Hedrick and Karl T. Fish defending. Prymas's trial in Courtroom No. 5 featured Judge Frank Phillips, Edward Stanton, Henry Williams, and David Kramer prosecuting, with court-appointed attorneys J. P. Mooney and William G. Gibbons handling the defense. Much time was consumed in finding jurors tolerant of capital punishment; of the more than 200 jurors examined in both courtrooms, over 100 were dismissed because of their opposition to the death penalty.

Nothing was left to chance in sweetening the foul public image of the accused men. By the time Holt's trial opened on Monday morning, November 17, Margaret Horton was a non-person. Indeed, virtually nothing was ever again reported about the hapless mother, who had been released without charges and was never called as a witness by either side. "Forget that Margaret stuff!" said a miffed Red Holt to reporters, as he obligingly posed in court for photographers with his loving wife, Marie, and smiling children. Spectators in the standing-room-only courtroom were especially touched by the sight of little Alberta Holt handing a red carnation to her beleaguered daddy. But such happy-face behavior didn't impress Katherine Meyers, Hahnel's sister, who attended Holt's trial, sitting right behind his family. "I'm not cold-blooded but that doesn't move me," she said. "My brother was shot down in cold blood. That is just a show to get sympathy. I'm not revengeful. I simply want to see justice done. The killers should not be shown any greater mercy than was showed my brother."

Judge Kramer, perhaps because of adverse comments like this, ordered a stop to such sweet domestic tableaux on the second day of the trial. Undiscouraged, Holt kept up his public-relations campaign with reporters, pleading that they call him Albert instead of "Red": "It sounds too rough. My name is Albert E. Holt. I'm not a hard guy." Prymas, for his part, was sympathetically flanked in court by the weeping, verbose Stella, and a no less lachrymose if more dignified Maggie Laskowski, his aged, adoring mother.

Both trials lasted a little more than a week, and both of them hinged on the same legal questions. With each man accusing the other of the fatal deed, much depended on the admissibility of Joe Prymas's suicide note as evidence. Was it a sincere confession, made in the belief that its author was dying? Or was it, as J. P.

Mooney argued, evidence of a noble if fleeting impulse to shoulder the blame for Prymas's erstwhile friend? Mooney also argued that Prymas had been refused medical treatment until he signed another confession that he shot Hahnel. Holt's attorneys, naturally, insisted on the contrary that Prymas's confession was valid and a complete exoneration of their client. Ultimately, the confession was allowed as evidence but did little to clear up inconsistencies in identifying the actual gunman in the Peerless. Hahnel's deathbed statement was that the red-haired man shot him; yet Frank Dietrich claimed that the red-haired man was the driver. The version that Prymas eventually stuck with was that Holt had kicked his foot as a mutually understood signal to shoot Hahnel.

More critical for both of them was the question of whether Hahnel had been shot while his killers were committing a robbery, a first-degree murder offense. Both Hedrick and Mooney argued that the robbery was consummated before Hahnel stopped the Peerless, and that his murder was a separate offense. Paradoxically, Judge Kramer ruled the robbery was over, while Judge Phillips decided it was not. Both defenses failed in their attempt to claim that Michael Hahnel was not on duty when he was shot, leaving Holt vulnerable to two death-penalty counts and Prymas to one. Lacking supporting medical testimony, Mooney's attempt to portray his client as brain-damaged—the alleged result of a 1919 beating—went nowhere.

The most dramatic moment of the two trials came on Monday, November 24, during Stanton's final argument against Prymas. His own attorney had already characterized Prymas as a "weak and vacillating creature," but Stanton, calling him a "sly, cunning, yellow coward," finished his death sentence plea with a riveting, grandstanding gesture. Picking up Michael Hahnel's badge, which Prymas had torn off the wounded officer in the backseat of the Peerless, Stanton held out the badge and thundered: "Then you, Joe, stole that badge—took the law into your own hands. You violated the badge that is emblematic of the authority that protects every one of us. You stamped on the law."

With that, Stanton vigorously threw the badge down on the floor, and spectators, lawyers, the defendant, and the jury watched in shocked silence as it loudly clattered across the floor before stopping at a deputy's foot 10 feet away. The jury of four women and eight men went out at noon on November 24 and returned at

9:30 p.m. with a verdict of guilty of first-degree murder on the second count of the indictment. Immediately, Judge Phillips sentenced Joe Prymas to die in the electric chair on March 10, 1925. Prymas took both verdict and sentence with the same taciturn, stoical indifference he had displayed since being caught. Perhaps Stella spoke for him, sobbing to reporters: "My Joe never would have gotten in trouble if he hadn't known Holt."

The luck of Red Holt held. The case went to the jury of six men and six women just before noon on Tuesday, November 25. After 34 hours (15 of actual deliberation), they were dismissed by Judge Kramer at 3 p.m. on November 26 after announcing that they were hopelessly deadlocked and had not yet even balloted. It was reported that seven members were for conviction, with five opposed and no one in favor of a death penalty without mercy. Foreman Reverend J. W. Giffin, no foe of capital punishment himself, reported that the jury disagreed on matters of fact rather than the applicable law in the case. Judge Kramer immediately set a new trial date for December 15. Holt, for his part, attributed his good fortune to a rabbit's foot sent to him by a fan but complained that he had expected to be exonerated in time to have Thanksgiving dinner with his brother's family.

Holt's second trial, which eventually took place in January 1925, was a relatively sedate affair. Lasting a little over a week, it was presided over by Judge Carl Weygandt, with Prosecutor Cassidy and defense attorney Louis Hedrick repeating their roles. Joe Prymas was brought from death row in Columbus to testify against Holt but refused to answer any questions. Holt himself was not much more cooperative, refusing to give the details of his alibi and telling Cassidy repeatedly, "That's none of your business." On January 17, a jury of six men and six women found him guilty of first-degree murder—with a recommendation of mercy. En route two days later to a life term in the Ohio Penitentiary, Red Holt made his final comment to reporters on the unfairness of his fate with the hackneyed words, "Give me liberty or give me death!"

Holt's bravado was no doubt a pose, but Prymas didn't enjoy this opportunity to disparage a life sentence. Death is exactly what Joe Prymas got, albeit postponed for six weeks by a stay of execution while his sentence was appealed. Happily, perhaps, this modest delay allowed further public entertainment ensuing from the birth of his son, "Little Joe," in a Salvation Army shelter to his still-faithful Stella on March 18. This blessed event stimulated Stella to plead with penitentiary warden P. E. Thomas to allow her to espouse Joe before his execution, so Little Joe could bear his father's name. Joe himself was unenthusiastic, sensibly observing, "What good would my name do the kid when it means that the guy who carried it was knocked off in the electric chair?" Warden Thomas, alas no sentimentalist, put the final kibosh on this idea made in tabloid heaven with the tart comment: "I won't permit such contemplated mockery. There is no legal prohibition against marriages in death row. But there is my own prohibition." Stella's last appearance in the public realm came on March 31, when she insisted on keeping "Little Joe," against the wishes of Joe's mother, who wanted to raise her doomed son's namesake herself.

Joe Prymas went to his end with the same indifferent silence he had ever shown. Attributing his fate to the hostility of Cleveland journalists, he volunteered no further comment, except to say that Red deserved to die with him: "Holt was as guilty as I am. He's a welcher." On April 23, 1925, he dined alone and heartily on squabs (young pigeons—once a popular dish), fried chicken, sweet pickles, a custard pie, a quarter-pound of butter, a dozen soft rolls, a pound of salted almonds, a quart of ice cream, coffee, and 10 cigars. His request that Red Holt share his last meal with him was denied. At 1:02 a.m. the next day he walked calmly and quietly to the execution chamber and was electrocuted without mishap two minutes later. So much for the advice given to him in a letter sent by a well-wisher: "Brace up. Pray constantly: 'Jesus save me from the chair.' And if you mean it, you will not die in the electric chair. I know what I'm talking about. I have been through exactly the same thing myself. I am one of the boys who have tried both ways to get along."

Michael Hahnel sleeps to this day in St. Mary Cemetery on Cleveland's West Side. Shaker Heights is now an urbanized suburb, large and old enough to give some company to his badge in its front-office case. And the rest of the cast in the improbable melodrama of his foul assassination has disappeared into history.

Chapter 2

"MURDERER IN SHORT BREECHES"

The Gothic Doom of Maggie Thompson

It sounds so familiar and contemporary—the sickening murder of an innocent child; yet another child accused of the dreadful deed; a sensational trial, replete with dubiously "expert" testimony, suspicious "confessions," allegations of police "third-degree" methods, and charges of a biased press; not to mention "latchkey" children, systematic child abuse, saccharine sympathy for the guilty, and charges of ethnic favoritism. But it all happened in the "good old days"—1889 to be exact—and the murder of Maggie Thompson set a standard for sensationalism and cruelty still difficult to best.

Maggie Thompson was a delightful girl. Seven years old, pretty, affectionate, and winsome, she was the light of her parents' lives. She was one of four children of Jacob and Clara Thompson, living in a Merchant Avenue home in Tremont—then still known as the "Heights." Her precociously handsome appearance made her "windmill" walk—she habitually and vigorously swung her arms as she walked—a welcome sight in Tremont as she traveled back and forth each school day to the Tremont Street School, four short blocks away. She was also known as what we would now term a "streetwise" child: the Thompsons had lived in a number of large cities, and Maggie was trained to be wary of strangers.

Thursday, May 9, the last day of her life, began much as usual. Awakened, fed, and scrupulously dressed for school, Maggie left home shortly after 8 a.m., with the usual shower of kisses from Clara and Jacob, who had just returned home from his job as a night brakeman with the Valley Railroad. Just as Maggie reached the gate, however, she turned around and ran back to Clara, begging for another kiss. Clara embraced her, sent her off again, and

Otto Lueth.   Maggie Thompson.

turned to her household tasks. It was the last time she ever saw
Maggie alive.

We know Maggie got to the 1,200-pupil Tremont Street School
and began her school day promptly at 8:30. We also know that she
left there at 11:15 a.m., dismissed for lunch at home by her teacher,
Miss Cottrell. After that, the details become murky. It seems that
Maggie walked north down Pelton Avenue (now West 10th Street)
to Fairfield with her classmate Mary Hull, who wanted Maggie to
see some flowers at the back of the Hull house at 17 Fairfield. Maggie was next seen several doors west at 5 Fairfield, where she
played briefly with three-year-old Gracie Larsen, who wanted to
show Maggie her new tricycle. Maggie left the Larsen home about
11:30, turned the corner to walk the last block home to 24 Merchant—and vanished. As the *Plain Dealer* subsequently put it, it
happened so suddenly and silently, "the sidewalk might have
opened and swallowed the girl."

The hue and cry arose immediately. When Maggie didn't show
up for lunch, Clara awoke Jacob just after noon, and he went looking for Maggie at the school and at the homes of the many Thompson relatives who lived nearby in the closely knit neighborhood.
When she did not turn up, the Cleveland police were notified, and
detectives, abetted by many Thompson relatives and neighbors,
began a thorough search of virtually every street, sewer, cavern,
and waterway in Greater Cleveland. Twenty-four hours of frantic,
fruitless searching went by, and by Friday night Cleveland authorities had posted this notice all over the streets of Cleveland [the
notice misidentifies her as being eight years old]:

"On May the 9th, 1889, Maggie Thompson left Tremont street school to go to her home, No. 24 Merchant Avenue, this city, but failed to do so, and has not been seen or heard from since. She is eight years old, dark-complexioned, black hair, large black eyes, two front teeth on upper jaw gone; she is rather good-looking and smart for her age; she was dressed in a plaid woolen dress, trimmed with velvet down in front, white apron with small red dots, brown felt hat, new high-top button shoes. Any information as to the whereabouts of said child will be thankfully received. Address: Jacob Thompson, 24 Merchant Avenue, or J. W. Schmitt, Chief of Police."

As is often the case in tragic situations, the disappearance of Maggie Thompson did not bring out the best in everyone. Maddened with anxiety and sleep deprivation, Jacob Thompson conducted an agonized search, which deteriorated qualitatively during the week that followed and was further aggravated by his succumbing to the solace of strong drink. Cranks and busybodies, always the bane of efficient detection, hindered the police and further afflicted Maggie's crazed parents with wild tales of clairvoyant visions and mysterious prowlers. Self-proclaimed eyewitnesses proved no more helpful. Several persons claimed to have seen Maggie being dragged into a bakery shop on Fairfield by a man; investigation revealed that the shop was located at Gracie Larsen's Fairfield home, and that the the the baker, Peter Larsen, was not home on May 9. One of Maggie's classmates, Helen Pasternack, told police a chilling tale of seeing Maggie with a woman up by the Centralway bridge—several blocks from Maggie's house—about 12:30 p.m. on the fatal day. Helen said the woman, garbed in black and carrying a red parasol, was pulling a weeping Maggie along with her.

Other neighbors contributed the scurrilous, bigoted rumor that Jacob Thompson himself, a Catholic married to the non-Catholic Clara, had secretly spirited Maggie away to be brought up properly in a Catholic institution. And the terribly frustrated Cleveland police assiduously stoked the rumor mill themselves, with dark and repeated hints both on and off the record,

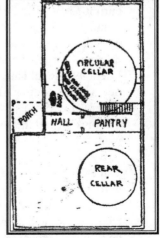

Diagram of Lueth cellar.

saying that Jacob Thompson knew more than he was telling about Maggie's whereabouts and fate. And so the search continued, the days went by, and May gradually turned into June . . .

May 1889 had been an unusually cool month, and the welcome warmth of June arrived none too early for the residents of Merchant Avenue—except for one, a Mrs. Clarissa Shevel of 42 Merchant Avenue, a two-family dwelling just seven doors away from the Thompson home. Clarissa liked the warming weather well enough, but the awful stench that arose around the house about the end of May was driving her crazy. Clarissa and her husband, Joseph, lived in the back part of the house, which the Shevels rented from owner Henry Lueth, who lived with his wife, Lena, and 16-year-old son, Otto, in the front. With Henry gone for most of the previous six months plying his cabinet-making trade in Fremont, and Lena Lueth in a private mental hospital off and on, it was difficult for Clarissa to find someone to deal with her smelly problem. Finally, however, about the beginning of June, she saw Otto and asked him to do something about the odor, which was starting to annoy other neighbors and passersby. Otto took a nickel from her, bought three boxes of chloride of lime, and put them down a ventilation hole in the Shevel parlor. He told Clarissa that the smell was probably caused by dead rats, or perhaps the house Maltese cat, which had not been seen for several weeks.

About a day later, Otto also purchased some sulfur from a neighborhood store and requested instruction from a clerk on how to burn it as an antidote for odors. The clerk showed Otto how to do it and even offered to help him, but Otto refused his aid. Several days later Otto was seen carrying some very badly stained and maggot-infested bedding into a smokehouse at the back of the Lueth lot. He told anyone who asked him about it that he had vomited on the bedding after drinking too much beer sometime in May. Several more days went by. There was still no trace of Maggie Thompson, and the smell at 42 Merchant Avenue waxed worse and worse . . .

By the evening of June 9, Lena Lueth had endured enough. Something had to be done about the terrible odor that had been bothering her since her return from Dr. C. B. Humiston's asylum at the end of May. So that evening about 8:30 she confronted her husband, Henry, and demanded that he go down, search the cellar until he found whatever was rotting down there, and get rid of it. Given

Otto's confession.

Lena's legendary reputation for having an uncontrollable temper, Henry dutifully disappeared down into the basement. Actually, though, it wasn't a real basement. Like many dwellings of the day, the Lueth half-house had a small circular cellar, about nine feet in diameter, which could be reached by a ladderlike staircase. Through a small window in that round cellar one could in turn gain access to the remaining, unfinished area beneath the house walls.

A few minutes later, Henry returned upstairs to Lena, his face ashen. In a trembling voice, he told her, "There's a corpse down there!" Henry went outside and found a policeman on his beat. Returning to the cellar, Henry went through the window into the crawl space outside and returned soon with the badly decomposed, nude corpse of Maggie Thompson. When found, she was partially wrapped in one of Mrs. Lueth's old housedresses, and her own clothes were heaped underneath her. The skin had rotted completely off her skull, her brain was missing, and her lower limbs disintegrated when the body was pulled from its dark resting place. Within minutes the house was full of police and neighbors, and a hysterical Jacob and Clara Thompson soon identified Maggie by the scars on her hips, the result of a childhood accident.

Henry and Lena Lueth and both the Shevels were placed under arrest, as was the Lueths' son, Otto, when he returned to the house about 9:30 p.m. from the local ice-cream parlor. "Do you know anything about this?" asked his distraught mother. Otto disclaimed all knowledge about it to both his mother and the police, but soon

the three Lueths and two Shevels were on their way to the nearby
9th Precinct police station on Barber Street for interrogation. Coroner Walz had already determined that Maggie Thompson had been
beaten to death with a hammerlike object. There were three holes
beaten in her skull, her nose and jaw were broken, and her teeth had
been driven into her palate by the force of the blows inflicted on
her. Her right arm was torn off at the elbow.

There were already cries of "Lynch the murderers!" arising from
the restive crowd in front of the Lueth house, and the Cleveland
police wanted some answers.

The ensuing "sweating" sessions with the five suspects went on
for some five hours. That was mainly for show, however, as the
investigating detectives were focused from the start on Otto Lueth
as the likeliest suspect. Between 10:30 p.m. and the wee hours of
June 10, Captains E. K. Hutchinson and A. S. Gates and detectives
Jake Lohrer, A. A. Lawrence, and Francis Douglass questioned the
16-year-old in isolation, constantly moving him around to various
rooms in the station. They knew that his parents had been largely
absent from home over the last month, and they were likewise
aware of his reputation in the neighborhood for bullying mischief.
Indeed, even before Otto had been taken in as a suspect, Clara
Thompson blurted out to the police, "Have they arrested that Otto
Lueth? The scamp, I want him arrested!"

Otto, who had initially been almost suspiciously cooperative
with the police, grew more sullen and nervous as the hours of questioning went by, and more and more inconsistencies developed in
his version of his whereabouts on May 9. The climax came at 3:30
a.m., when an agonized female shriek resounded from the floor
below the sweating room. "Who is that?" cried Otto to Detective
Francis Douglass. "Your mother, I believe," replied Douglass. "She
had nothing to do with it!" blurted out Otto. "Who did?" queried
Douglass. Otto: "I did it! I did it!" Douglass: "Did what, Otto?" "I
killed her! I killed her! Please give me your revolver so I can kill
myself!" screamed Otto. A minute later Coroner Walz came into
the room, wrote out Otto's verbal confession, and had him swear
and sign to it, and Otto was led away in manacles to a cell at the
Cleveland Central Police Station on Champlain Street (present site
of the Terminal Tower).

Otto's confession was brief and to the point. His story was that
he had been standing at the gate of his parents' house at 42 Mer-

chant Avenue at about 11:30 on the morning of May 9. Maggie was walking by and stopped to ask him if he had some buttons for the "button-string" she was collecting. He told her he would give her some if she came into the house. He led her upstairs to his bedroom, and as soon as they got into the room, he tried to assault her. She screamed, and he hit her with a hammer lying nearby, a small tinsmith's hammer with a blunt point, weighing about five ounces. He probably killed her with the first blow, but he kept on hitting her until she and the bed were covered with blood. He then renewed his attempt to rape her, unsuccessfully, and fled from the house. He returned briefly to the house that night and spent the next week at his brother John's house.

The following Wednesday, six days later, Otto returned to the murder bedroom. He knew his mother might get out of the hospital at any time, and he had to get the body out of the house. He didn't know what else to do, so he carried it down to the Lueth cellar, opened the window, and dragged it to a point 11 feet away. He said nothing to anybody about what he had done, and he returned to his daily activities as one of the most concerned and assiduous of the searchers who were combing the neighborhood for Maggie. Almost every day, he found occasion to ask Clara Thompson whether any word had been heard about her poor little girl.

Otto's arrest and trial were the most sensational criminal proceedings in the history of Cleveland up to that time. Incarcerated in "Blinky" Morgan's old cell at Central, Otto spent the days after his arrest weeping, reading the newspapers, smoking cigars, and participating with gusto in Sunday-morning services held at the jail by the ladies of the Women's Christian Temperance Union. The latter phenomenon greatly irritated the editorialist at the *Cleveland Press*, who commented sourly on the penchant of women of a certain temperament to be seduced by the charming wiles of psychopathically evil criminals:

> "They are invariably women of undoubted respectability who usually belong to the most favored orders of society. They generally take up the case a few days after the defendant has been arraigned and answered to his indictment. They usually go in flocks, loaded with sighs, flowers, and pitying glances, to the cell of the accused. Not infrequently, it is seen soon that the cell is carpeted and furnished like a well-ordered parlor, and that the accused is served with better fare than he perhaps ever indulged

in before. Perhaps there will be songs and prayers and in a short time the public will be informed through the columns of the daily papers that the accused has experienced a change of heart."

Another gothic detail was added to the horror when, as Clara and Jacob Thompson picked out Maggie's burial clothes in an Ontario Street store, their sad business was interrupted by the sound of newsboys braying the headline of the day: "Murderer in Short Breeches! Murderer in Short Breeches!"

Two days after she was found, Maggie Thompson was buried out of nearby St. Augustine Catholic Church. The original plan had been to have services at home, but the experience of the wake, where more than 2,000 mainly ghoulish Clevelanders filed past what the *Cleveland Leader* termed her "chaste" white—and open!—casket, dictated the larger venue. There, to a weeping congregation, Father O'Connor expatiated on the unknowable ways of the Deity and the comforting "consolation that . . . she died defending her purity." The interment followed immediately in St. Joseph Cemetery on Woodland.

Otto was indicted on four counts of murder on June 14, 1887, and booked for a quick trial in late June. Following legal fashion, the charges were somewhat redundant, but they boiled down to the accusation that Otto had murdered Maggie during a rape attempt. For a number of reasons, Otto's trial was delayed until December of that year. The initial difficulty arose from Otto's problems in securing legal counsel; there were few reputable attorneys who desired to defend a figure already known to newspaper readers as the "boy murderer-rapist." Finally, W. S. Kerruish agreed to take the case, but the incapacity of Jacob Thompson, who suffered a crippling injury—he fell between two railroad cars several nights after his daughter's body was found—followed by a paralytic stroke, further delayed the proceedings. The death of Kerruish's son and the illness of Clara Thompson put the date off yet again, and the trial did not open until Monday, December 2. Opposing Kerruish's defense were prosecutors Alexander Hadden and C. W. Collister with Judge George B. Solders presiding.

The state's case was powerful, brimming with circumstantial evidence, and sufficiently gory to satisfy the attentions of the packed audiences, mainly female, who crowded Judge Solders's courtroom on Public Square for day after day of the three-week trial. The jurors were led through the narrative of Maggie's last hours before she vanished, the discovery of her body in the Lueth cellar, and Otto's anguished midnight confession. Maggie's bloody clothes, her felt hat, the bloody bed headboard, and the fatal "button-string" were held up by Prosecutor Hadden for the jury to see, and they also endured Clara Thompson's heartbreaking testimony. The clinching argument came on December 10 with the attempted introduction of Otto's confession.

Kerruish objected. This shrewd attorney combined a healthy respect for the damning circumstantial evidence with a frankly avowed revulsion to his client, "This boy, who is a disgrace to humanity; for whom I have very little respect and no feeling . . ."

He was willing to concede the facts of Maggie's murder in return for saving his youthful client from the hangman—but he knew he had to keep Otto's written confession out of the record. That document, signed and sworn to by Otto (although never read back to him by Coroner Walz), included both the admission that he had killed her "because I wanted to have connection [intercourse] with her" and, perhaps worse, Otto's acknowledgment that he had also tried to rape her after he killed her. Sending the jury out of the room, Judge Solders listened carefully to Kerruish, and Hadden's arguments. His subsequent ruling that the confession was admissible sealed Otto Lueth's doom.

Kerruish didn't give up without a fight. Mercilessly grilling Otto's May 9 interrogators, he contrasted their insistence that Otto's confession was voluntary with the discordant picture that simultaneously emerged of a young boy increasingly bewildered and confused by hours of nonstop questioning. "Getting into a voluntary state of mind, wasn't he?" he repeated again and again, as Cleveland police detectives recalled how Otto's initial bland confidence dissolved over the hours into agitated nervousness. His strategy was to paint Otto's confession as the inevitable capitulation of a mere boy terrorized by bullying adults—but the bottom line was that he couldn't erase Otto's self-proclaimed guilt.

The other prong of Kerruish's desperate defense strategy was to paint Otto as the victim of tainted genetics. Arguing that Otto was an atypical epileptic, Kerruish examined a succession of Lueth relatives to document a pedigree of family insanity and epilepsy. According to Otto's family, his maternal grandmother, aunt, uncle, mother, and brother had all suffered from epileptic-like fits during their lives. Otto himself, Lena Lueth claimed on the stand, had suffered "spasms" and "night terrors" as an infant, endured frequent and debilitating headaches as an adolescent, and had a poor memory. The gist of Kerruish's argument, then, was that on May 9 Otto had suffered a sudden episode of his malady—"masked epilepsy," Kerruish termed it—and acted without even knowing what he was doing.

Kerruish didn't get very far with his fanciful medical hypothesis. Although he brought forward several eminent physicians to support his diagnosis of "masked epilepsy," none of them was able to say whether Otto really suffered from it. He did get Dr. Reuben Vance to testify that he had examined Otto and found a depression on his skull, probably the result of an injury that could have caused brain damage. But the attempt to sell Otto to the jury as a brain-damaged idiot with a poor memory foundered on testimony by Otto's teachers at the Tremont Street School—where he dropped out at the age of 13—who well remembered his general mental acumen, his ability with figures, and his gift for playing the violin. And municipal records that Prosecutor Hadden entered as evidence provided a legal demonstration of Otto's excellent memory at the time he testified in an 1888 lawsuit brought by Lena Lueth against the city of Cleveland.

Otto's attorney might have done better, and certainly no worse, if he had subpoenaed the many phrenologists who were fascinated by Otto Lueth from the moment he came to public notice. Many people throughout his life had already noticed the oddly flattened shape of Otto's skull and his unusually low brow. That's all that was needed by the many local phrenologists, all of whom believed that skull conformation determined destiny and lusted after the chance to personally examine the boy murderer's skull. Typical was a Cleveland physician quoted in the June 13, 1889 *Plain Dealer* to the effect that Otto's "organ of destructiveness was abnormally developed." And the murder of Maggie Thompson came as a perfectly logical, indeed, inevitable event to Conrad Mizer, a tailor who had once employed Otto in odd jobs. Mizer had actually examined Otto phrenologically, and he modestly admitted to a *Leader* reporter that he "was probably the only person in town who wasn't surprised at the news of his crime . . ." Mizer continued: "If phrenology is true, he was bound to make mischief of one kind or another . . . He had a very low forehead. The region of benevolence, kindness, and reverence were [*sic*] very deficient, while he had large self-esteem and stubbornness. He carried out the instincts implanted in him as naturally as a bull dog does his disposition to fight."

Interestingly, Kerruish did not pursue a line of argument that lawyers of the present day would likely have seized upon with ferocity. In the trial testimony concerning Otto's mental heritage, it was well established that his mother, Lena Lueth, suffered—if that is the right word—from an ungovernable temper. As her husband, Henry, her older son, John, and she herself swore under oath, Lena went into veritably demonic fits of rage, during which she was in the habit of physically abusing her children, especially Otto. From an early age, she blandly admitted, she had pulled his hair, kicked him, beaten him, walked on him, and often hit him with any object that came to hand. Once, when Otto was eight, she had beaten him with a chair leg and, when Henry tried to intervene, stabbed Henry twice with a convenient butcher knife. Just a few months before Maggie Thompson's murder, Lena had repeatedly slammed Otto's head into a wooden door, the origin, perhaps, of the skull injury detected by Dr. Vance. It is an illuminating token of attitudes regarding parental discipline during Otto's era that the only comment made about Lena's maternal brutality was to excuse it on the grounds that she was poor, and her methods were in "the German style." One can only imagine what capital contemporary defense attorneys would make of such Dickensian cruelties.

Lena didn't help Otto much by her behavior in the courtroom either. Ashen-faced at best, and constantly muttering to herself, Lena had a number of "spasms" at climactic moments of the trial and had to be removed until she returned to her normal tense demeanor. Nor did she help the defense—or, for that matter, ethnic tensions in Cleveland—with her repeated comment: "Had Maggie Thompson been a German girl and Otto an Irish boy, instead of a German boy and an Irish girl, they would not be so hot about it and if he were a few years older he would have been acquitted and placed on the police force."

With evidence presented and cross-examinations completed, Kerruish and Prosecutor Hadden made their closing arguments. Holding up Maggie's bloody garments, hair, and "button-string" one more time, Hadden reminded the jury that the law assumed every person sane until proven otherwise—and that the defense had not produced a single physician who would certify Otto as insane. He once again characterized Otto's confession as voluntary and cited the four buttons found in Maggie's bloody dress as the evidentiary link in proving that Otto's primary motive was rape. Over Kerruish's strenuous objections, Hadden recalled trial testimony that indicated Maggie Thompson had not possessed the four buttons found with her corpse when she left her parents' house on the morning of May 9. The inference to be drawn by the jury was unavoidable: Otto Lueth had lured Maggie Thompson into his house with those buttons, and he deserved to die for it, the penalty being death for anyone found guilty of a murder committed while attempting to rape a girl under 14 years of age.

Kerruish followed Hadden's emotional summary with a florid peroration of his own. Painting Otto again as the "bad seed" of a genetically cursed family and the unwitting victim of an uncontrollable spasm, Kerruish excoriated primitive public attitudes about insanity and compared the atmosphere in the courtroom to Salem Village in 1692. Otto, he pleaded, was "crippled in intellect; crippled in every way, crippled by his inheritance from his ancestors and crippled by the beatings received from his mother. The maniacal outburst was bound to come . . . " And as to why Otto had allowed Maggie's body to rot for a week, well, it was just another index of Otto's subnormality: "Why, a dog knows enough to bury a bone, yet this boy leaves this body in the cellar to fester and smell and tell its story to the community." Otto had not tried to rape Maggie before or after he hammered her; it was Detective Douglass, not naive Otto, who had planted that fatal word "connection" in his so-called confession to supply a motive for what was actually a motiveless crime.

Wisely or not, Kerruish reserved his most special scorn for the press. Like Sam Sheppard's defenders would do 65 years later, he blamed reporters and editors most of all for unfavorable public opinion about his client: "It isn't the papers that make the opinions but the boys here who write these articles and who don't earn over $5 a month—I beg your pardon, $5 a week, I believe. I don't want to refer much to these papers and reporters but if I ever got on the judge's bench . . . I know I would find a way to prevent a common, scurrilous newspaper from interfering in the trial of a case. I think that there [should] have been power enough in the law of the state of Ohio to have that paper [the *Cleveland Leader*] from trying this case in their columns. If you send this boy to the gallows," Kerruish finished, "you will live to decide in calm and passionless reflection that you probably did wrong." Hadden followed, repeating the elements of the prosecution's case, and Judge Solders charged the jury, which went out at 1 p.m., Friday, December 27.

To probably no one's surprise, the 12 men good and true returned four hours and 27 minutes later with a verdict of guilty on the third count. Otto took the news with white-faced calm, but Lena refused to leave the room after Judge Solders dismissed the jury, and she began a singsong rant: "No, I will not go. I might as well die here as outside. If they kill him, they kill me. If he is guilty, so am I. They are murderers. They will hang my poor boy though everybody says he is wrong in his head. I have no more use to live."

Four days later, on New Year's Eve, Judge Solders sentenced Otto to hang on April 26, 1890, in the Columbus Penitentiary. Otto merely sank back in his chair, but Lena was good for another impassioned outburst: "Damn! Damn! Damn! The jury be damned! All 13 men be damned! They are fools. It is a damned shame to hang a child of 16 years. They all be damned, their children and grandchildren. I damn them, I, the mother of the murdered boy."

When bailiffs Harry Lancefield and Peter Hill tried to restrain the crazed woman, she screamed, "Don't touch me. I will kill you! I will kill you!"

For the next few months Kerruish's motion for a new trial crawled through the appeals system, before Justices C. C. Baldwin, W. H. Upson, and H. J. Caldwell of the Ohio circuit court unanimously upheld the jury's verdict on June 13, 1890. Otto's death date, which had already been delayed to allow for his appeal, was now moved back to August 29, allowing still more time for the Board of Pardons and Governor Campbell to consider Otto's merits for clemency. The circuit court's decision came just three days after the death of Jacob Thompson, who succumbed to his infirmities and a broken heart exactly a year and a day after his daughter's body was discovered.

Otto's options dwindled. On August 22 the Board of Pardons turned him down, despite the pleas of former president Rutherford B. Hayes and four of the members of Otto's original jury. Mrs. Lueth took the news badly and threatened again to kill herself— and did not.

Four days later, Governor Campbell refused to grant clemency, and preparations for Otto's execution went into high gear. Otto himself did not take the news in genteel fashion, first cursing everyone he could think of (except his mother) and then whining, "I just want to see the governor and tell him what I think of him! If he came down to see that nigger Blythe [an African-American death-row candidate] he might come to see me." Unwilling as always to be upstaged, Lena Lueth confronted Deputy Warden Porter, screaming that she was going to shoot and poison Governor Campbell.

Otto died pretty gamely, considering his general career as a loutish poltroon. After a few tears in his last hours, he pulled himself together, requesting only that the newspaper reporters not "give it too hard to me" in their accounts and that the hangman do his business briskly and well. Which the latter did: Just after the black-hooded, black-suited, and white-tied Otto said, "All right, let her go," at 12:05 a.m., August 29, the trap was sprung, and he died a second later from a broken neck. After 17 minutes, he was cut down in front of the 29 witnesses and hustled off on a stretcher. It was a ghastly spectacle: his eyes were bulging out, blood oozed from his mouth, his face was a livid purple, and the mark of the noose left an angry circular scar around his neck. He left behind a final statement in which he admitted the murder but denied attempting to rape Maggie Thompson.

Following an aborted funeral—because of a misunderstanding the church doors were locked—Otto's body was shipped off to Fremont, Ohio, for funeral rites and burial.

As one might expect, Otto Lueth's demented mother had the last word. A week after her son was executed, she sent a letter to Cuyahoga County sheriff Sawyer in which she once more cursed all those who had participated in Otto's trial and death: "The jury was bribed. Consequently, no other verdict could be expected, and when the Irish element is arraigned [sic] against the German then everything is lost. But I tell you, I, the mother of the murdered boy, cursed be you all. May his shadow pursue you by day and by night and in the hour of your death may you suffer the pangs that I now suffer. He was a murderer against his will. You murdered him with premeditation. Therefore, once more, all be cursed that lent their hands, you murderers. Lena Lueth."

It is not known whether Mrs. Lueth was aware of the fact that the Thompson family was not, in fact, of Irish extraction.

Chapter 3

THE INCREDIBLE VANISHING KILLER

Cleveland's "Black Widow"

Black Widow. The two words provoke several images, none of them cheery. Most people are aware, at least by repute, of the female black widow spider, the most lethal arachnid native to America, notorious for occasionally dining on her male partner after mating. Some, too, are familiar with the archetype of the female serial-killer spouse, memorably rendered in a number of films, most recently by Theresa Russell in *Black Widow* (1987). Few Clevelanders realize, however, that almost four score years ago their city riveted the attention of the nation for almost a fortnight with sensational news of a serial husband murderess. They should probably be readily forgiven for not knowing: the "Black Widow" story came out of nowhere, burned fiercely in the public mind for two weeks, and then, just as suddenly, disappeared forever.

Edward C. Stanton was probably the most interesting, aggressive, and effective prosecutor in Cuyahoga County history. During his tenure as county prosecutor (1921–1929), Stanton sent eight men to the electric chair and earned a deserved reputation as a publicity-savvy, cunning, and relentless lawman. Propelled into office by his avidity in prosecuting the alleged May Day rioters of 1919, Stanton quickly gained the public's favor with his unexpected conviction of municipal judge William H. McGannon for perjury, for his dramatic pursuit and prosecution of those involved in the infamous murder-for-hire demise of Lakewood printer Dan Kaber, and for the long-awaited guilty verdict that ended the chilling criminal career of Cleveland's Public Enemy No.1, George "Jiggs" Losteiner. (All of these trials are covered in the pages of the author's previous volume, *They Died Crawling*.) Stanton's zealous

Woman's Poison Alibi Denied

From the *Cleveland Press*, May 3, 1922.

efforts also sent three men to the electric chair for their role in the brutal payroll robbery and murder of businessmen Wilfred C. Sly and George K. Fanner on the last day of 1920. (The author has chronicled the Sly-Fanner murders in another previous book, *The Maniac in the Bushes*.) It is likely, however, that none of Stanton's celebrated cases was more bizarre, more chilling and yet paradoxically inconclusive than the ephemeral "Black Widow" phenomenon of 1922.

The story erupted on May 1, when Stanton announced that a 37-year-old Cleveland woman was under investigation on suspicion of multiple murder. Held in the county jail on an unrelated larceny charge, she was suspected, Stanton told reporters, of having poisoned two of her four children and perhaps as many as three of her five husbands in order to collect on various substantial insurance policies. The next day's newspaper headlines left nothing to the reader's imagination. The *Plain Dealer* blared, "Suspect Woman Killed Husbands For Insurance," while the *Press* shouted, "Body Exhumed In Poison Plot." Interestingly, neither Stanton nor the newspapers revealed—then or ever—the identity of the accused distaff Borgia.

Stanton, as usual, was in deadly earnest. Early the very next day, county coroner A. P. Hammond showed up at staid Lake View Cemetery to oversee the exhumation of the suspected poisoner's fifth husband, a machinist who died in May of 1921. After removing the corpse to the county morgue on Lakeside, Hammond's physicians quickly extracted the vital organs and turned them over to city chemists Harold J. Knapp and George Voerg for analysis. Pursuant to Stanton's orders, they were looking for signs of metallic poisons: Stanton publicly vowed a murder indictment should so little as even a tenth of a grain of arsenic show up in the cadaver.

Meanwhile, the background story luridly unfolded in the pages of Cleveland's three daily newspapers. And what a story it was.

The woman, it seems, had originally come to Stanton's notice a year before, when she sought his aid in collecting on her recently deceased husband's insurance. Her sad story to Stanton was that her late spouse was a World War I veteran whose health had been fatally ruined by poison gas in the trenches of France, and that the heartless United States government had refused to pay off on his $5,000 war risk insurance. Stanton couldn't help her, but he turned her over to the Cleveland offices of the American Red Cross.

This proved an imprudent move for the grieving widow. Not only did the Red Cross fail to expedite her insurance problem—it seems that Husband No. 5 had been remiss in his premium payments—but Red Cross official Esther Knowles became suspicious as she learned more and more details of the high-living widow's lifestyle. Several months later, in April 1922, the widow would be arrested on unrelated larceny charges, and Esther would renew their acquaintance when the Red Cross took over care of the woman's two teenage daughters. After talking with the daughters, Esther went to Stanton, and he went to the media on May 1.

STANTON AND AIDS FAIL TO SHAKE STORY

Prisoner Smiles as Prosecutors Hurl Questions; Admits She Planned Sixth Marriage.

SPENT $5,000 IN MONTH, INVESTIGATION REVEALS

Woman Had "Mania for Collecting Insurance," Declares Ex-Husband.

From the *Cleveland Press*, May 3, 1922.

Over the next week, the strange saga of the "Black Widow" unfolded in the newspapers. Her trail led back to Pittsburgh, where nearly 20 years before she had wed her first husband and produced two daughters. They did not last long: the heavily insured girls died after eating "poison tablets" in what was assumed to be an unfortunate household "accident." The Black Widow soon divorced and married Husband No. 2, a Pittsburgh druggist. That marriage produced another two daughters, born in 1907 and 1908 but, alas, not nuptial felicity: the couple divorced during World War I. Husband No. 2 survived his experience with the Black Widow, but he would later recall that she did seem to have "a mania for collecting insurance."

The pace of her marital adventures now picked up steam. She married Husband No. 3 in Pittsburgh, and she and her daughters moved with him to Cleveland, where he had found a splendid job opportunity. Indeed, it was so good that it even included a free

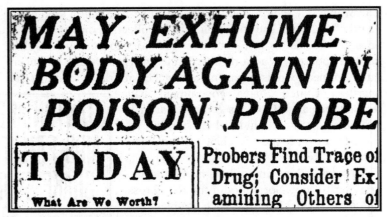

MAY EXHUME BODY AGAIN IN POISON PROBE

TODAY *What Are We Worth?*

Probers Find Trace of Drug; Consider Examining Others of

From the *Cleveland Press*, May 5, 1922.

$1,200 insurance policy as an employee benefit. Unfortunately, No. 3 didn't stick around to enjoy it, as he died very unexpectedly only a week after it took effect. Described as in "perfect health," he nonetheless fainted at work one afternoon and was dead within 24 hours. After cashing in his policy, the Black Widow took her family back to Pittsburgh.

There, she wasn't lonely for long. Within the year she had snared Husband No. 4, a wealthy man likewise described as being in "perfect health." Shortly after the nuptials were celebrated, however, he began to fail alarmingly and died in May of 1919. The Black Widow had by now begun to attract the attention of local lawmen, and an autopsy was conducted on her late No. 4. Robert Brauh, the Allegheny County chief of detectives, was not surprised when the autopsy turned up traces of arsenic in the stomach. But nothing further was done, because Husband No. 4's physician testified that he had prescribed medicines for the deceased containing the potent metallic powder. The late No. 4 left $5,000 to his stricken widow, who now shifted her base of operations back to Cleveland.

As ever, the new widow did not pine long. Seven months after No. 4 shuffled off his mortal coil, she met Husband No. 5, an ex-soldier just returned after the Armistice. After a whirlwind courtship, which was by now her wont, the newlyweds settled down to marital bliss in an expensive flat on East 40th Street.

Probably more is known about the corpse of Husband No. 5 than about the living man, but it is fair to surmise that his brief married life was not a felicitous idyll. Unlike his immediate predecessor in the Black Widow's mercurial affections, Husband No. 5—known to inquiring newspaper readers only as "Joe"—was not a wealthy man, and his machinist's wages were not adequate to underwrite the lifestyle to which his spouse had become accustomed. Sad to say, very soon after tying the knot, his wife took to wistfully voicing her discontent aloud to her bosom friend Jessie Burns. It began with subtle wishes, modest daydreaming hints like: "Wouldn't it be nice if Joe died? Think of the fun and parties we could have if Joe died." Within a few more weeks, as the 25-year-old Jessie later reminisced, the Black Widow's coy remarks became more direct and concrete: "I would like to get rid of him. I would like to give him arsenic."

But all was not Lady Bluebeard gloom-and-doom at the East 40th Street love nest. Various roomers who sublet premises from the couple would later testify that Joe's wife not only insisted on cooking all of his food herself but was shrewishly insistent that not a tasty morsel go to waste, often screaming profanely, "--- ---- you, eat that food. I'm not going to cook for you and have you leave everything!"

Perhaps more ominously for Joe, there were increasing hints that his wife had not lost her "mania for collecting insurance." He complained to friends that she was constantly nagging him to join lodges that offered insurance benefits, and she attempted, unsuccessfully, in the weeks just before his death, to get his veteran's insurance raised from $5,000 to $10,000. And to friends to whom she owed money, she promised that she was just about to come into an "expected windfall" of $5,000—the exact amount of Joe's G. I. death benefit.

Although the Black Widow would later claim that Joe's abrupt demise stemmed from longstanding health problems caused by his gassing in France, neither War Department records nor the recollections of Joe's brothers supported her assertion. Indeed, Joe's fatal crisis must have come unexpectedly. The couple's only remaining roomer would recall leaving Joe in perfect health on a May day in 1921—and returning only three days later to find him laid out in a casket.

For her friends, who remarked that the new widow seemed rather jolly under the circumstances, the Black Widow had a ready explanation, encrusted with convincingly mundane detail: "Joe ate a hearty meal last night and drank six bottles of loganberry juice. At about 10 p.m., he went to take a hot bath. Eating, drinking and the hot water must have affected his heart, I guess, because when I got up the next morning I found him dead on the bathroom floor."

Perhaps custom by now had steeled Joe's widow to the familiar pain. But it is likely that she had already realized ready cash from his unexpected departure, as a mere 48 hours after her spouse's funeral she was throwing parties and spending her substance in what a disapproving Stanton later characterized as "riotous living." Moving to a luxurious East Side apartment, the Black Widow decorated with expensive furniture, splurged on $1,400 in diamonds, and bought herself a new car.

Also pampering her aesthetic side, she acquired a piano and, along with it, a new beau. His name was L. P. Farrell, a widowed 53-year-old, and he met the Black Widow when he delivered the piano to her new digs. They had a few drinks and struck up a conversation that soon developed, he would ruefully recall, into her "making violent love" to him after she discovered he was a man of some property. Over the next few months she wooed Farrell assiduously. The result was a wedding date set for April 24, 1922.

That problematic union never came off. The Black Widow was arrested that very morning on multiple charges of larceny brought by her neighbors, who connected her with the recent disappearance of their cherished valuables. After she was taken to the county jail, her children were turned over to the Red Cross, leading ultimately to Esther Knowles's fateful conversation with Edward Stanton and the ensuing nationwide sensation.

The story peaked on May 5. That afternoon, Stanton announced that the autopsy of Husband No. 5 had turned up traces of both morphine and arsenic in the vital organs. Simultaneously, word came from Pittsburgh authorities that they had been trying to build a murder case against the Black Widow for three years. There was talk of impending murder indictments and the possibility of digging up husbands No. 3 and No. 4 and her two dead children from their graveyard homes. Yet another talkative friend came forward to tell police of an additional, now vanished child the accused had given birth to. A search of East Side drugstore records disclosed two purchases of arsenic in the spring of 1921 that bore her surname. The discovery of a cache of suggestive newspaper clippings at the Black Widow's flat further inflamed police and public suspi-

WOMAN POISON SUSPECT ANSWERS ACCUSERS

From the *Cleveland Press*, May 8, 1922.

cions. One was a report of a judge's charge to a jury, which seemed to have a lurid bearing on her present predicament: "Bear in mind that suspicion was an entirely different thing from legal proof, and it was in accordance with proofs and not suspicion that their verdict must be given."

A second item provided a juicy rationale for the much-married suspect's alleged modus operandi: "As to loving more than once, it certainly can be done. No love is so great that no one else can come along and take the place of the former love."

What more did the authorities need to hear?—except, perhaps, this remark from the widow, kindly recalled by one of her friends: "Wasn't Mrs. Kaber foolish to have her husband stabbed? Why didn't she give him ground glass instead of poison?"

Excited Clevelanders didn't know it, but the sensational story of the Black Widow was about to implode and disappear. Within five days it would vanish from the newspapers, Cuyahoga County coroner's files, and police records forever. Almost everything known after May 5 consists of negative facts: We know that the supposedly infamous Black Widow was never indicted, never brought to trial, and never publicly exonerated from the terrible charges made against her. What happened?

In the absence of documented fact, conjecture rules—but it's a pretty good guess that Stanton's impressive case against the Black Widow was not so impressive after all. After the initial stories about the finding of arsenic in the corpse of No. 5, word leaked out that the amount was laughably insignificant. In fact, city chemist George Voerg at first reported that he could find no arsenic at all. Ordered to take a more scrupulous look, he eventually found the sought-for poison—at a concentration of one per three million parts in the dead man's vital organs. This was considerably less that Edward Stanton's indictment threshold of a tenth of a grain, so the body of No. 5 was once again dug up from Lake View Cemetery on the morning of May 6. Apparently, nothing more was found.

Nothing has been heard of the Black Widow since May 10, 1922, when Cuyahoga County authorities promised reporters that there would soon be "startling developments" in the flagging investigation. It is not known where she went, and whether she recovered her two daughters—whom the Red Cross had placed in foster homes—when she was finally let out of jail. Whether she was just a crass, unlucky gold digger or a fiendishly heartless serial killer remains an open question. It is only fair, however, to let her have the last word, considering the unproved charges against her. When she was first arrested, reporters could hear the Black Widow screaming from Stanton's interrogation room, "It's a lie! It's a lie! I won't answer another of your questions!" Her final word on her situation was issued through her attorney, G. W. Gurney, on May 8:

> "I am the unnamed woman in County Jail. Much has been said unfavorable to me. I know the public wishes to know the truth . . . I am here because of false charges. It has been intimated that I may have poisoned my husband. The desire of public officials to gain applause for themselves soon opened the floodgates. If any of my accusers had any evidence that I had poisoned my husband, they kept it to themselves for nearly a year . . .
> "I did not murder my husband. He died of natural causes. I loved him dearly . . . I have had many offers to marry since his death and some of the offers have come from wealthy men. If my business is to marry and kill for the love of gold, is it not a bit strange that I should have allowed a year to pass without any further pursuit of my profession? . . . There is no evidence of my guilt, for I am innocent. The county officials are merely trying to weave a chain of circumstances in my life that might make it possible for me to have poisoned the man I loved. How much easier it would be for them to weave a dozen chains to prove my innocence. My innocence would not please them. Meanwhile I must suffer . . . My greatest solace is that there must be someone who will believe me innocent, at least until some real evidence of my guilt has been discovered."

Whatever her guilt or innocence, that "someone" was certainly not her one-time fiancé, piano mover L. P. Farrell. Upon learning of the charges against her, he replied, "When I read of her arrest, my blood turned cold. I am a lucky man to have escaped her . . . I had a feeling that I would meet a terrible end."

Chapter 4

MURDER ON MILLIONAIRES' ROW

Herbert Noyes's "Danse Macabre"

One of the most glittering and cherished chapters of Cleveland's past is the legend of "Millionaires' Row." However democratic one's feelings, there are few Clevelanders who do not respond with pride and an almost saccharine nostalgia to visions of the haughty, luxurious lifestyle that characterized the Euclid Avenue homes of the Forest City's social elite in the half-century following the Civil War. Many have lamented the demise of those houses and that lifestyle and wondered how what visitors admiringly called the "most beautiful street in the world" could have deteriorated so quickly and so irretrievably in the years after the turn of the last century. The reasons for its demise, as brilliantly illuminated in Jan Cigliano's beautifully produced book on the phenomenon (*Showplace of America: Cleveland's Euclid Avenue*, 1850–1910; Kent State University Press, 1991), were brutally mundane: inexorable commercial development and confiscatory real estate taxes. Maybe that's the whole story, maybe not. This romantic likes to think that it was the curse of Herbert Noyes—vengeance on the adopted city and street that disdained to discover and punish his cowardly assassins. His strange death is something to think about the next time you're stuck in traffic on Euclid Avenue in front of the relentless concrete blocks of Cleveland State University—that, and the very odd links between his brutal death and another mysterious assassination involving some of the same dramatis personae.

By all accounts, Herbert N. Noyes was a perfectly likable, perfectly respectable, and perfectly competent young man. Thirty years old in May 1900, the Illinois-born stockbroker had come to Cleveland in 1897 to work at the J. F. Harris & Company brokerage in the Williamson Building (site of the current BP building on

SCENE OF THE EUCLID AVENUE MURDER.

From the *Cleveland World*, May 25, 1900.

Public Square). With hard work, he became the office manager within a year, and in his leisure hours pursued an active, if not intemperate social life. His stated ambition from the moment of his arrival in Cleveland was to mix with only the best society—the "Forest City 400" whose palatial homes lined Euclid Avenue—and he succeeded rapidly and completely during his few years here. Rooming initially with lawyer Frank H. Ginn, the personable, bespectacled Noyes found himself frequently hobnobbing with well-known leaders of the Cleveland elite: Frank B. Meade, William. J. Starkweather, F. L. Gilchrist, Max Reiber, J. E. Ferris, John A. Green, L. H. Fox, and Dr. Hamilton Biggar Jr. Prospering, if not yet wealthy, Noyes roomed with W. J. Starkweather in a pleasant flat at the residential Croxden Hotel, took his daily lunches at the Century Club, and spent his evenings enjoying the respectable pleasures of Cleveland's theaters and concert halls with like-minded members of the upper class. As a token of his quick social advancement, by May 1900 Noyes belonged to both the Cleveland Golf Club and the Century Club and had agreed to take up quarters in a bachelor summer cottage on Lake Shore Boulevard in company with five other similarly situated young men. Uncharitable souls might have called Herbert Noyes a social climber, but, if so, he was a very successful one and had done pretty well for the son of a respectable, if unremarkable, Presbyterian parson from Evanston, Illinois.

As frustrated investigators subsequently found, there was little to be publicly known beyond the bland surface of Herbert Noyes's social profile. Apparently winning in personality, he was popular with many Cleveland men but close with few of them, and with no women at all. In his watch, it is true, he carried the small photo-graph of a distinguished-looking woman. When queried about it, however, Noyes would simply smile wistfully and say that it was the portrait of "another young woman who liked me well enough to give me her picture and then marry another." Some of his acquaintances thought he had a quick temper, but they also allowed that he cooled down fast, and it is probably a good index of his general winsomeness that he was popular with the numerous servants that were part of his casually pampered lifestyle. Although known to be economical, he was not stingy, yet he rarely carried more than a few dollars on his person, lest he be tempted into unnecessary expenditure. He was abstemious with regard to alcohol, and the fact that he had never brought a woman to his rooms cemented his virtuous repute at the Croxden Hotel.

Herbert N. Noyes.

May 24, 1900, Herbert Noyes's last day on earth, was a typical one. After laboring at the offices of J. F. Harris & Company, Noyes returned home to the Croxden at 5:30 p.m. Mrs. Vincent, the manager's wife, saw him come in, and she also witnessed his departure about an hour later. In the interim, he had telephoned Miss Flora Smith, a Euclid Avenue debutante, and asked her whether she and her mother, Mrs. Catherine G. Smith, would be his guests at a Gray's Armory concert that evening. The Smith females already had tickets for the concert, so the three agreed to go together. After din-ing out, Noyes, attired in full formal evening dress, including a light spring topcoat and silk hat, showed up at the Smith residence at 690 Euclid, and the three left for Gray's Armory in the Smiths' horse-drawn carriage.

What a phenomenal concert it must have been. Featuring three of the best-known pianists of the day, Russians Mark Hambourg and Alex Petschnikoff and Frenchman Aimé Lachaume, perform-ing on two concert grands, it included arrangements of Beethoven's "Kreutzer" sonata and the "Fantasia Appassionata," by Vieuxtemps. The program ended at 10:10 p.m., following a stunning rendition of Saint-Säens's demonic "Danse Macabre" (Dance of Death). Afterwards, the Smiths' carriage driver picked up the threesome, and they went to Bismarck's, a fashionable cafe on Huron Street, for some refreshment. They left there shortly after 11 and were on the way to the Croxden, on Prospect near Case Avenue (next to the old Rockefeller home, just west of present-day East 40th Street), to drop Noyes off when he insisted on escorting them home. It was probably about 11:15 when the carriage came to a halt at the side entrance to the Smith home. Catherine Smith wanted her driver to take Noyes home, but he insisted on walking the few blocks. It was a fine, warm spring night, he noted, and, anyway, he wanted to smoke a cigar. So after a final goodnight, Catherine and Flora Smith closed the door behind them, and Herbert Noyes walked down the drive to Euclid Avenue and turned right for the walk east and home. He was on the south side of the many-mansioned avenue, and it was about 11:30.

There was much subsequent dispute over whether the streetlights in the area were functioning that night. There was one located in front of the Smith home (just east of the current East 24th Street) and another several doors up the street outside John V. Painter's mansion at 706 (currently 2508 Euclid). Some witnesses claimed that the lights were off, others that they were on—and some that they were alternately lit and darkened. The only thing certain is that about 11:32 p.m. quite a number of persons in the vicinity heard the distinct sound of a single pistol shot.

Catherine and Flora Smith heard it inside their home. Thinking it came from the direction of Prospect Avenue to the south, Flora stepped out on the back porch and asked the Smiths' carriage driver, who had just finished stabling the horses for the night, whether he knew what the sound was. He didn't, and the Smiths thought no more about the mysterious noise until the next morning.

Two other persons who heard the shot were Morris Morrow and Hal D. Banks, young *Cleveland Leader* reporters, who were walking west on the north side of Euclid just east of Oliver Street (East 24th). They had just passed three men on the opposite side of the street when they heard the report and saw a muzzle flash there, in front of the Painter residence. Seconds later they saw two men running from the scene of the flash. One, a medium-sized man with a soft hat, crossed the street and turned up Oliver, running north toward Payne Avenue. The other, short, slight, and attired in dark clothes and a derby hat, ran down the Painter driveway and disappeared in the direction of Prospect Avenue.

Morrow and Banks initially thought that "someone was firing a revolver for fun" or shooting at a stray dog. Hearing a groan, however, the two reporters crossed the street and found the body of a man lying on the sidewalk in front of the Painter front gate. The street light there was out, but they could see that he was well dressed. His hat, cane, and eyeglasses were lying beside him, and he was covered with blood, more of which was steadily gushing from a head wound. Cradling Noyes's head and pouring some brandy from a flask he carried on his person, Morrow asked the unknown victim who he was. Apparently delirious, the bleeding man replied, "What was that noise?" (Most accounts of the Noyes murder, then and later, would focus on Noyes's question as evidence of his disorientation; it is likely, however, that what he said was "Noyes," and they misinterpreted his remark.) The only other information they could get out of him was that he was alone and that he couldn't remember where he lived. He murmured, "What happened? Oh, my head!" and lapsed into unconsciousness. At this point, young Fayette Brown Jr., who lived nearby, came upon the scene, returning from a University School drama club rehearsal. Joined soon by a private policeman, John Bruder, the group tried to flag down a cabman, who refused to stop.

Leaving Brown and Banks to tend Noyes, Bruder went to get a pail of water to wash off the blood, and Morrow went for help. At the nearby home of Harvey H. Brown (757 Euclid), Morrow telephoned for a Black & Wright ambulance and then talked to Captain Madigan at the central police station on Champlain. Madigan promised to send the police, and Morrow returned to the crime scene, where Brown and Bruder had moved Noyes's body to the Painter tree lawn.

Just how long it took the cops to get there subsequently sparked great and bitter controversy. Madigan later claimed that he immediately notified the 2nd Precinct station at Oregon and Oliver streets (present-day Rockwell Avenue and East 24th Street). Bruder, Banks, and Morrow, however, testified at the coroner's inquest that it was a good 45 minutes before a patrol wagon and several policemen arrived at the scene. (Most observers estimated that it should have taken 5 minutes for the wagon and 10 minutes for a pedestrian). After the witnesses' statements had been taken, Noyes's body was loaded into the Black & Wright wagon and taken to Cleveland General Hospital on Woodland Avenue. The only pieces of evidence garnered by the police at the scene were Noyes's hat, his cane, his partially smoked cigar, and a man's black leather belt found lying on the sidewalk nearby—which police

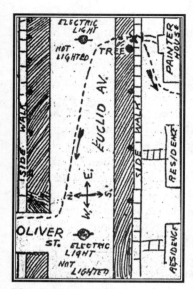

**Murder map and
route of murderers.**

somehow managed to lose before they returned to the 2nd Precinct station.

Noyes lived until 3:00 the next morning, May 25, but never regained full consciousness. The attending nurses thought he muttered a woman's name, either "Mary" or "Bertha," but they couldn't be sure. In his clothes they found $3.50 in cash, a set of gold shirt studs, a pair of gold cufflinks, and an expensive gold watch containing the picture of an unknown woman. On his body, the doctors found 14 major bruises—4 on the face alone—several minor abrasions, and a gunshot wound behind his left ear. Fired from behind, and so close to Noyes's head that it had burned his hat and singed his hair, the fatal bullet pierced the brim of his top hat, entered his head just about an inch above and behind his left ear, broke a small piece off his skull, passed along the top of his head just below the skin, and lodged just under the skin over his right eye. The bullet fractured his skull from ear to ear and triggered a massive cerebral hemorrhage, which caused Herbert Noyes's death at 3:00 a.m. Doctors and police finally learned the victim's identity just minutes before he expired, when Dr. Hamilton Biggar Jr. arrived at the hospital and identified his friend. Noyes's roommate, W. J. Starkweather, was with him when he died but heard nothing to help identify Noyes's killers.

The investigation of Herbert Noyes's death was one of the most botched murder investigations in Cleveland police history. From the moment Chief of Police George E. Corner's finest arrived on the bloody scene, they refused to consider any motive for the shooting other than premeditated assassination. James Doran, the dean of Cleveland detectives and the official in charge of the case, expressed the consensus of the Forest City men in blue with his magisterial dismissal of alternative theories: "Every circumstance surrounding the case points to the fact that Noyes was taken by surprise and had no idea what had happened to him." The killers, Doran and his fellow sleuths surmised, had lain in wait for the young club man behind a tree near the Painter residence and had, perhaps, stalked him since the moment he and the Smiths had departed for the Armory at 8 p.m. Picking a darkened area, shielded by the shadow of the tree, and possibly tampering with the streetlight, his assassins had pounced at a time and place of their choosing. The entry point of the bullet, Doran argued, suggested that he had been shot from behind without even being aware of his assailants, and his considerable bruises and injuries were caused by the fall to the ground. Declining to consider the possibility of a robbery attempt, Doran and Company adamantly refused to look for guilty highwaymen, or "footpads," as they were called in the romantic parlance of the day. That being the case, Chief Corner added, it was no use offering a reward for information about the killing. Treating it, like Doran did, as a personally motivated, Social Register rubout, Corner darkly hinted that "Noyes's murderers will be found among persons who move in the better class of society." Such persons, Corner reasoned, would not be "tempted to 'peach' by any reward within the power of the authorities to offer." Given this constrictive theory and the fact that there were no real witnesses to the shooting, the Noyes investigation never even got off the ground.

Practically no one else seems to have agreed with this glib dismissal of the alternative robbery theory. After a close examination of Noyes's considerable bruises, Cuyahoga County coroner John C. Simon expressed the conviction that Noyes had put up a "terrific struggle" against his assailants, and that the bruises on his knuckles were inflicted before he was shot and in the course of vigorous fisticuffs. Moreover, Simon argued, some of the bruises—especially on his forearms and hips—could not have resulted from his fall to the pavement. That hypothesis was strongly supported by Edward Seward, from whom Noyes had taken rigorous boxing lessons over the past year. Noyes, Seward related, had been an aggressive pugilist—a "hard hitter"—determined to resist robbery attempts and, in fact, had been trained intensively to disarm and defeat armed assailants. It was true, of course, that the putative highwaymen's failure to relieve Noyes of his studs, cufflinks, watch, and petty cash implied other motives, but seasoned investigators were quick to cite instances of experienced footpads leaving such minor swag behind them. But Cleveland police would have none of it; for them, the only possible motive for the crime had to be some unknown thread in the non-gambling, non-wenching, near-teetotaling young stockbroker's personal life. Maybe it was some disappointed stock speculator, they hinted to the gentlemen of the press, who had held Noyes responsible for his unfortunate investments—an inference for which the police had no evidence. And to Noyes's friends, who unanimously denied that he had any personal enemies, Detective C. E. Parker riposted for the department with a high literary flourish not commonly found in the annals of Cleveland's finest: "Neither Othello nor his friends were aware of Iago's villainy, and yet Iago secretly hated Othello and plotted to overthrow him. May we not entertain the possibility of a fear that this man had a secret enemy who plotted against his life?"

In lieu of a serious investigation, the citizens of Cleveland and Noyes's grieving family were treated instead to a fortnight-long festival of recrimination, name-calling, and petty spite from Forest City officialdom. Coroner Simon, convinced from the outset that Noyes was the victim of highwaymen, and backed up by county prosecutor Harvey R. Keeler, reacted scathingly to police criticism of his conduct of the Noyes inquest, which opened Tuesday morning, May 29. The *Plain Dealer* reported that, he was "doing his duty as he saw it and that if the police attended to their affairs as well as he, there wouldn't be so many murders in Cleveland." Chief Corner responded with further criticism of Simon's short witness list—Banks, Morrow, Bruder, Cleveland General Hospital house physician Henry Crumine, autopsy doctor Robert Williams, and Fayette Brown Jr.—and plaintive excuses that his investigation was hindered by uncooperative Social Register witnesses. "If Noyes was murdered by 'nabobs,'" he whined to a *Cleveland World* reporter, "and they keep their mouths shut there will be no possibility of apprehending the murderers." And his final comment, made at the conclusion of the inquest, might well serve as an epitaph for the Noyes case: "Either some people know a great deal about the case, or no person knows anything. We have questioned every person who was intimately acquainted with Noyes and we have followed every clew possible—and the mystery is as deep as when we started."

Not surprisingly, Corner and his men also insisted, against the testimony of all the other witnesses, that his patrol wagon and detectives had arrived promptly on the murder scene. To which captain of detectives Jake Lohrer added his glib two cents: the witnesses to Noyes's shooting—presumably Morrow and Banks—"should have made an effort to stop the escaping murderers."

THERE IS NO CLEW!

From the *Cleveland World*, May 26, 1900.

Corner's critics weren't having any of it. Noyes's grieving family—his mother, sister, and five brothers—was outraged by the refusal of the police to search for highwaymen, and architect Frank B. Meade, Noyes's oldest friend in Cleveland, spoke for them and all who cherished the dead stockbroker when he said: "It makes me mad that the police cling to the theory of murder from jealousy or revenge, when the evidence of a 'hold up' is so complete." Police director Michael F. Barrett excoriated the police protection provided Cleveland citizens as a "glittering farce," but placed the blame on scandalous civic underfunding, which caused some individual beat patrolmen to cover areas of up to six square miles. The *Cleveland World*, gleefully echoing Coroner Simon's public jeering, criticized Corner's handling of the Noyes investigation and unflatteringly paired it with a previous and comically botched manhunt:

> That a man with but one leg, but one hand, and with a defective eye should escape from the police after committing murder is one of the strange things connected with Cleveland's murder mysteries. Yet John Hulf, who killed his wife on Franklin Avenue, was so marked, and failure to capture him is a serious reflection upon the ability of the detective force.

To which Chief Corner could only reply: "The public is too quick to criticize, for we are doing our best." All that was lacking in this grotesque carnival of bureaucratic backbiting was a droll Gilbert and Sullivan song.

Within two weeks the Noyes murder quickly devolved from the consuming sensation of the day to just another of Cleveland's growing list of unsolved murder mysteries. Herbert Noyes was buried by his sorrowing relatives in an Evanston, Illinois, churchyard. The gawking crowds disappeared from the front of the Painter residence, where the bloodstains could still be seen for some time, and the investigation became dormant, infrequently flickering to life with fleeting and unsubstantiated theories that

Noyes had been murdered by a woman disguised as a man, or that he had been the unwitting target in a case of mistaken identity. No one ever found out who "Bertha" was, but "Mary" proved to be the name of the dead man's sister, and Dr. Hamilton Biggar eventually disclosed to police the name of the female whose picture Noyes carried in his watch—a Chicago woman of "considerable prominence," but with no connection to his murder. There was a brief flurry of excitement in Norwalk, Ohio, at the end of May, when young John Tenny, the son of a local minister, told his impressionable friends that he had witnessed the Noyes killing; a long session in the police "sweatbox" soon cured him of an overactive imagination. A year later, another supposed denouement ensued from a Chicago jailhouse confession of one Henry Kearney, a petty criminal who claimed that Noyes had been killed during an attempted robbery by one "Lightfoot." Lightfoot, alas, was not to be found or even clearly identified, and the attention of investigators dissipated as Kearney repeatedly changed his story and undermined his usefulness with multiple suicide attempts.

The Noyes murder had one last and very loud reverberation. On August 5, 1910, wealthy lawyer and socialite William Lowe Rice—a founder of Blandin, Rice & Ginn, the forerunner of Jones, Day, Reavis & Pogue—was shot, stabbed, and bludgeoned to death while walking home to his Cleveland Heights mansion on Euclid Heights Boulevard. The circumstances of his slaying were remarkably similar to the killing of Herbert Noyes, and his murder remains likewise unsolved. (The Rice murder is fully chronicled in the author's *They Died Crawling*.) As in the Noyes case, there was little evidence of a robbery attempt. There were also charges that the streetlights were out and details suggesting that the victim— likewise an amateur pugilist—had put up a terrific fight before falling to the street, not to mention an odd constellation of uncanny personal coincidences connecting the two almost identical murders. Rice's law partner was Frank H. Ginn, Herbert Noyes's old roommate from the Croxden and also the lawyer who handled matters for Noyes's Illinois family at the time of his killing, a role Ginn sadly repeated 10 years later for his friend and partner Rice. In an uncanny further connection, Judge E. F. Blandin, Rice's other law partner, who helped execute Rice's will, represented the Noyes estate in its successful fight with the United States Casualty Company. Coincidence? You be the judge.

Chapter 5

"WE ARE GOING DOWN!"

The Ashtabula Bridge Disaster

The world was a howling, smothering white wasteland that fateful night in Ashtabula. It was Friday, December 29, 1876, and for two days an intense winter blizzard had been pummeling the small country town, located in the northeast corner of Ohio, with up to 20 inches of snow and winds up to 55 miles an hour. Nevertheless, the town train depot was crowded and bustling that Christmas week evening, with some awaiting incoming trains and others about to depart. And the most anxious in the throng were those waiting for the No. 5 "Pacific Express," due in from Erie, Pennsylvania, on the Lake Shore & Michigan Southern railway. It was already two hours late, and the word was that it had not gotten out of Erie until after 6 p.m.

Things were more cheerful and relaxed on the No. 5 train. Drawn by two powerful locomotives pulling two express cars, two baggage cars, two passenger cars, one smoking car, and three sleeping cars, the No. 5 was chugging steadily through the white winter night at 10 miles an hour, its comfortable passengers oblivious to the frigid fury outside. Many of them were conversing or eating, some were playing cards, and yet others were nestled in their sleeping berths. Others prepared themselves for their imminent departure at Ashtabula or warmed themselves at the coal-fired Baker steam heaters that provided warmth to all cars except the smoker, which was furnished with an old-fashioned wood stove. No one afterwards could ever be sure, but there were at least 128 passengers and 19 crewmen aboard at 7:23 p.m. as the No. 5 roared onto the railway bridge spanning Ashtabula Creek.

Daniel McGuire, the engineer of the "Socrates," the lead locomotive, was the first to realize there was a problem. As he entered the bridge, he pulled the throttle out, increasing his train's speed to

Ashtabula Bridge design sketch.

about 12 miles per hour, the acceleration needed to drive the train through the two feet of snow on the tracks and the stiff, gale-force winds. As the "Socrates" approached the western abutment of the 154-foot bridge, McGuire suddenly had the terrifying sensation that his engine was "running uphill." Turning his head, he looked back and gaped in horror as he saw the rest of his train—the second locomotive "Columbia" and the 11 cars—falling with the collapsing bridge toward the creek, 82 feet below. Almost simultaneously, McGuire pulled the throttle out again, giving the "Socrates" a surge of power that broke its coupling with the "Columbia" and pushed it the last critical 80 feet uphill to the western abutment and safety. As he hit the brakes on the other side, McGuire heard a frightful crashing noise behind and below.

William Asell, a telegraph operator, was the first person at the depot, only 1,000 feet east of the bridge, to realize what had happened. Hoping to hitch a ride through town with the train, he had heard the whistle of the No. 5 as it entered the bridge and was walking toward it to see whether it was a passenger or freight train. When he saw that it was a passenger train, he turned around and began walking back to the station. Seconds later, he heard a terrible crash, and, turning around, he saw the lights of the sleeping cars as they fell and disappeared into the darkness below. He ran back to the bridge—and was thunderstruck to find that it was gone. Later that fatal night, he would notice that there was an engraved reproduction of Rembrandt's *Court of Death* on the wall of the train depot telegraph office.

The experience of the passengers and crew, of course, was far more dramatic and painful. Miss Marian Shepard, a survivor, remembered her first hint that something was wrong in her sleeper—the bell rope snapped in two, one piece smashing a whale-oil lamp and the other knocking over a burning candle. A split second later, she heard a bumping noise, as if the train had jumped the tracks and was riding on the wooden ties. Then there was a smashing noise, as if every piece of glass on the train had been shattered to smithereens at once. As all the lights went out, a voice cried, "We are going down!"—and there was a sickening falling sensation. As Miss Shepard braced herself, the air was suddenly filled with flying splinters and dust, as fixtures, seats, lamps, and human bodies were flung about the car, now falling fast, perpendicular to the ground. Seconds later—Marian recalled that it seemed like "two minutes"—her sleeper hit the rest of the No. 5 cars, already wrecked in the frozen waters of Ashtabula Creek.

Marian's experience in the smashed car was a typical one for the terrorized passengers still left alive in the ruined train. Surrounded by the dead who had been killed on impact, she struggled to get out of the dark car, stunned by shock and traumatized by the screams of the wounded. "Every one alive was scrambling and struggling to get out," she recalled. "I heard someone say, 'Hurry out; the car will be on fire in a minute.' Another man shouted, 'The water is coming in, and we will be drowned!'"

It was only too true. Most of the passenger and sleeping cars had fallen like upended dominos, stacked and smashed atop each other, with the bottom layer impaled on the broken ice of Ashtabula Creek. Within five minutes of the crash, the last car, its Baker heater broken but still burning, caught on fire. Dazed, bleeding people staggered out of the pulverized cars, and the winter night was illuminated by flames as, one by one, the No. 5 cars began to burn. Within 15 or 20 minutes, what remained of all 11 cars was a scorching inferno, triggered by the Baker heaters and fed by the train's oil lamps and thickly varnished woodwork.

Many of the survivors were unable to ever forget the terrible scenes they saw that night. As the survivors and rescuers from Ashtabula labored frantically to extricate the wounded and dead from the wrecked train, the flames inexorably moved through the cars, setting one person after another on fire as, foot by foot, their would-be rescuers were driven back. Ironically, at the same time, some of the wounded or trapped passengers were drowning, as the melting waters of the creek crept upward through the mass of bloody, burning debris. Some, perhaps mercifully, would drown before their bodies were thoroughly cremated. Daniel McGuire, who had stopped the "Socrates" 150 feet beyond the bridge and returned to render aid, remembered an especially pitiful sight. A woman trapped by debris screamed over and over as the flames moved toward her, "Take an ax and cut off my legs! Take an ax and cut off my legs!" No one got a chance to perform this awful service for her before she went up in flames and was burned to a crisp. A similar fate awaited a little girl who screamed, "Help me, Mother!" repeatedly as the flames claimed her. Her mother, who already had been pulled from a burning car, could do nothing but watch her child incinerated. Another child was luckier: passed overhead from man to man through a wrecked car, she was eventually handed out of a window to safety. In another case, six men, several of them badly wounded, labored heroically and successfully to free an extremely obese woman who was trapped in a sleeper. They could do little for Peter Levenbroe, the fireman of the "Columbia"; trapped and crushed under a quarter-ton of iron when his engine fell end down and flipped over on its back, he died on the way to a hospital in Cleveland.

The passengers of the "Pacific Express" were not alone in their torment for long.

William Asell, the telegraph operator who had seen the cars fall, immediately made his way to the wreck, half-running, half-falling down the steep, snow-covered hill to the burning railroad pyre. Kicking out windows, he began to pull wounded and often unconscious passengers out, desperately dragging them from the path of the flames. Meanwhile, engineer Daniel McGuire, having brought the "Socrates" to a screeching halt west of the bridge, sprinted the remaining 900 feet to the crowded depot with the terrible news: "Great God, the train is over the bridge, all but us!" A minute later, brakeman A. L. Stone, who had escaped from the last car, limped into the depot. He was hurt and bleeding but frantic that a telegram be sent to Erie in case another train was coming behind. Meanwhile, within minutes, every bell in Ashtabula was sounding the alarm for firemen and rescuers to come to the scene.

The progress of the fire, which ultimately killed more people than the initial crash, has been a source of acrid controversy ever since the moment the first tongues of flame sprang up in the rear car. Although the Ashtabula fire department managed to drag at least one engine down the difficult terrain to the fire, no hoses were ever connected to any available hydrants, and no water, except for a few random buckets of melted snow, was ever thrown at the burning wreck. It was rumored then and afterwards that Lake Shore & Michigan Southern officials, some of whom were on the train or at the depot, expressly forbade anyone to put out the fire. The reason, according to the rumor, was that the company's insurance liability would be less if the passengers were not only dead, but burned beyond recognition. There was no truth to the rumor, but it added a special nastiness to the nightmare of recrimination that followed. The less dramatic truth lay in the confused conditions at the unprecedented conflagration. When Ashtabula fire chief G. A. Knapp arrived at the scene, at least 45 minutes after the crash, he found a scene of pandemonium. (Knapp's personal perception was possibly affected by what a contemporary chronicler characterized as his addiction "to the constant use of intoxicating liquors.")

There was no organized effort to do anything: Passengers and rescuers were simply trying to save such persons as they could, harried as they were by fire, smoke, water, snow, and the difficult terrain. Efforts to deal with the situation were further impeded by hundreds of spectators who crowded the stone abutments above and thronged the panic-stricken spectacle below. Not to mention the activities of thieves, including some who boldly robbed the wounded and helplessly crippled passengers. The terror of those at ground zero was increased by a terrible snapping noise produced by the

HORROR UPON HORROR.

TERRIBLE RAILROAD ACCIDENT.

The Ashtabula Iron Bridge Broken

Eleven Cars and One Engine Plunge Seventy Feet Down Into the River and are Burned.

Sixty Persons Killed an d as Many More Wounded.

Description of the Scene.

PARTIAL LIST OF THE WOUNDED.

ASHTABULA, Dec. 29—8:50 P. M.—A terrible accident has occurred at Ashtabula. Train No. 5, bound West, went through an iron bridge, down seventy-five feet to the river. Eleven coaches went down.

From the *Plain Dealer*, December 30, 1876.

paint on the train cars as it ignited. Knapp looked around at the chaos and then asked the L. S. & M. S. station agent George Strong which side of the burning wreck he and his men were supposed to throw water on. On hand were 1,500 feet of hose that could be connected to hydrants from 1,000 to 1,200 feet away. Strong, mindful that the advancing flames were consuming more and more people even as they talked, replied that he "didn't want any water, wanted help to get people out." It was probably the right decision. By the time both fire apparatus and personnel were on the scene, the wreck—most of it compact in one sloppy stack of burning cars—was a fully engaged inferno. Without any effort to throw water, the firemen and bystanders concentrated all efforts on trying to pull the wounded from potential watery or fiery graves. No actual orders by Knapp, Strong, or any Ashtabula city officials were issued at the disaster site throughout that long, agonizing night. The fire eventually burned itself out, by morning leaving only a blackened mass of bent iron, festooned with scraps of burned baggage and human flesh.

It took almost a week to clean up the mess. Although railway officials quickly had 150 men on the scene to tidy it up and replace the bridge, they never did find or identify the bodies of everyone missing. The chief problem was no one actually knew how many were on the train; the conductor's records showed 128 passengers, but other observers claimed upwards of 200 were aboard when the cars went down. The best guess is that there were 89 killed and 63 wounded, of whom five died later. Nineteen corpses or parts thereof were never identified at all, which is just as well, as the opinion of contemporary spectators was that those found looked like "charred logs" or "Egyptian mummies." A temporary morgue was set up in the Lake Shore & Michigan Southern freight depot, where for several weeks sobbing relatives searched through rows of boxed human remains for their missing loved ones. Many of them could be identified only from earrings, rings, and other items of jewelry that had escaped the attention of thieves attracted to the disaster scene. After funeral services were conducted at two Ashtabula churches on January 19, 1877, the 19 unidentified dead were buried in nearby Chestnut Grove Cemetery. In the 1890s a movement sprang up to memorialize the victims, culminating in the dedication of an impressive 37-foot gray Vermont marble obelisk. Among those who donated to cover the cost were Governor William McKinley and Lucretia Garfield, widow of the murdered president.

The recriminations and investigations began while the fires were still smoldering in Ashtabula Creek. At 9 a.m. the day after the accident, an inquest convened under the authority of justice of the peace Edward W. Richards. Sixty-eight days and dozens of witnesses later, the jury reached a series of eight verdicts, all highly critical of both the Lake Shore railroad and the rescuers at the scene. The controversies generated by their findings still reverberate passionately 130 years later.

The inquest jury found the railway company entirely responsible for the accident, and the consequent deaths and injuries. The jury charged that the L. S. & M. S. had willfully designed, constructed, and erected a fatally flawed bridge and then failed to adequately inspect it over the next 11 years, leading to an inevitable disaster. Additionally, they found that the railway company, in direct violation of an Ohio law of May 4, 1869, had failed to heat its passenger cars "by heating apparatus so constructed that the fire in it will be immediately extinguished whenever the cars are thrown from the track." Lastly, the jury blamed fire department and railway officials at the disaster scene for many of the fire deaths, claiming that they should have concentrated on putting the flames out, rather than rescuing the trapped victims.

None of those accused of malfeasance took it lying down. The Lake Shore and Michigan Southern Railroad eventually paid off about $500,000 in damage claims with little haggling or dispute. But it refused to admit responsibility for the bridge failure, arguing from the first that the wreck was caused either by the "Columbia" leaving the track, a broken rail, or, even more implausibly, a tornado which swooped down to detach the bridge and swooped away again. Most vociferous in rejecting blame was Amasa B. Stone Jr., Cleveland millionaire and railroad mogul—the man who had designed and erected the fatal bridge. Until the day he died, he insisted that it was a sound bridge, flawlessly executed, and that it must have been human error or an act of God that took the "Pacific Express" and his bridge to their ruin.

Stone was wrong, but the truth was a little more complex than either side was willing to allow. The original L. S. & M. S. Ashtabula Creek bridge was a wooden one. In 1863, Amasa Stone made plans to replace it with a new design of his own. The key section was the middle span, a 154-foot section that sat on two stone abutments put up after extensive fill-in narrowed the river valley. It was a variation on the widely used Howe wood-and-iron truss, but Stone's radical redesign made it an all-iron structure, a type that had never been tried and, indeed, would never be replicated. The new structure, installed in the fall of 1865, was a series of 14 panels, protected against the force produced by the weight of the trains

Stereoscopic view of the wrecked train.

by enormous diagonal I-beams, 21 feet in length, which were
anchored by three-foot-wide bearing blocks. All of the steel for the
bridge was produced at the Cleveland Rolling Mill owned by
Amasa Stone's brother Andros. There were many difficulties
encountered in installing the bridge, and it had to be completely
taken down and put back up again at great expense. When Joseph
Tomlinson, an engineer working for Stone, cautioned him about
the stress on the trusses, Stone responded by firing him, a move he
later blamed on Tomlinson's "inefficiency." The bridge was finished in 1865, tested by the weight of six locomotives, and pronounced perfectly safe. The stage was set for the 1876 tragedy.

As a number of persons later remarked, the strange thing about
the fatal bridge was not that it eventually fell, but that it stayed up
for 11 years. It was inspected four times a year by L. S. & M. S.
officials, who reported no defects, except for an unexplained
"snapping" noise train engineers sometimes heard as they sped
over the bridge. Among the details missed by the inspectors, no
doubt, were the ends of the beams and lugs, where metal had been
crudely filed down to make them fit. The bridge was looked at by
Charles Collins, the engineer in charge of that stretch of the railroad, just 10 days before the calamity, and he found nothing amiss.
What he might have discovered, if he had gotten down among the
I-beams, is what Joseph Tomlinson saw when the ruined bridge

was lying on the ground 70 feet below two months later: Several of the diagonal I-beams were as much as three inches out of alignment at their juncture with the bearing blocks. Given that the essence of the bridge's design was the interreliance of all its parts, the displacement of the I-beams meant it was just a question of time before something terrible happened.

Charles McDonald subsequently conducted an examination of the tragedy for the American Society of Engineers. His study pinpointed a flaw in one of the large bearing blocks—probably a large, hidden air pocket produced in the casting process—that led to the failure of the supporting beams.

Stone would have none of it, and was his usual adamant, arrogant, and choleric self when interviewed by a special investigative committee of the Ohio legislature on January 18, 1877. Not only was the bridge safe, he insisted to his questioners, it was probably stronger than it needed to be. And as for the Baker stoves that set the cars afire in direct violation of state law, he blustered that he had examined some of the alternative patent stoves available and dismissed them as unsuitable. "My opinion," he stated to his respectful audience of Gilded Age legislators, "is that no stove could be provided which would extinguish its fire in case of accident." "I never shirk responsibility," he concluded, but his final opinion was that the train had simply jumped the track and smashed the bridge to pieces.

There was at least one Lake Shore official with a more tender conscience. Charles Collins, the chief engineer who had recently inspected the failed bridge, "wept like a baby" when he saw the human and material wreckage still smoking in the Ashtabula River valley. Although he testified in public that he had always thought the bridge safe, there were rumors that he had told a different story to his friends. One anecdote had him cynically remarking the year before, "If it goes down, I trust it will be with a freight and not with a passenger train." A more likely public statement was attributed to Collins in the wake of the tragedy, when he felt himself the target for all of the blame hurled by the public at the L. S. & M. S. officials: "Here I have been working 30 years for the protection of the public and now they turn right around and kick me for something which I have had nothing to do with."

Whether Collins actually said these things is debatable, but there is no question he took the bridge disaster uncommonly to heart.

Three days after he testified to the special committee, he was found dead in his bed at his residence at Seneca Street (West 3rd) and St. Clair Avenue. Armed with two pistols, he had blown his brains out by firing one of them through the roof of his mouth sometime in the hours just after he finished his testimony. The decomposed state of his body suggested that he had come right home from his ordeal and killed himself.

There were, fortunately, some positive long-term effects from the Ashtabula Bridge disaster. Although there was a brief flurry of agitation for more stringent regulation of railroad safety, nothing ensued immediately except some studies and recommendations authorized by the Ohio legislature. Eventually, however, the beginnings of government oversight, based in part on insights gained from the 1876 accident, were incorporated in the Interstate Commerce Act of 1887. In the meantime, moreover, railway bridge construction had taken a safer, more conservative turn, with most engineers relying on the more reliable Pratt truss. They may not have been impressed by the threat of government interference as much as they were by the half-million dollars in liability paid out by the L. S. & M. S. after the accident.

Destiny finally caught up with irascible Amasa Stone Jr., also. Although he fiercely disclaimed responsibility for the accident and avoided personal legal consequences for it, there is no question that he was hurt by public perception of him as a murderer. His temperament, never a happy one, soured further as ill health and business reverses pressed him harder and harder in the years after the Ashtabula disaster. By 1883, he had endured enough: On the afternoon of May 11 he locked himself in the bathroom of his palatial Euclid Avenue mansion and fired a .32 caliber bullet through his heart.

There is little trace today of the terrible events of December 29, 1876, in the Ashtabula River valley where it happened. The dirty river flows sluggishly under a modern and quite undistinguished viaduct, and it is almost impossible to envision that incredible night of pain, terror, and death. There is a man named Bill Yenne, though, who sees glamour where others might find just a boring landscape. According to his book *Hidden Treasure* (1992), the "Pacific Express" No. 5 train may have been carrying two million dollars in gold bullion that frigid December night. If so, it was all lost in the valley below, waiting still for the right person to find it.

Chapter 6

CITY HALL CADAVER

Robert Mercer's Unquiet Grave

"He knows where the bodies are buried." It's a common catch-phrase denoting an insider, usually with the police, city hall, or local newspaper, who knows, guards, and selectively exploits the secret details of suppressed but still lethal scandals and public mysteries. Many policemen, reporters, and politicos throughout Cleveland's colorful history have enjoyed the attractively lurid repute the phrase carries. But if anyone ever literally earned the compliment, it was Detective John T. Shibley. The illustrious Cleveland policeman scored many deductive coups in his score of years as a Cleveland sleuth, garnering merit for his work on such sensations as the 1909 Billy Whitla kidnapping, the 1920 Sly-Fanner payroll murders, and the 1921 Foote-Wolf double homicide. But his greatest feat, and the one that made him famous in his day, was his 1914 discovery of murder victim Robert Mercer—under four feet of dirt in the sub-basement of the new city hall on Lakeside Avenue.

There must have been some peculiar personal circumstances in the malign fate that brought Robert Everal Mercer to Cleveland in June 1913. Twenty-seven years old, Mercer was the only son of an illustrious Pennsylvania family. An ancestor, Hugh Mercer, was a famous Revolutionary War general who founded the city of Mercerberg and the Mercerberg Academy. Robert's deceased father, J. Carson Mercer, was a successful, respected Republican politician in Pittsburgh who served 15 years as an Allegheny County commissioner.

Adored by his doting mother, Jennie, and three married sisters, Robert had graduated from Mercerberg Academy and entered Lafayette College in his early twenties. But for reasons unknown, he left college after a year. By the time he showed up five years later

in

From the *Plain Dealer*, December 27, 1913.

Cleveland, Robert, despite inheriting generously from his father's estate, was working at what must have seemed casual labor for one with his ancestry. He was employed as a timekeeper by the Woodbury Granite Company, which was doing stonework on the new Cleveland city hall rising near the corner of Lakeside Avenue and East 9th Street. Robert spent his free time with fellow construction laborers who lived at the Mittleberger Hotel at Prospect Avenue and East 40th Street and frequenting the saloons, dives, and fleshpots of pre-Prohibition Cleveland. And by December 1913, only six months after coming to the Forest City, Robert Mercer already had a reputation as a hard-drinking fellow who tended to get ugly when in his cups.

There was, no doubt, another, softer side to the young, five-foot-nine-inch, 160-pound, smooth-shaven, dark-haired, and blue-eyed "Bob" Mercer. When he wasn't drinking, his friends found him amiable company, and there was at least one person, his Pittsburgh fiancée, a perfectly gorgeous girl named Alma MacMillan, who believed him the very paragon of personal charm and gentlemanly virtues. "Bob was a clean-cut, high-minded boy, he was pure of heart," is the way she liked to remember him. Sweethearts since high school, Robert and Alma had planned to marry the previous year but had delayed their plans when Alma's father died. But

Robert was coming home to Pittsburgh for Christmas 1913, and the two lovebirds hoped to marry soon after that.

That, anyway, was the story sweet Alma gave out later in the wake of the Mercer tragedy. Whether her hopes were realistic is yet another matter. During the last week of his life, Robert Mercer didn't act much like the Christian knight of Alma's description. Hard-drinking, and habitually somewhat irascible the morning after, Robert was fired by his foreman on December 16 for uttering "vile words" to an architectural inspector at the City Hall building site. Agreeing to stay on for another four days to train his successor, Mercer continued the pattern of his boisterously thirsty evenings through the week. And although it was well known that his mother Jennie and Alma expected him for Christmas Day dinner in Pittsburgh, Robert told his best friend John Cooper that he wasn't going home for the Yuletide.

Robert Mercer's last day of work ended at four o'clock on the afternoon of Saturday, December 21. As soon as he punched out on the clock, Mercer repaired to the office of the James L. Stuart Construction Company, a temporary structure at Lakeside Avenue and East 3rd, where there was a poker game in progress. The other players, all laborers on the new city hall, included John Cooper, William Boettjer, John Maurer, Ernest Linden, Herman Pennstrom, and the night watchman, 23-year-old Norman Stanley. There was quite a lot of whiskey going around the table, and Mercer, it was later recalled, imbibed his usual generous share. He also managed to lose a hefty portion of his Christmas present from Jennie Mercer—a $100 roll that he frequently flashed on that long afternoon. For five hours he drank, lost, and became, as was his wont, increasingly sullen and ill tempered. As his friend John Cooper would recall, "Saturday nights were always his bad nights."

About 9 p.m., Mercer left the Stuart company office and walked over to Herbert Strauss's saloon at Ontario Street and Lakeside. There, Mercer continued to imbibe, diminish his bankroll, and increase his distemper. Everyone in the joint, it seems, was buying bottles of champagne at $4.50 a pop, and at least seven or eight bottles were consumed during the next three hours. Some time during that period Philip Oakes and George Stanley (no relation to Norman) came into the saloon with a pet fox terrier, boasting at length about its ability to perform various amazing tricks. The woozy

Mercer, taking offense for unknown reasons, argued with the two men about the dog. Eventually, he flashed what was left of his roll and offered to buy the dog. The men refused and left. Mercer returned to his drinking in company with Norman Stanley, John and Fred Cooper, Harvey Sheets, and several other men who had fled the poker game for more powerful diversion.

MERCER'S BODY UNEARTHED AT NEW CITY HALL

Police, Urged by Mother, Find Body of Missing Youth Under Two Feet of Dirt.

MAN WHOSE BODY IS FOUND AT CITY HALL

BELIEVE HIM MURDERED

Declare Suspect Who Has Disappeared Buried Body to Hide His Crime.

The body of Robert E. Mercer, young timekeeper on the new city hall construction work, who mysteriously vanished Dec. 21, under suspicious circumstances, with more than $1900 worth of jewelry on his person, was found Wednesday noon buried under three feet of dirt in the southwest corner of the new municipal buildings.

The discovery was made by workmen, acting under instruc-

ROBERT F. MERCER.

From the *Cleveland Press*, February 4, 1914.

The evening's merriment broke up when the Strauss saloon closed at midnight. Purchasing a case of beer and a quart of whiskey, Mercer left the saloon with Norman Stanley and Peter Kalig, the saloon porter. By this time Mercer had apparently quarreled with Stanley for reasons never divulged, and Kalig and Stanley carried the beer up Lakeside to the Stuart company office, while Mercer sulked and skulked along the opposite side of the street. Kalig left Stanley and Mercer together at the office, however, and saw them go inside. It was the last time Robert was seen alive—except by Norman Stanley . . . or his murderers.

Stanley's story, told in unvarying detail during innumerable interrogations and "sweatings," was that he and Mercer began to play penny-ante poker when they returned to the office. They drank a couple of bottles of the beer, and then Stanley left the office about 1 a.m. to check and clock in at various points throughout the extensive city hall construction site. When he returned 20 minutes later, Mercer was gone. He had left his handsome fur coat behind on a chair, but he did not return during Stanley's shift that cold December night. Nor did he go back to his room at the Mittleberger Hotel. His friends, like John and Fred Cooper, simply assumed that he had decided to keep his Christmas day dinner date with Jennie and Alma and thought no more about it.

Four days went by. When Robert failed to show up for dinner, Jennie Mercer got in touch with John Cooper, who was in Pittsburgh to see his own family. Learning that Robert had not returned to his hotel after December 20, Jennie called Alma, and the two women took a train to Cleveland that same night. The next day they began an agonizing search for the missing son and lover. During the next 48 hours, working without sleep or food out of a hired touring car, they searched every hospital bed, jail cell, morgue, and funeral home in Cleveland. They found nothing, not even the merest trace of Robert Mercer, after he left the Stuart office at 1 a.m. that frigid Sunday.

Jennie and Alma also went to the Cleveland police. Although the latter were uniformly sympathetic to the silver-haired widow and beautiful Alma, their pessimism about finding Robert was soon borne out by a complete failure to learn his whereabouts. After all, they reasoned with the devastated women, Robert Mercer was the 247th "missing person" in Cleveland for the year 1913—and the police had yet to turn up a clue as to any of the other 246 disappearances.

And so the days went by, the police sincerely went through such motions as they could perform, and Alma and Jennie went back to Pittsburgh, convinced that Robert had met with foul play. They posted a $500 reward for information about Robert's whereabouts, but Jennie was already convinced that Robert was dead. The more optimistic Alma held to the theory that he had been "drugged" and was being held somewhere against his will. Cleveland police detectives John T. Shibley and C.W. Norton, who had charge of the open case, promised to stay in touch with Jennie and Alma.

Detective John Shibley.

Shibley did much more than that. Although the carefully cultivated legend about the Mercer case has been considerably romanticized, it is nevertheless true that the mystery would have remained unsolved without Shibley's stubborn persistence. The legend is that Mrs. Mercer, after her return to Pittsburgh, was haunted by persistent dreams—dreams in which she saw her son's body buried in the sub-basement of the new Cleveland city hall. The grief-stricken mother immediately informed the Cleveland police—who, understandably, initially refused to act upon the spectral "evidence" of her pathetic nightmares. Except, of course, for the doughty Shibley, who promised Jennie Mercer that he would follow up on her hunches, even if he had to do it on his own time. Which he did, astonishing his peers and all of Cleveland by finding the murdered man in the very spot suggested by Mrs. Mercer's macabre dream. The *Cleveland News* pithily summarized the Mercer myth in its February 4 story about the case:

> Premonition? Intuition? She didn't try to classify it or go into its psychology, but she knew her son had been murdered and buried in the cellar of the city hall at Cleveland.

The actual truth was a bit more mundane, if still high tribute to Shibley's keen investigative instincts and dogged persistence. Jennie Mercer had been back in Pittsburgh for three weeks when, on January 26, Charles Roof, the day watchman at the city hall site, confided to deputy city building inspector Ora Coltman his suspicion that night watchman Norman Stanley had murdered Mercer and buried the body in the sub-basement. Coltman mentioned this tidbit to Stuart company construction superintendent A. Fred Walther, who in turn told Shibley a few days later. Shibley moved fast. He knew that the dirt sub-basement floor was soon to be covered with cement, and he got on the telephone to Pittsburgh. Two days later, Jennie Mercer was in Cleveland, insisting to everyone, especially newspaper reporters, that her beloved son's body would be found in the sub-basement. When she even offered to pay the cost of the excavation, Cleveland police chief William S. Rowe caved in, and inspector Norman Shattuck scheduled the dig for Wednesday, February 4.

Once begun, the grisly search, conducted by the flickering light of gasoline torches, did not take long. After a trial dig was made in the sub-basement's northeast corner to ascertain how long it might take a murderer to dig and fill in a grave, Shibley ordered his digging crew to the northwest corner. After probing with steel rods to find any loose pockets, crew chief Andrew Calabrese found one. At about noon the men attacked the area with their shovels; within minutes, four feet down, they turned up a wood scrap, then a piece of cloth. The next shovel of dirt exposed a human arm and then the body of Robert Mercer. Wrapped in a shabby coat, Mercer lay on his back. His right arm was bent over his face, which was turned left. His left arm was over his head, extended as if to ward off a blow. Attired in the dark gray suit he was last seen in on December 21, Mercer still sported his diamond tiepin, his gold cufflinks, a large diamond ring, a diamond stickpin, and a monogrammed silver belt buckle. The billfold in his pocket contained a number of business cards and five letters from Alma and Jennie. The gold watch in his pocket had stopped at 4:13. John Shibley took the bad news to Jennie Mercer, who had waited patiently in the Stuart Company office. She shuddered once and returned to the Mittleberger Hotel to begin arrangements for Robert's Pittsburgh funeral.

Robert Mercer's autopsy, performed that evening by Dr. Wenzel Medlin, established the cause of death. Although bruises and a small skull fracture indicated that Mercer had been beaten, Medlin located a bullet wound just above the left breast. The .32 caliber bullet had entered there, between the second and third ribs, passed through the apex of the heart, ranged downward through the diaphragm, drilled the liver and left kidney, bounced off a rib, and come to rest in the lower back muscles. The path of the bullet wound suggested that Mercer had been lying down or crouching when he was shot. Medlin assured the grieving Jennie Mercer that her son had been dead when he was buried, although there were morbid and lingering suspicions that his killer had buried him and then fired a slug into the soil to make sure he was dead. Twenty-four hours after his body was found, Jennie took Robert to Pittsburgh in a mauve casket to his permanent home.

RESISTS PLAN TO TAKE STANLEY TO SCENE OF MURDER

STANLEY BEFORE JUDGE

From the *Cleveland Press*, February 6, 1914.

There was never any question about a prime suspect. Norman Stanley, the night watchman, was the last person known to have seen Mercer alive. He was also responsible for noticing what went on at the building site, so it was inevitable that he would become the focus of investigation when Mercer's corpse turned up there. The police had already talked to Stanley on December 27 for several hours, at which time he had given them the fur coat allegedly left by Mercer at the Stuart office. In fact—additional evidence that the police knew far more than they admitted—warrants to pick up Stanley had been out several days before Mercer was exhumed. He had quit his watchman's job in mid-January and returned to his parents' house in Wheeling, West Virginia. Lieutenant George Matowitz, a future Cleveland police chief, caught up with Stanley at his parents' Wheeling home only 12 hours after Mercer was found and arrested him in the wee hours of February 5. Stanley initially tried to hide in the attic but, when flushed out, denied his guilt and agreed to return to Cleveland without formal extradition. That night he entered a Cleveland jail cell, repeatedly blustering his innocence ("My arrest is ridiculous and absurd!") but refusing to add any details to anxious police or hungry reporters.

Stanley was fortunate in his choice of legal representation. John A. Cline, a former county prosecutor, was a veritable junkyard dog in the zealous defense of his clients. His partner in Stanley's case was William E. Minshall, another capable lawyer, who was at the beginning of a distinguished career that would be capped by his many years as a member of the U. S. House of Representatives. They decided the best defense was a good offense, and they never let up from the moment they took on Stanley's case.

The police claimed to have overwhelming evidence of Stanley's guilt, but the inquest, which opened Friday, February 6, proved otherwise. Coroner P. J. Byrne furnished the details of Mercer's careful autopsy but refused to speculate about his killer, stating only that it was "death by a bullet fired by a person or persons unknown to me." A parade of witnesses from the Saturday evening card game at the Stuart office and the drinking party at the Strauss saloon added nothing to details already known to any avid reader of Cleveland newspapers. Before the inquest was over, Jennie Mercer herself announced that she believed Stanley had nothing to do with her son's death.

The police countered that they had the murderer, the motive, and the murder weapon on hand. It was well established by inquest testimony that Stanley and Mercer were quarreling on the night of December 21 and that Stanley was the last person seen with Mercer. It was also known that Mercer had possessed a big roll of cash, yet only a single penny was found on his body. Stanley, on the other hand, had borrowed $5 from Fred Cooper that Saturday night yet apparently had ample cash the next day. Moreover, the records of the time clocks Stanley had punched on his 1 a.m. round suggested the night watchman had been in one hell of a hurry—a hurry to get back to the sub-basement and bury the body of Robert Mercer, the police argued. And if it wasn't Stanley, they argued, who else could it have been? Stanley, after all, was the night watchman, the only one with unfettered access to the sub-basement during the period when the body was probably buried there. Even the case of undrunk beer was presented as telling evidence against Stanley; Mercer's cousin George argued that the consumption of just two bottles was highly suspicious:

> When Bob was drinking he would not let up on a case after only two bottles had consumed. When I talked with [Stanley] he told me that he and Bob carried the case of beer into the building at 12:05 o'clock on the morning on which Bob is supposed to have been killed . . . The fact that the two had drank only two bottles of beer . . . caused me to become suspicious.

Wrapping up their case, the police produced the murder weapon, a rusty Harrington & Richardson .32 pistol Lieutenant Matowitz had found and pocketed while searching the Stanley house in Wheeling. They also had several bullets taken from Stanley's pocket at the time of his arrest, which they insisted could have been fired from his weapon. It was true, the police admitted, that the ancient and damaged gun could not be fired by pulling the trigger. But their firearms experts, W. C. Andrews and Colonel Hubert J. Turney, assured the court that the fatal shot could have been discharged from the gun by pulling back the hammer and letting it fall. Summarizing the evidence against Stanley, Shibley said, "The two were there. One of them is alive. The other was found buried in the city-hall sub-basement. If Stanley didn't do it, no one did."

By the time matters moved to a subsequent hearing before Municipal Judge George P. Baer, the police case was unraveling. Cline and Minshall were in fine, fulminating form, and they delighted reporters and the many spectators with forensic fireworks aplenty. Beginning with the corpse, they challenged the basic assumption that the body found in the sub-basement was that of Robert Mercer. That tactic accomplished no more than delaying the proceedings while witnesses who had viewed Mercer's remains were rounded up, but Cline and Minshall quickly moved on to other matters. Denying that some suspicious spots on Stanley's coat were bloodstains, they eventually got City Chemist Wilbur

White to admit in court that he couldn't identify the origin of the spots. In any case, Cline jeered, Stanley had a perfectly good excuse for the stains, a thumb injury that he had already told the prosecutors about.

Cline and Minshall reserved their heaviest artillery for Detective Shibley and his peers. Charging that Stanley had been the victim of a merciless "third-degree" procedure, Cline accused police of torturing his client because they wanted a "goat" to excuse their inept investigation of the Mercer case. It was incredible, Cline screamed, what the cops had done to his client: denied him access to his lawyers, kept him up at all hours for endless grilling sessions, moved him around from room to room to increase his fatigue and disorientation, and even shouted epithets like "Murderer!" and "Liar!" at the frightened Stanley. As a former and skilled county prosecutor—Cline had handled the probing, if futile inquest into the 1910 murder of William Lowe Rice—he doubtless knew that such techniques were standard procedure in virtually all police departments, whatever the publicity given out to the contrary. But that didn't stop him from screaming in highest outrage at Shibley: "You are willing, are you not, to hang that boy if your reputation as a detective can be sustained?"

Although Cline and Minshall had a high old time flaying their opponents, Judge Baer decided on February 11 that there was enough in the charges against Stanley to turn him over to the grand jury. Although it was true that there was no direct evidence against Stanley, the circumstances—he was the last one seen with Mercer and had unfettered and unseen access to the burial site—told heavily against him. Judge Baer also provided the sole moment of comedy in the acrid, drawn-out proceedings. Noting that he had decided to completely ignore the expert testimony about the condition of the alleged murder weapon, he picked up the rusty weapon . . . and pulled the trigger, quite easily, to the astonished laughter of the courtroom audience. At the same time, however, Baer discounted Shibley's damaging admission, forced from him on the witness stand by the aggressive Cline, that gun expert Turney had actually told Shibley, after looking at the weapon, "You may have the bullet and the man, but not the gun."

Neither County Prosecutor Cyrus Locher nor Cline and Minshall knew it, but the investigation into Robert Mercer's death had already climaxed. Beginning on February 17, the grand jury went over the evidence produced by the inquest and the hearing before Judge Baer but added little to the relevant evidence. The prosecution's gun experts eventually testified that Stanley's rusty pistol could not have been the murder weapon, and virtually everyone agreed that the night watchman's conduct after Mercer's disappearance was inconsistent with a guilty conscience. Meanwhile, Stanley remained in jail, proclaiming his innocence and repeating the sober avowal he had made to Matowitz at the time of his arrest: "Drink was the cause of it all. If I ever get out of this, I'll never drink again." His gun and the stains on his coat were retested—with the same results—and both Shibley and Cline had .32 pistols fired in the city hall sub-basement to see if the reports could be heard in the Stuart Company office. (They could not.) Finally, at noon on Thursday, March 5, 1914, the grand jury voted a no bill on Norman Stanley, and he was free after a month in jail.

No one ever did figure out who killed Robert Mercer and buried him at the bottom of architect J. Milton Dyer's Beaux Arts civic monument. Jennie Mercer returned to Cleveland for a few days of sleuthing after Stanley's release because one of her daughters had a dream about three men killing and burying Mercer in the sub-basement. There were continual rumors that there was a woman mixed up in the case—rumors partially fueled by the faded picture of an unknown female that turned up in Robert Mercer's billfold—but nothing ever proved out on that line. Seven months after Stanley was released, Miss Cora Marble, a self-described Cleveland detective, garnered brief headlines with her tale to reporters that she was trying to solve the case. She was said to be aided in her efforts by Norman Stanley, who was conducting his own investigation. Nothing came of all this, and most of the principals in the Mercer case disappeared from the public limelight forever, save for John T. Shibley. Seven years later he resigned from the Cleveland Police Department to become the head of security for the Cleveland Trust bank. He gave them good service, most famously with his apprehension of Fred Colladay, who attempted to cash a $48.50 check, a document that the enterprising Colladay had altered to read $26,148.50. But in the public memory none of Shibley's feats in the private sector ever eclipsed his discovery of Robert Mercer's corpse in the new city hall. He didn't solve the case, and he may—just may—have fingered the wrong suspect. But he sure knew where the bodies were buried.

Chapter 7

MEDINA'S WICKEDEST STEPMOTHER

The Garrett Tragedy

Stepmother. There are few words in the English language—perhaps none denoting relationship—with more negative overtones. It's one of those unfortunate nouns that unfailingly arrives with the explicit or implied modifier of *wicked* attached. And, whether brought to unquiet mind by the indelible archetype of Hansel and Gretel's nemesis or the Disneyfied image of Snow White's witch/queen, the mere word itself—*stepmother*—seems to have the evil power to evoke shudder-inducing stereotypes and irrational judgments. The next time you hear the word, though, you'll likely consider the tragic tale of Mary Garrett and her unlucky stepdaughters. Maybe Mary Garrett was the wickedest stepmother in Medina County history. Maybe she was as bad as the judge, jury, and public thought she was—and she was probably pretty bad. But one can't help concluding, after sifting the bizarre evidence, that Mary Garrett came chillingly close to an Ohio hangman's noose really because of that fatal word—*stepmother*—which clung to her like a bad smell.

There seems little to be known about Mary Garrett until the mid-1880s, when the then Mary Heffelfinger, a fortyish widow from Tiffin, Ohio, met and married Alonzo Garrett, a 63-year-old widower and farmer from Carlisle Township, Lorain County. The daughter of a Kentucky slaveholder, the plump and prepossessing Mrs. Heffelfinger brought two daughters from her first marriage to her new union: Anna, 16, and Elnora, 11. Alonzo, for his part, brought a grown son and daughter, neither living at home, and, more importantly, two imbecile daughters. The elder daughter, Anna, 44, was at least several years older than her new stepmother,

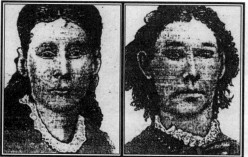 

The Victims: Anna and Eva Garrett.   The Accused:
Mary Garrett.

and her younger sister, Eva, was about 28. Although both Anna and
Eva had been institutionalized in state facilities for the feeble-
minded at various times, they were both living with Alonzo at the
time of his remarriage and had kept house for him for several years.
Mary Garrett, astonishingly, would later claim that she did not
know of the existence of Anna and Eva until the day she married
Alonzo. If her assertion was true, she probably also didn't know
that Alonzo's first marriage, to his cousin, almost 50 years before,
had produced yet another imbecile daughter who died in infancy.
In any case, whatever she knew and whenever she knew it, two
years after Mary and Alonzo's marriage in September 1885, the six
members of the Garrett family moved to a 101-acre farm in
Spencer Center, Medina County, just a half-mile south of Dun-
lock's crossing on the Wheeling and Lake Erie road.

The Garretts' neighbors in Spencer soon sensed that all was not
harmonious with the new family living on the old Kramer homestead. Mrs. Garrett made it brutally clear even to strangers, neighbors, and hired hands that she could not abide her adult stepdaughters, Anna and Eva. The two girls were constantly belittled by their
father's new wife: put to work at incessant manual chores like
chopping firewood, toting water, and digging garden plots; prohibited from eating at the family dinner table; forced to live on slops;
and made to wear clothes that amounted to little more than filthy
rags. Restricted to sleeping in a small 7-by-13-foot room, a converted kitchen at the back of the house, Anna and Eva were denied
shoes even when at their gardening tasks, as evidenced by the ugly
scars the metal shovel left on their feet. And when they weren't
slaving away at menial household work, they were often forced to

stay in their bedroom from 3 or 4 in the afternoon until 9 or 10 in the morning. More ominously, as the summer of 1887 waned toward autumn, Mary Garrett could more and more often be heard saying things like "I would give a nice colt to anyone who would help me get rid of these girls," or even, after Alonzo apparently reneged on a promise to send the girls away, "If the old man goes back on me there will be another corpse in the home before night." As November arrived, tensions in the Garrett household had clearly achieved critical mass—and on the night of Tuesday, November 1, that mass exploded in terrible tragedy.

The Garrett mystery proper began at 11:30 p.m., when W. D. Dimock, the Garretts' nearest neighbor, on a farm about 1,000 feet away, was awakened by shouts. Peering out the window, he saw Anna and Elnora Heffelfinger. They screamed something about their house being on fire and disappeared into the night. Pulling his clothes on, Dimock awakened his adopted son, Harry Warner, and the hired man, Anthony Nicholas, and the three men rushed to the Garrett house. As they departed, Dimock's wife, Annie, was already ringing their heavy farm bell to spread the fire alarm throughout the Medina countryside.

DEAD IN THEIR BEDS.

Brutal Murder of Two Poor Girls in Medina County.

A Bonfire Started in Their Sleeping Apartment and Both are Suffocated to Death—Their Unnatural Stepmother Accused of the Crime and Everything Points to Her Guilt—A Sensational Case at Elyria—Other Neighborhood News.

MEDINA, O., Nov. 2.—[Special.]—The people of Spencer, this county, were aroused from their usual quiet and. hundrum existence today by the startling information that during the solitude of the night two harmless and unfortunate creatures, to whom a sound mind and clear intellect had been denied, were cruelly murdered by a vicious and. inhuman stepmother. Your correspondent was the first newspaper man on the grounds, and the following are the facts as

From the *Plain Dealer*, November 3, 1887.

The scene Dimock and his companions found at the Garrett place was a strange one. Although they could smell smoke, there was little visible flame coming from the one-and-a-half story house, and Dimock and his companions were astonished to find most of the heavy furnishings and household goods—tables, chairs, a stove, a melodeon, a sewing machine, a new rug, and numerous other items—neatly piled on the front lawn. Indeed, while Alonzo ineffectually wept, raved, and wrung his hands, Mary and her daughter Anna were bringing yet more items out. Taking in the scene, Dimock shouted, "Where's the fire?" The elderly Alonzo was hysterical and could only reply, "Put out the fire! Put out the fire!" But Mary, altogether self-possessed, pointed to the small southeast bedroom at the rear of the house and said, "I am afraid that those girls are smothering in that room." Staring at Mary with her hands full of household items, Dimock sensibly replied, "My God, save the girls and let the house go to the devil." Then, dashing through the front door, Dimock got to the rear bedroom and pounded frantically on the door. Finding that it was locked from the inside, he tried to kick it in. His first kick smashed the lower panels, and his second knocked the door right off its hinges. Running inside, he quickly emerged with the lifeless body of Anna Garrett. Seconds later, Anthony Nicholas brought Eva's corpse out, and the two bodies were laid on the grass outside. The fire, such as it was, was soon extinguished with a surprisingly small amount of water.

There were many oddities to that horrific midnight scene at the Garrett house, and everyone present seems to have remembered them vividly at the eventual trial. One peculiarity was the odd far-rago of items on the lawn, virtually all the heavy furniture and most prized belongings of the Garrett household. Another odd thing was the fatal fire room itself: the blaze had burned very little of the walls or floor. More suspiciously, there appeared to be a quantity of kerosene spilt on one corner of the floor and a great mass of rub-bish strewn about the room: leaves, rags, lint, newspaper, broken boards, dirt, and a pile of partially burnt paper.

The story that Mary Garrett told her neighbors that night was the story her lawyers repeated in court and the same story she stuck to for the rest of her life. She claimed she had been awakened about 11:30 p.m. by a noise coming from the barn. Thinking it was the mischief of a fractious horse, she dressed herself and went out to investigate. Finding nothing amiss at the barn, she decided to return by way of the back garden fence to check on some clothes left there on a clothesline. (In November?) It was then that she smelled and saw smoke coming from the window of Anna and Eva's back bedroom. She pounded on the window, but it was locked. Getting no response, Mary rushed inside the front door of the house, only to find the inner back bedroom door likewise locked. Rousing Alonzo and her own daughters, she sent Anna to spread the alarm, and she and Alonzo began throwing small buck-ets of water at the outside bedroom wall. To anyone who asked why she had not persisted in trying to save her trapped stepdaughters, she insisted that she thought they had already escaped from the burning bedroom.

Neither her neighbors nor the Medina County authorities liked

Mary Garrett's story very much. The evidence of flammable litter and kerosene in the bedroom strongly suggested arson, and the presence of the household valuables on the lawn—apparently placed there before the fire started—suggested criminal premeditation.

Only one more piece of evidence was needed to put Mary Garrett in a murderer's cell, and it came when the bodies of the two dead girls were closely examined by Mr. Dimock and B. F. Lewis, another Garrett neighbor who had arrived to put out the fire. Both stepdaughters had died of suffocation, specifically carbon monoxide inhalation, and Anna's lower body was badly scalded, so much so that the burned skin came away at a touch. In addition, Anna had a terrible bruise on her forehead and another one on her side. Most shocking, however, was the appearance of her throat: Clearly visible around her neck were the finger marks of two hands, indicating that she had been strangled before the fire started. Before daylight on November 2, Lewis and Dimock telegraphed Justice Lyman Daugherty in Medina and requested that he come to hold an inquest into the suspicious deaths. It began at 10 a.m. the same day with six jurymen, two doctors, a crowd of witnesses, and Justice Daugherty presiding. At its conclusion 24 hours later, Mary Garrett was arrested on charges of arson and murder.

After an official, painstaking postmortem examination of the girls on Thursday afternoon, and a brief funeral service held for them at the house on Friday morning, November 4, the girls' remains were taken back to La Porte, Ohio, for burial in the Garrett family plot. Meanwhile, at the jammed Spencer town hall, Mary Garrett, to the audible pleasure of the "suffocating" crowd, was arraigned on counts of first-degree murder and arson and ordered away to the county jail in Medina. Her request for bail was abruptly brushed aside by Justice Daugherty, who replied with this bit of rural folk wisdom to a *Cleveland Press* reporter's query, "This affordavit sez murder in the first degree and I ain't goin to go agin' it. The appropriate court can tend to the bail matter." Mary was spirited out of the courtroom immediately, in part because of rumors that a lynching would be attempted by the unruly, partisan crowd. Her dignified composure broke only once, as she realized, while leaving the courtroom, that her husband, Alonzo, shared the popular conviction that she was guilty. Laying her head on his shoulder, she murmured, "Did you agree to this, husband?" Receiving no answer, she entered a plea of "not guilty" and was led away. To a *Cleveland Press* reporter who inquired as to his thoughts on his wife's guilt, Alonzo said, "Oh, I can't say, I can't say. But I have my opinions." In a move perhaps more eloquent, Alonzo advertised his farm and goods for sale a few days later. Meanwhile, Spencer residents were left to reflect and to recover from the unprecedented crowds and attention the Garrett tragedy had brought to their modest town. Justice Daugherty probably spoke for all with his characteristically folksy comment, "Well, that's the blamedest, everlastin'est, most amazin' crowd I ever see. Why, boys, I'll bet a dollar there were more'n 400 people in that little room. Beats all, don't it?"

After several weeks of delay and maneuvering, Mary's trial was scheduled for the May term of 1888. By then she had secured seemingly astute legal representation in the persons of E. G. Johnson of Elyria (already famous throughout Ohio for his 1887 defense of "Blinky" Morgan), J. H. Dickson of Wellington, and the firm of Bostwick & Barnard of Medina. A further delay, however, became unavoidable when it was discovered that the accused murderess was in a "delicate condition." Delivered of a healthy baby boy in July, the new mother was sufficiently recovered to allow for the opening of her trial on Monday, September 17, 1888. Opposing her defense team were prosecutors J. W. Seymour, John C. Hale, and Frank Health, with Judge G. W. Lewis presiding.

The state's case against Mary Garrett was simple and directly presented, with a large cast of talkative supporting players. A parade of eyewitnesses described the strange goings-on at the Garrett home on the night of November 1, with particular emphasis on the localized scope of the fire, the presence of the household goods on the lawn, and Mrs. Garrett's eerily calm demeanor throughout the excitement. More witnesses, many of them neighbors and friends of the family, testified to Mary's hatred and ill treatment of her stepdaughters from the moment they came into her life, and to the many occasions on which she had expressed a fervent desire to be rid of them. Various witnesses detailed the repeated attempts she had made over the two-year period of her marriage to have divers state, county, and private charitable institutions take the girls off her hands. One such scheme involved a veritable abduction of the witless girls to the county poorhouse during the previous summer while their father was away. Another was Mary's mendacious attempt to place Anna at the Home of the Good Shepherd in Cleveland (later the temporary abode of "Lakewood's Lady Borgia," Eva Kaber, during her erring adolescent years) on the premise that

Anna, then in her forties, was a "fallen" girl likely to again go astray. It was an awful picture of perverted maternal treatment and neglect painted by the prosecutors. The defense did little to counter it, other than call a couple of witnesses to deny that they had personally seen any maltreatment.

The cumulative and disturbing details of Mary's systematic cruelty to Eva and Anna no doubt told heavily with the jury. But, after all, the state's charge was not that Mary Garrett was a bad stepmother but that she had maliciously and with premeditation committed "arson, strangulation, scalding, and suffocation" as a means of ridding herself of the girls. The evidence on record, however, shows that the state did a lousy job of proving that any of those acts occurred, much less presenting any direct evidence that Mary Garrett planned and perpetrated them. The jury, for example, never even visited the scene of the alleged murder. If they had, they might have laid more emphasis on the fact that the death-room door and windows could be locked only from the inside. How could Mary Garrett have set the fire and then escaped through the door or window? The prosecution never addressed the issue, relying on Mary's heavily documented and unspeakable conduct toward the girls to carry its case forward.

The evidence of the dead girls' corpses, moreover, added little strength to the state's case, despite an exhumation and second autopsy performed in December of 1887. As the defense claimed, the scalding below Anna's hips was likely caused by the action of the fire on the water that Alonzo and Mary were throwing at the blaze. Anna's two bruises were inconclusive as to their origin, and as for the finger marks on her throat (as Mary's attorneys attempted to prove with expert testimony by Dr. E. G. Hard), they could well have been the marks of Anna's own hands, the result of her death struggle as she frantically fought to get air into her lungs. The fire itself, attorney Johnson argued, was started by the girls themselves, who had locked the door and window in order to play with matches unobserved. Although they were not allowed to have a lamp in their room, he reasoned, they must have smuggled in some kerosene without the knowledge of their stepmother. The leaves, which had done much to feed the fire, were explained as Anna and Eva's attempt to make a bed for their cat.

There was that suspicious matter of the furniture on the lawn, which the trial testimony did little to explain. Some of the witnesses claimed that it had been removed to the lawn prior to the fire to facilitate housecleaning; others claimed that Mary and her children spent most of their time on that fatal night moving out more furniture rather than trying to save Anna and Eva. Even if the latter was the case, it would support only a charge of criminal indifference, rather than premeditated murder.

The state rested on Wednesday, September 26, and Judge Lewis soberly and carefully charged the jury of 12 men, mostly farmers. Lewis properly dwelt at length on the question of what constituted premeditation and on the need to afford Mrs. Garrett "the benefit of every reasonable doubt." He was also appropriately cautionary about the enormous volume and value of the hearsay testimony that had done superb service in the blackening of Mary Garrett's character during the trial: ". . . no class of testimony is more unreliable, and a more frequent cause of error in courts of justice than the narration of conversations real or pretended."

MRS. GARRETT IS PARDONED.

Woman Who Committed Double Murder in 1888 Given Freedom.

Set Fire to Room in Which Two Step-Daughters Were Sleeping.

Mrs. Mary Garrett, one of the most noted women prisoners in the Ohio penitentiary at Columbus, was pardoned yesterday. She entered the prison Oct. 5, 888, under a sentence of death, but her sentence was commuted to life imprison-

From the *Plain Dealer*, December 26, 1899.

Mary's jury retired at 3 p.m. the same day and returned after only five hours with a verdict of guilty on both the murder and arson counts. A week later, on October 4, Judge Lewis sentenced Mary to death by hanging. As ever, Mary maintained her remarkable composure through both her verdict and sentencing ordeals, and during her subsequent journey to the Ohio Penitentiary in Columbus to await execution. In the privacy of her cell there, however, she unburdened herself by letter to her estranged husband:

> "God only knows I am clear. I ain't afraid to die. I pity my family, poor husband lonely and no one to care as I did. I want him to look for the children . . . I am going to meet those I did not abuse.... I can stand all. God is my strength, help in all. I glory in his name. I am wronged here. I am rewarded in heaven, I feel it."

Several weeks later, Alonzo Garrett filed for divorce.

The date set for Mary's execution was January 24, 1889, but no one ever expected her to actually hang. No woman had ever been executed by the state of Ohio, so no one was surprised when Governor Joseph Foraker commuted her sentence to life imprisonment in late January. Typically, because it was a capital case involving a woman, the petition for executive clemency was signed by Judge Lewis, the prosecuting attorneys, and all 12 of her jurors. By this time Mary had settled pretty well into the rhythms of life on death row, the same special annex in the Ohio Penitentiary where Blinky Morgan had spent his final days, and she was so taken with Warden E. G. Coffin that she named her baby boy, christened Warden Garrett, after him. (This despite the fact that Coffin was quoted in print characterizing Mary as "a dangerous and wicked woman," and expressing his opinion that "she was no doubt guilty.") Following the commutation of her sentence, Mary was removed to the female prison wing and began her fight to win freedom and clear her name. Her son Warden was returned to his father's custody in Medina County in January of 1890, after more than a year of life in prison with his mother.

Mary's "life imprisonment" lasted but 12 years. After her lawyers' motion for a new trial was denied by the circuit court, she and her few supporters began a vigorous campaign to obtain an executive pardon. Their ranks gradually swelled, and by 1895 even ex-warden Coffin was working on behalf of Mary Garrett's release. She won that release in December of 1899, when the governor of Ohio granted her a pardon as a Christmas present and she returned to a life of obscurity and, one hopes, happiness.

So, the question remains: Did Mary Garrett do the deed—did she deliberately set her stepdaughters' bedroom on fire as a means of getting rid of the unwanted girls—or did she not? Well, there's no question that, whatever the varying veracity of the many gossipy witnesses at her trial, Mary Garrett never would have been named Medina's Mother of the Year. Beyond the shadow of a reasonable or unreasonable doubt, she treated her stepdaughters worse than animals, greatly assisted and enabled, it should be mentioned, by the doormat complicity of her doddering mate, Alonzo. But it's very improbable that she murdered them with malice aforethought. Harriet L. Adams of Cleveland, who worked mightily in the successful campaign to free Mrs. Garrett, put the case for her innocence persuasively in a letter to the *Cleveland Leader* published just after Mary's release from prison. Commenting on the circumstances of the fire, Adams noted:

> As the room was small and the one door and one window closely fastened, there was not sufficient air for the fire to burn readily,

but it finally charred a space about three feet long and one and a half feet wide on the floor and burned through the baseboard, thus getting between the walls and burning a few small holes in the siding outside. That was the entire extent of the fire. . . . To be brief, no human agency could have set this fire but the girls themselves. The door was securely fastened from within by sliding bolt and the window by shutters with drop catches on the inside. . . . I am confident, from an interview with the foreman of the jury in the case, that had the defendant's counsel taken the jury to the scene of the supposed murder there never would have been a conviction.

Two minor points are worth mentioning before bidding adieu to the story of Medina's worst stepmother. The first is that we don't know just how "feeble-minded" or retarded Anna and Eva Garrett really were. Mary herself termed them impossibly "idiotic" and "imbecile" and claimed they were incorrigible, untrainable, and virtually unhousebroken. Her martyred comment to a *Cleveland Leader* and *Herald* reporter was, "God alone knows what a trial those girls were to me, with their terrible tempers and vicious habits. Language cannot describe it." The testimony of the Garrett neighbors at Mary's trial, however, consistently portrayed the unfortunate girls as "slow," "stammering," and "fluttering" but tractable and of mild disposition. The other matter is the reason Mary Garrett claimed she barred the girls from the family dinner table: Like many superstitious people of her time, the pregnant Mary believed that her coming child might turn out "ugly" if its mother were continually exposed to the faces of her "ugly" stepdaughters while in her delicate condition. But whatever the true nature of the doomed girls or the complexity of Mary Garrett's maternal motives, it is hard to protest the fate that brought her 12 years behind bars after everything she did to her suffering stepdaughters. She may not have been an actual murderess, but it seems she got what was coming to her anyway.

Chapter 8

STAND BY
YOUR MAN

The Joe Filkowski Story

You could call Joe Filkowski a lot of things. His contemporaries, both admiring and not, didn't stint on names for this memorable 1930s Tremont-area gangster. In his formative years as an incorrigible juvenile delinquent and neighborhood bully, his bad complexion earned him the sobriquet of "Pimples" Filkowski. He graduated from childish petty thefts to the more adult concerns of armed robbery, auto theft, and murder, and acquired nicknames befitting his eventual status as Cleveland's Depression-era Public Enemy No. 1. By 1930, surely his prime year, he was luridly known to newspaper readers as "The Phantom of the South Side," "The Jefferson Hill Tough," "The Sheik of Literary Avenue," "The Powder-Puff Bandit," and "Smiling Joe." True, some called him a "love thief" and "yellow," most especially Cleveland's Finest, whose standing orders regarding Joe were to "shoot first and then ask questions." Call him what you will: Any sober assessment of Joe Filkowski's improbable career must lead to the conclusion that he was the luckiest hoodlum who ever called Cleveland home.

For those soft-souled readers who believe people are depraved because deprived, Joseph Filkowski was a textbook paradigm. One of the 13 children born to an unstable, violent slum family (three sets of children born to various and ephemeral parents), Joe grew up in the Jefferson Avenue/West 5th area overlooking the Flats. His father was killed in a lumberyard accident while he was an infant; his first stepfather committed suicide. A wild, surly youth, Joe was weaned on the temptations of the grimy dance halls and poolrooms of his native turf and began his recorded criminal career in 1914, when he and his brother were arrested for stealing air rifles and BB ammo from a grocery store. Two years later, he was caught stealing six bicycles from a Flats boxcar; a subsequent theft of 2,000

Joe Filkowski mug shots.

pounds of copper from a B. & O. boxcar that same year earned him a stretch in the Mansfield Reformatory. Paroled in 1918, he robbed John Butler of $41.50 on Fairfield Avenue on December 28. That charge was no billed by a sympathetic grand jury, but stealing Neal Anderson's automobile on January 26, 1919, brought him back to Mansfield. Paroled in 1921, he returned to Mansfield that same year on yet more boxcar and auto theft raps. Out in 1923, he whiled away the tedium of freedom with a couple of 30-day terms in the Cleveland workhouse (for auto theft and license plate alteration) before his arrest on August 20 for stealing H. W. Herriman's automobile.

The 24-year-old Joe was by now a hardened career felon, and it was inevitable that he would take things to a higher level. That came on January 12, 1924, while he was free on appeal of his sentence for stealing Mr. Herriman's car. Anthony Bublo, a bank security guard, was shot to death during an attempt to capture a gang robbing Walter Fedrick's butcher shop at 2515 West 10th. Before he died, the 25-year-old Bublo identified the triggerman as his childhood chum and schoolmate Joe Filkowski. When the grand jury refused to indict Filkowski for the murder, the irate county prosecutor, Edward C. Stanton, insisted that Joe serve the full six years of his impending theft sentence.

Joe publicly swore that he would "get" Stanton for such vindictiveness. But subsequent events proved that he had some reason to be grateful to the implacable lawman. While in the Ohio Penitentiary, Joe met a number of the experienced criminals with whom he would later work to spread a reign of terror among the merchants and payroll couriers of Greater Cleveland. More concretely, he used his labor stint in the penitentiary's license-plate plant to become an acknowledged expert in the illegal alteration of automobile plates.

Joe's public career really began in 1930, just after his April 15 release from prison. He got together with Charles Frisco, a hoodlum he had met in prison, and Joseph Stazek, a childhood friend from his Tremont days. The trio laid plans for a series of brutal, lucrative stickups. By the end of 1930 they were known as the "Flats Gang," and their criminal activities were the envy of their peers, a mocking reproach to the police, and a feast for sensation-addicted newspaper readers.

Joe began his reign as gangster chief, oddly enough, with a solo job. On the afternoon of June 6, 1930, contractor Anthony Veryk was distributing a $1,500 payroll on the fourth floor of an apartment under construction at 10017 Lake Avenue. He was nearly finished when a gunman entered and demanded his satchel of money with the words, "Hands up!" Joe Filkowski gave no warning: when Veryk momentarily hesitated, Joe shot him fatally in the chest, grabbed the satchel, and fled west in his car in a hail of bricks thrown by Veryk's outraged laborers. That night, the cautious Joe burned the car in an isolated area of Broadview Heights to destroy any lingering fingerprints. But the senseless killing of Veryk would come back to haunt him.

On June 9, the Flats Gang launched their corporate work—and never looked back. That evening they broke into the John Meckes & Son department store at West 25th and Lorain, bound and gagged the watchman, and escaped after blowing the safe. Several minor street robberies and safe jobs followed, interrupted by Filkowski's involvement in the murder-robbery of a Buffalo garage owner. His return to Cleveland was announced by a stickup of the Piper Brothers Shoe Company on October 4; nine days later, the Filkowski trio robbed jeweler Einar Abrahamsen of his wares as he was leaving his West 25th store. On November 3, they robbed, bound, and gagged sewer contractor Sam Amata in his automobile in the Flats; 18 days later they slugged Dr. Louis C. Kintzler of $40 at Broadview and Pearl.

The best was yet to come. On November 24, Filkowski, Stazek, and Frisco held up the Capitol Clothing Company at 6317 St. Clair. It was a routine job—but two nights later they committed the first of the crimes that would make them the rancorously hunted prey of the Cleveland police. About 6 p.m. on Thanksgiving eve, in the middle of a blinding snowstorm, the trio entered the Dixie Shoe Company. While ransacking the register, Charles Frisco, the lookout, saw patrolman Harry Keating outside. He alerted Joe, who hustled Keating inside with a gun to his ribs, stripped him of his uniform, badge, and gun, tied him up, and—no doubt laughing in his notoriously high-pitched, hoarse voice—put a wastebasket over Keating's head as they were leaving the store with their loot. The hapless Keating was exonerated of blame in the affair, but the wastebasket was the kind of thing the Cleveland cops would never forget.

Not that Joe and his friends were allowed to slip their minds for long: Two days later the threesome hit the Chandler & Price Company on payroll day to the tune of $8,100. Rubbing it in even more, Joe's men hit the Commonwealth Oil Company at West 3rd and Jefferson Avenue—right in the middle of "Smiling Joe" Filkowski's well-known stomping grounds—on December 3.

Joe didn't know it, but his luck was about to take a downward swing. As if his blood feud with the police were not enough, he was about to create an additional enemy who would prove to be an even more deadly nemesis. George Kekic, of 2467 West 5th Street, an unemployed factory worker and sometime bootlegger, had grown up with Joe Filkowski on the rough streets of Tremont. Both had been smitten by the charms of a girl named Mary Stazeki, a schoolmate about five years younger than Joe and a half sister of fellow gangster Joseph Stazek. George had married Mary and fathered two children, eight and two years old. But the bloom was off their romance by December 1930, as George discovered when he came home on the afternoon of December 5 to find his childhood pal making love to his wife Mary.

George didn't take the news of his wife's defection well. Maybe the marriage had failed; maybe, as Joe later claimed, George beat Mary and made her life hell. But George felt bad about it, and just how bad he felt was revealed the next night, when Joe returned to his hideout home at 861 Jefferson. Acting on a tip by the disgruntled husband, the Cleveland police had a squad of heavily armed men waiting inside as Joe turned the handle on the side door at

11:45 p.m. As he pushed it open, Detective Edward Trsek jammed a .38 into his ribs and said, "Hands up!"

Joe Filkowski liked to boast that he could "draw a revolver faster than you could wink." He proved it that moment, reaching for his gun even as his left hand obeyed Trsek's command. As the door opened up, Joe whipped around with the gun and fired it at the surprised Trsek. The detective pulled the trigger of his .38 as Joe started to run away, only to find that he had left the safety on. As Joe ran by the side windows of the house toward the back fence,

Detective Walter Keary fired both barrels of his shotgun through the closed windows at the fleeing Filkowski. He missed Joe but managed to cut Trsek badly as the pursuing detective was showered by falling glass. Filkowski leapt for the back fence and ran to West 14th. There he commandeered a car at gunpoint and forced driver Anthony Abraham to "drive like hell" over the Central Viaduct to the East Side. At 657 Broadway, Joe jumped from the automobile and disappeared.

To say the least, the Filkowski fiasco on Jefferson Street was a major humiliation for the Cleveland police. Keary and Trsek were busted to West Side patrol beats, and

Filkowski at bay.

the word came down from the top that Filkowski and his gunmen were to be shot on sight. That draconian policy paid off well, at least initially. The next afternoon police picked up Charles Frisco at a house on Tremont Avenue. A few hours later—on the night after Joe's Jefferson Street escape—the police, acting on a tip that may have been furnished by the angered Kekic, staked out the second-floor apartment of Edward Stazek, father of Filkowski henchman Joseph Stazek, at 2061 Monroe Court. Detectives Patrick McNeeley and William Dempsey were waiting for Stazek, and when he opened the door they blasted him with three slugs to the head, chest, and abdomen. His father, forcibly detained and thus a passive witness to his son's execution, just silently turned his face away as they loaded his son's corpse into the police ambulance. Two days later the police picked up Mary Kekic, who had fled to Detroit just about the time Joe disappeared over the back fence.

From the *Cleveland Press*, April 29, 1931.

She claimed she knew nothing about his whereabouts, but the police didn't believe her.

Cleveland chief of police George Matowitz's "shoot first" policy bore bitterer fruit on December 9. Thinking he had spotted the pockmarked fugitive at East 65th Street and Carnegie, Detective Patrick McNeeley, fresh from the killing of Joseph Stazek, followed a young male down to East 55th Street and Euclid Avenue. Although he later admitted the man did nothing suspicious, McNeeley peremptorily shot the man to death, under the impression that he was "Smiling Joe" himself. He was not: McNeeley's innocent victim was Joseph Fortini, a 22-year-old *Plain Dealer* circulation man who just happened to be in the wrong place at the wrong time. McNeeley was quickly found guiltless by his superiors in the awful mishap and returned with renewed hatred to the quest for Filkowski.

As if to imply that he wasn't impressed by the intense manhunt—all Cleveland detectives were working 12-hour shifts—or the loss of Frisco and Stazek, Joe returned to his wonted activities at his old pace. On Sunday, January 4, 1931, Cleveland patrolman John Maple noticed something amiss with the license plate of an automobile parked on Superior Avenue. A closer look revealed a 1930 plate that had been clumsily altered to resemble a 1931 tag.

Dogged inquiries revealed that the car belonged to a recently arrived roomer at 10816 Superior, a young man named "Charlie" who only went out at night and intimated to his landlady that he was a Prohibition agent engaged in hush-hush investigations. "Charlie," of course, was really Joseph Filkowski, and he was already on his way out the back door of the building when a shotgun-wielding squad of police showed up. No one was demoted this time—Chief Matowitz characterized the episode simply as an "unfortunate occurrence"—but once again the elusive "Smiling Joe" had made the police look like idiots.

They didn't feel any better about it, no doubt, when Joe and a companion hit the City Savings & Loan Company on Hayden Avenue for $3,100 five days later, and the Belkin Neckwear Company at 710 Prospect Avenue for about $5,000 worth of loot a few days after that. Not that Joe's life was unalloyed success and joy: at the end of January compatriot Charles Frisco was sentenced to a life term, thanks in part to the testimony of George Kekic. By now Kekic had also revealed to the police some of his erstwhile friend's indiscreet confidences about the Veryk killing, and the police had a desirable Murder One charge to add to their Filkowski file.

After the Belkin Neckwear job, Filkowski seemed to vanish from the streets of Cleveland. Or so the police thought. In fact, Filkowski, long concerned about the recognizability of his bumpy, misshapen nose had decided to do something about it. In late February of 1931, he entered the Cleveland Clinic for a nose job. Operated upon by an unsuspecting Dr. William V. Mullin, Joe stayed several weeks in the comfort of the hospital while the dragnet swirling outside it sought one of the most publicized faces in Cleveland. He had a few close calls: He came out of the ether murmuring "Mary! Mary!"—the name of his illicit paramour—and he would later claim that he shared a room for 45 minutes with Prosecutor Ray T. Miller. Subsequently, his new beak was well publicized in the Cleveland newspapers, much to the chagrin of the humiliated police. But such exposure was not all to the good, for both the reporters and the police, unable to find him, took to publicly goading the sensitive Joe. Attacking his masculinity, they took to calling him "The Powder Puff Bandit" and accused him—retailing scurrilous stories provided by a vengeful George Kekic—of eluding the law by masquerading as a woman in powder, rouge, and dresses. As he told a credulous *Press* reporter:

"Two weeks ago I saw Filkowski in women's clothes in a small
coupe at Professor Avenue and Literary Road. He was hatless.
He'd had his hair marcelled. Joe was wearing a dark dress. His
face was powdered and roughed and his lips were painted bright
red. . . . Joe is a powder puff bandit; he always carries a powder
puff because of his strawberry nose. He's yellow. I'd like to run
across him."

Maybe it was because of the taunts, maybe it was in retaliation
for George's treatment of Mary. (Joe would always maintain that
George beat and mistreated Mary.) She had been hiding somewhere, probably Detroit, with Joe for most of the first nine months
of 1931, and George filed child neglect charges against her when
she returned to Cleveland in September. (Interestingly, Mary's
legal defense was handled by Edward C. Stanton, who had apparently forgiven Joe's 1924 threat to "get" him and who didn't inform
the authorities of a little consulting visit Public Enemy No. 1 paid
him in the fall of 1931).

Whatever his motivation, Joe surfaced with a vengeance on the
night of October 17. In the wee hours he broke into George Kekic's
home at 2467 West 5th Street and made his way to the room where
George was sleeping with his son and two-year-old daughter. The
enraged "Smiling Joe" smashed a gun butt across George's forehead and screamed, "Take that, you ----!" Apparently, George had
been educated in the same tough school as Joe, for as he pushed the
baby away from his pillow, he reached underneath and pulled out
a pistol. Both men shot simultaneously, both missed in the darkness, and Joe fled out the door. George got off another round
through the door, and he heard Joe scream "He got me!" as he ran
out of the house.

No one knew it, but the Filkowski Reign of Terror in Cleveland
was over. Even as Mary was put on probation, Joe healed from his
back wound at a Webb Road speakeasy and then left for a new
career in Chicago. Apparently he did pretty well there, especially
after Mary joined him and provided her wonted comforts. Once
again, though, his luck ran out, just as he and a crook named Morris Cohen were about to rob the Liberty Trust and Savings Bank.
But the Chicago police yet had lessons to learn from their Cleveland peers. As Joe was accosted by Chicago detectives Harry Land
and Harry Miller outside the bank, he got the drop on them, level-
ing no fewer than three guns at the surprised lawmen. He and Mor-

ris took them several miles away and turned them loose without their guns. Chicago had become too hot for Joe, and he and Mary decided to go for the big time in New York City.

Two months later, Joe Filkowski was captured by a large squad of Cleveland and New York detectives as he walked down West 47th Street in New York City in front of the Hotel America. Entrapped by a bogus correspondence with Cleveland detectives Patrick McNeeley and Bernard Wolf, who convinced him they were stolen jewelry "fences," Joe had set up a meeting with them at the Hotel America, just a block from Times Square. They spotted him from their stakeout at the Hotel Somerset coffee shop, and they wrestled the desperate gangster to the pavement a minute later in front of hundreds of amazed spectators. Joe's take on this downturn in his fortunes was typically insouciant and differed remarkably from that of his captors. He claimed he had been brutally beaten: "How the hell was I to know what them dicks were doing? They come up behind me and grabbed me. I thought it was a stickup. You never know about this town."

A physician's business card in Joe's wallet soon led them to his Long Island gangster lair, where they found Mary Kekic, an "arsenal" of guns and ammo, and $100,000 in stolen diamonds. As the newspapers happily reported, Mary stoutly insisted the guns and gems were her sole personal property. Joe, for his part, was dressed for his apprehension in a wardrobe even James Cagney could not have faulted: a new gray suit, a light gray fedora, and a blue double-breasted overcoat. Even in captivity, it was noted almost admiringly, he still had his widely publicized swagger and an angry insistence that the reports of his makeup and wardrobe of women's clothes were widely exaggerated: "What do you think I am? A sissy? I never did anything like that. You got a lot of nerve asking me a thing like that. I'm no sissy. I never had to hide behind a woman's skirts."

He didn't get a chance to hide behind Mary's. She wasn't kidding when she said, "I'm no squealer," and she was packed off to a two-to-four-year term at New York's Auburn State Prison on a charge of possessing stolen jewels the week before Joe's murder trial opened on April 11. His lawyers, Maurice J. Meyer and Walter S. Plotrowicz, did their best, but they didn't have much to work with. Two of the laborers who saw Anthony Veryk gunned down identified Joe as the triggerman, and a third, Oliver Raeder, although initially uncertain, exclaimed "Sho! That's the man!" when County

Prosecutor Frank T. Cullitan made the six-foot Filkowski stand up in the courtroom. Joe was visibly unhappy about having to identify himself, and his palpable resentment deepened as witness Louis Kelly described him as "looking like he just came from a beauty parlor" as he fled the Veryk murder scene.

Joe repeatedly took the Fifth Amendment regarding his numerous robberies, and the best counterwitness the defense could offer was Charles Silver, who swore Joe wasn't the man he saw running from the Veryk murder scene. The jury was probably more impressed by anonymous threats made against two of the prosecution's witnesses. They may also have noticed the unprecedented security measures taken with Joe, who was surrounded in court by seven burly deputies with more guarding the doors. As expected, Joe Kekic testified with special relish against his former friend.

Joe himself did not make a good impression, testifying on April 15 in what hostile reporters described as a "high-pitched, hoarse voice . . . a little boy's voice coming from a six-foot muscular man." The climax came the next day, as Prosecutor Cullitan made his last, impassioned pitch to the six-man, six-woman jury: "This dirty dog despoiled the wife of his best friend. . . . Human life is a precious thing. Joseph Filkowski, when you put a gun against the body of poor Anthony Veryk and pulled the trigger hurling him into eternity unprepared and unshriven, you usurped the power of God with your dirty hands!"

The sensitive Joe couldn't take it anymore. Leaping to his feet, his face twitching and his eyes streaming with tears, he shouted at Cullitan, "You—you're guilty—more guilty than I am!" Maurice Meyer tried to repair the damage, noting that he had once prosecuted the state's chief witness—George Kekic—for rape and asserting that his client was simply paying the price for so long and so successfully humiliating the Cleveland police:

> "A man can't go to the electric chair to satisfy the whims of the Cleveland police department. The police bungled the Veryk murder like they bungled so many other murders but they should not take their unsolved crimes from the mystery book and pin them on Joe Filkowski. The state is out for blood. They want their pound of flesh. The police got mad at Filkowski because he made fools of them, but death should not be the penalty for making fools of the police department."

From the *Cleveland Press*, December 8, 1930.

The jury went out that afternoon and returned after two hours and 45 minutes with a verdict of guilty of first-degree murder—with a recommendation of mercy. Two days later Judge Frederick P. Walther sentenced Joe to life in the Ohio Penitentiary, with an additional condition that he spend every June 6—the day he killed Anthony Veryk—in solitary. Joe expressed amazement that he hadn't been found innocent and was packed off to Columbus under heavy guard.

A betting man might have wagered that this was the penultimate chapter of the Joe Filkowski story, and that he would soon end up on a slab like John Leonard Whitfield, the daring 1923 Cleveland cop killer whose abortive 1928 prison escape ended in a fatal blast of gunfire. If Joe didn't, it wasn't for lack of trying. An incorrigible prisoner, he participated in no fewer than three plots to break out of the Ohio Penitentiary. The first came in 1934, when Joe and Howard Beauman, another lifer, conspired to blast their way through the wall with seven or eight other cons. It was a harebrained, dangerous scheme involving lots of nitroglycerin, an underground tunnel, and the help of Howard's psychopathic brother, an escapee from Lima State Hospital for the Criminally Insane. It came to naught when a visitor to the prison found an elaborate cryptogram that, when decoded, gave away the plan. Shots fired by a prison guard on the night of February 28, 1936, halted an attempted breakout over the wall by Filkowski and two accomplices, armed with improvised knives and fake pistols made from machine-shop metal. A similar plan ended in fiasco in December of that same year, when an unsympathetic fellow prisoner alerted prison authorities by setting his bed on fire at the critical moment. The odds on Joe dying in prison or trying to get out of it just kept climbing.

But the years went by . . . and then something wonderful, something amazing and almost unbelievable began to happen. George Kekic had divorced his faithless wife Mary in the wake of Joe's trial, and when Mary got out of Auburn State in the mid-1930s she discovered she was still in love with "Smiling Joe" Filkowski. She wrote to him in prison and told him to go straight, and, after seven years, he began to change under her affectionate suasion. The years went by, and Joe left one parole hearing after another a disappointed man, but Mary never gave up. While he was learning a new trade as a first-class baker in the prison kitchen, she nagged each succeeding governor of Ohio on Joe's behalf. Warden Ralph Alvis was the first man of authority to believe in Joe's rehabilitation, and he made him a trusty, eventually allowing him to work on the construction of the new prison in Marion.

Astonishingly, Mary's perseverance and Joe's authentic regeneration paid off. On April 15, 1963, Joe was released from prison after serving 30 years, 11 months, and six days. Three months later, on July 6, 1963, Joe and Mary were married at St. John Cantius Catholic Church in Tremont, within sight of his childhood haunts and the scenes of his bloody deeds. The Phantom of the South Side had at last been tamed by something even stronger than his guns or the law: the enduring love of a good woman.

Chapter 9

A SHOT IN THE DARK

The Rayner Tragedy

The past—with its antique "good old days"—is always closer than you think. It's especially true in Cuyahoga County. Although it was settled more than two centuries ago, most of its inhabitants long lived lives little changed from early pioneer days. A century ago, the Heights area just east of Cleveland was just beginning its suburbanization phase, while the area to the west of the city was still mainly a district of farms and empty land. Men and women still living could recall Native Americans in the area, and the automobile was not yet supreme in the townships, villages, and hamlets that began where Cleveland ended at West 117th Street. And for all the talk of newfangled modernity, you could still see sights little removed from the earliest days of the Western Reserve.

The scene on Lorain Road at Kamm's Corners on the night of August 27, 1910, presented just such a premodern tableau. Just before midnight, a string of horses drawing wagons wearily plodded westward along Lorain Road, in front of the Rockport racetrack, 150 yards east of Kamm's Corners in the village of West Park. It was a caravan of market garden farmers, residents of Rockport, Dover, and points west, returning home from a long Saturday selling their produce at the West Side Market (located on West 25th, but across the street from its present location). In the lead was Earl Dunford, a Dover florist, driving a covered van drawn by a single horse. About 100 feet behind him were Walter J. Rayner, his wife, Clara, and their eight-year-old daughter, Blanche, riding in a wagon with a canvas top drawn by two horses. About 100 feet behind the Rayners came a rig carrying Miss Mabel Dunford and a friend, followed by farmer Merrill Snyder, his wife, and two children making up the rear guard. It was a tired group, most of them exhausted from the day's bustling toil, with little to divert them

Place on Lorain-av where highwaymen murdered Mrs. Rayner.

Walter Rayner, husband of slain
woman.

Scene and victims of Rockport murder and hold-up.

other than the clip-clop of the horses' hooves and the passing scene
visible in the meager light shed by the lanterns that swung from
each wagon.

The trouble came without warning. Just as Earl Dunford's lead
wagon got to the race track, two shadowy male figures leapt out
from the left (south) side of the road. One grabbed the head of the
rig's horse, while the other poked a revolver at Dunford and said,
"Halt. Give us your money!" But Dunford wasn't in the habit of
giving in so easily. Grabbing his reins, he flailed them violently,
and the animal wrenched its head free and began to gallop away.
Dunford heard the sound of a revolver firing behind him, and a bullet smashed into the side of his wagon. He spurred his rig forward,
westward toward safety.

Although he couldn't see what was going on 100 feet ahead,
Walter Rayner heard the gunshot. Alarmed, he began to turn his rig
around, just as the two men came abreast of his wagon, their guns
drawn. Apparently they didn't even try to rob him; no one could
later remember either of them saying "Halt!" or demanding money.
But as Walter came out of the turn, they started firing and continued their fusillade of bullets as the Rayner rig, accelerating with
every second, pulled away eastward. Suddenly, Clara Rayner, who
was sitting next to Walter, groaned and slumped against his side.

"Did they hit you?" he asked. "Yes!" she replied in a choked voice. It was her last word; a second later blood gushed from her nose and mouth, and she died from the bullet that had smashed into her side just below her left shoulder blade and entered her heart. The next thing Walter remembered hearing was his daughter Blanche's voice as she sobbed, "Daddy, my foot hurts!" Looking down, Walter saw that she had been shot in her left leg, just above the ankle. It was only later that he realized she would have been killed if she hadn't been dozing with her head in his lap. One of the horses, too, had been shot, in the flank.

Frantically whipping his team, Walter brought his rig to the house of his brother-in-law, August J. Herrington. Carrying Clara and Blanche to the porch, he pounded on the door until he aroused the household. As Walter carried his dead wife to a bed in the front room, August was already calling Rockport mayor W. W. Nichols, town marshal William Stocker, and Cuyahoga County sheriff Gus Hirstius. Within 15 minutes, citizen posses of "minute men," a policing concept encouraged and developed by Hirstius for the rural townships, fanned out over the far West Side in search—"dead or alive"—of the mysterious, murderous highwaymen.

THIS SHOWS HOW MRS. RAYNER WAS MURDERED

From the *Cleveland Press*, August 29, 1910.

Sad to say, Hirstius's "minute men" seem to have created more sound than light that fearful night. Combing the roads and fields on foot, on horseback, and in automobiles, they stopped and interrogated quite a number of people. But the only suspect they turned up was a 19-year-old half-wit named Harry McDougall, found sleeping in a nearby barn.

The authorities didn't know it, but the clues that would ultimately lead them to their prey were already in their hands. Among the reports that reached Sheriff Hirstius and Marshal Stocker that long night were five incidents that they failed to put together in a coherent criminal theory. The first was a reported barn burning at the home of Ellis Herrington, another of Rayner's in-laws, on Herrington Road on August 26, the night before his wife's murder. Two apparent tramps had requested permission to sleep in his barn and when ordered off the property had set it on fire in retaliation. The second incident occurred the same night, also near Ellis's house. Two men, after unsuccessfully attempting to rob Myron Hughes of Columbia Station, had fired a shot at him, drilling his top hat but leaving him unhurt. The third involved two men seen driving a surrey, "aimlessly and recklessly," on Lorain Road about an hour and a half after the murder. The fourth was the theft of a dark bay horse and rig from the home of Chris Christiansen on Riverside Road, not far from the murder site. Apparently stolen about 1:30 a.m., only 90 minutes after the murder, the horse and rig were found about dawn at Fred Minot's saloon at West 104th Street and Lorain. Pinned to the seat of the surrey was a note that read: "This rig belongs to a man on the Riverside Road." It was signed, "Two pals."

The fifth incident was related to the police on August 28, just hours after the killing. Charles Herrington, a member of the posse looking for the killers (and yet another Rayner in-law), was accosted by two men about 3 a.m. near Bosworth Hill (about West 117th Street and Lorain). Seemingly quite drunk, the two men asked Herrington if he knew where they could get a drink. He noticed the horse seemed nervous and said, "Horse balky?" One of the men slurred in reply, "He's drunk, as drunk as we are," and drove off toward Cleveland. Later—too late—Herrington would identify the rig found at Minot's saloon as the same one driven by the two drunken men. There were some who thought the various strands of this veritable Rockport crime wave might be connected. But they were shouted down by others, most prominently county detective James Doran, fresh from the debacle of his failed investigation of the murder of prominent lawyer William Lowe Rice on August 5. "Coincidence," sniffed Doran, and precious days slipped by while he searched for professional highwaymen and supposed chicken thieves.

Meanwhile, after a funeral at the Rayner home, Mrs. Rayner was buried in Coe Ridge Cemetery, just three miles from the site of her midnight assassination. By that time Dr. C. W. Stoll of Dover had dug a .32 caliber slug out of Blanche Rayner's leg, and the motherless little girl was on the mend. The entire western half of the county was seething with hatred for Mrs. Rayner's unknown

William Van Gelder.   Earl Pender.

killers: the Rayner clan was one of the oldest families in Cuyahoga County. Their neighbors and elected officials demanded that the police find the culprits and end the reign of terror in Rockport's streets. The day after the murder, the Cuyahoga County commissioners offered a $500 reward for the arrest of the killers.

The much-hoped-for break in the case came almost a week later. Detective Doran and other lawmen hadn't been impressed by the peculiar incidents occurring in Rockport on August 26 and 27, but Cleveland detective Gideon Rabshaw thought they might be connected. Cleveland police chief Fred Kohler had loaned Rabshaw to the Rockport investigation, and the detective supplemented his investigative stint with many additional hours of his own time. A fact-finding tour of local saloons eventually brought Rabshaw to Wyatt's tavern in Rockport. The proprietor there told him that two young men had been drinking there Saturday, late in the afternoon on the day of the murder. They had left at 8 p.m., but the barkeep thought he could identify them again. Better yet was the tip given by Joseph Kundtz, owner of a tavern just a half a mile from the crime scene. He told Rabshaw there had been two suspicious-looking young men drinking at his place about 9 p.m. on August 27. They had been drinking beer while sitting on a horse-watering trough in front of the saloon, and he had last seen them walking west on Lorain toward the race track.

A few more visits to West Side bars gave Rabshaw the names he was looking for: Earl Pender and William Van Gelder. A lot of barkeeps in a lot of saloons had seen these two young men many times as they caroused into the wee hours of many a morning, and what they told Rabshaw about them only intensified his suspicions. When a check at their West Side dwellings disclosed that they had vanished the day after Mrs. Rayner's murder, Rabshaw was sure that he had made his killers.

Finding them proved more difficult. A check at the home of Pender's father in Lorain County and a sweep of his mother's West 52nd Street home simply confirmed his hasty flight from Cleveland, and both William Van Gelder and his mother had disappeared from her West 45th Street home. But Rabshaw's peripatetic persistence paid off once again when he ran into William Schaff, a West Park butcher. Van Gelder's mother, Lillian Grummitt, had left Cleveland without paying her bill to Schaff. Eventually, the bill was forwarded to her new address, which Schaff now furnished to Rabshaw.

Rabshaw's well-armed flying squad caught up with the fugitive Van Gelder on the morning of September 8. He was sleeping in an upstairs bedroom at the home of Samuel Duck in Richmond, in Lake County, when Rabshaw's squad surrounded the house, and he surrendered meekly. Also there were his mother, Lillian Grummitt, and his grandmother, Mrs. Sickle; the two woman were working as domestics at the Duck house, where they had fled with William the previous Sunday. On the long ride back to Cleveland, Van Gelder told his version of the Rayner murder to Gideon Rabshaw.

Parts of the story were untrue, but on the whole it formed a persuasive narrative of feckless youthful folly ending in tragedy. The 19-year-old Van Gelder told his audience that he had been a hardworking, thrifty West Side laborer since he quit the 4th grade at the age of 15. The sole support of his worshipful mother and younger sister Hazel, and of Mrs. Sickle, William let it be known that he was an earnest, church-going fellow who never drank, never smoked, never read trashy dime novels, and never palled around with bad companions. Until, of course, the unhappy day six months before, when he met "the fiend": Earl, alias Hawley Pender. Under the worldly Pender's sinful tutelage in vice, the long-fatherless William soon discovered the pleasures of alcohol and was staying out all night in drinking bouts at the many saloons of West Side Cleveland. As in some teary temperance tale, William Van Gelder soon lost his sobriety, his job, and his self-respect.

Earl Pender was a real hard case. Thirty years old in 1910, he had begun his career in crime early. Enlisting in the U. S. Army in 1900, he had served in the Philippine campaign, until a bullet directed at his commanding officer put him in Alcatraz military prison. He graduated from there to Leavenworth when he attempted to burn his way out of his island durance by setting his prison bed on fire. Paroled in 1904, Pender bummed around the country for the next six years, working as a professional strike-breaker and accumulating dossiers in many metropolitan police departments. By the time he met Van Gelder in early 1910, he had served a term in the Mansfield Reformatory and at least one term in the Cleveland workhouse for stealing bicycles. All in all, he was a terrible influence on William Van Gelder—a point the latter repeatedly and emphatically stressed after the toils of justice closed upon him.

As William told it, it was Earl Pender's idea that they become highwaymen. He bragged to William that he had already held up a man in Collinwood and another on the West Side, and the normally inarticulate Pender waxed romantic as he wove verbal fantasies of their careers as the modern Tom Turpins and Jesse Jameses of Cuyahoga County. As is often the case, words are father to deeds, and on the afternoon of Friday, August 26, 1910, they decided to realize their high-flown criminal ambitions.

There were no restrictions, to say the least, on their sacred Second Amendment rights in that era. At an Ontario Street pawnshop, William bought a .32 revolver and bullets for $2, while Pender purchased a similar gun for $1 and the pawning of his watch. After a few fortifying drinks to warm their courage, the two took the western suburban trolley. Alighting on Lorain just past the Cleveland boundary at West 117th, they boldly embarked on their new profession by trying to rob Myron Hughes, a Columbia Station man who was walking on the street. But as they leveled their guns, he ran away, and they had to content themselves with putting a bullet through his top hat. They then spied August Herrington at his nearby barn. Their initial plan was to rob him, but chickening out, they asked if they could sleep in his barn. Accurately sizing them up, August swore he would horsewhip them if they didn't leave. They did eventually leave, but only after stealing a horse and buggy from Herrington's barn. As they trotted away, Pender looked behind them and said, "Do you see that light?" When Van Gelder assented, Earl replied, "That fellow will have to work; I set his barn afire." They had a good laugh about that and eventually abandoned Herrington's rig on Madison Avenue near West 117th Street and Madison, where it was found and returned the next morning.

Frustrated by their Friday-night fiascoes, they decided to try again on Saturday. Earl picked William up at his mother's house about 4 p.m., and they began drinking their way through various West Side taverns and saloons, working their way westward, where Pender said he knew a rich man named Colburn whom they could rob. They never found Colburn, so they continued drinking, first in Wyatt's saloon and later at Joseph Kundtz's bar, just a half-mile from the Rockport racetrack. They also attempted a few more highway robberies, but everyone just ran away from them.

Tragedy beckoned about midnight as they approached Kamm's Corners. Their initial thought was to burglarize either the racetrack or the nearby Fischer clubhouse. But they were frightened away and decided instead to wait in the bushes on the south side of Lorain and rob the first person who came along. Except for the entrance to the racetrack and the suburban trolley tracks, it was a deserted stretch, and they could hear the bells of the farmers' market caravan as it plodded westward on Lorain toward the drunken, armed twosome. William and Earl had been drinking beer and whiskey for seven hours when Earl Dunford first saw them from his wagon, and his first thought as they staggered toward him was that they were drunken farmhands. Pender and Van Gelder later would each insist that all of the bullets fired at Dunford and the Rayners came from the other's gun.

Regardless of who fired, it was clear that neither of the "highwaymen" realized what they had done. As Rayner's rig galloped away, Earl and William ran northeast across darkened farmers' fields toward the Rocky River and Cleveland. As they ran, Earl muttered, "Did you hear a groan?" "I don't know," replied William. By the time they got to the river, the countryside was already swarming with gun-toting farmers, so they stole Chris Cristiansen's horse and surrey and drove it to Cleveland, where they abandoned it about 4 a.m. at Minot's saloon. Still drunk and exhausted, they crashed in the Lorain Avenue streetcar barns. When Van Gelder woke up at dawn, Earl was gone.

Later that day, Pender's mother, Susie Zmich, and his stepfather came to Van Gelder's West Side home. Brandishing a newspaper whose headline trumpeted their crime, Susie told William that he would have to get out of town if he didn't want to be arrested. That same night William left for Richmond with his mother and grandmother.

Although he was well defended by attorneys Charles Snider and Eugene Quigley, Van Gelder's case was hopeless from the start and much jeopardized by his own behavior. Although he soon "got religion" via his noisy participation in Sunday morning jail services and an edifying, confessional essay in the *Cleveland Press* on the evils of drink, his public demeanor both before and during his trial was sullen, indifferent, and uncooperative. Repudiating his multiple oral and verbal confessions as "coerced," he refused to talk after his arraignment, whining, "I'm tired of hearing about it. I've told all I know." Meanwhile, his mother and grandmother let it be known that they would fight to the last for their innocent lamb. "He never done it!" said Grandmother Sickle, while tearful Lillian recalled the pious, hard-working son who "stayed home evenings usually reading. He didn't read trashy novels." She also let it be known that the insanity defense card would be played, claiming that "Willie" was the defective issue of her marriage to a first cousin.

Willie's stratagems and laconic sullenness proved all in vain at his October trial. His attorneys' attempt to suppress his "involuntary" confession was undermined by his eventual admission that he had been repeatedly warned by Hirstius, Rabshaw, and Madison that any of his statements could be used against him. His own attorney, Charles Snider, became so enraged by his balky behavior that he finally told him in court to "sit up, take your hand away from your face, and talk so you can be heard!" His insanity defense was degraded to a mere plea that he had been crazy from the "booze" and "misled" by his sinful companion. There wasn't much left of his case by the morning of October 19, when he finally admitted to firing at least one shot at the Rayner wagon. (He insisted it went harmlessly into the air.) In his closing plea Snider wisely dwelt on William's alleged boyish virtues before the coming of Earl Pender:

> The weak 19-year-old boy, living quietly with his mother, working and giving her the money he earned, nursing her when she was sick and spending his evenings at home . . . Then the coming of the "fiend Pender," the bad influence he had over the

younger boy, the effect of drink on the youth, with which the
elder companion tempted him, his sinking lower and lower, and
the final tragic episode of the hold-ups and murder . . . .

The jury didn't buy it. Retiring at noon on October 22, they
returned nine hours later with a verdict of manslaughter. But Van
Gelder actually had good reason to feel fortunate at the outcome.
Not only did he escape the first-degree penalty for killing during a
robbery—the electric chair—but he avoided a one-to-twenty sentence in the Ohio Penitentiary. Because of his age, Judge H. B.
Chapman had to content himself with giving Van Gelder an indef-
inite term in the Mansfield Reformatory. Several days later William
left for that institution, vowing to eschew alcohol and to make a
man of himself.

Before leaving Cleveland, however, Van Gelder committed yet
another crime for which he should be remembered. The day after
his conviction, the *Plain Dealer* released the text of a poem written
for his mother from his cell in the county jail:

> Nineteen years ago
> I was brought into this world,
> Cold, and white with snow.
> On the twenty-fifth of December,
> Well you will remember,
> That it was on the Christ's birthday,
> If God had taken me out of her arms then,
> How much better it would have been—
> I was her idol, her joy,
> To God she gave thanks for her baby boy.
> How many broken hearts would be happy today,
> Had I never seen the light of day.
> Little did she, my mother know,
> That in years to come,
> I would be in a worse place
> Than the lower one.
> And today I am in the county jail,
> Bound over, with $20,000 bail.

One pleasantly poignant episode relieved the sad and grim
tedium of the trial. Among the spectators were Walter and Blanche
Rayner. Walter took in the trial with ashen mien and frequently
clenched fists, but the 8-year-old Blanche seemed oblivious to the

tragic proceedings around her as she clutched a pink carnation in her hand. One day, as she was leaving the courtroom, she unknowingly dropped it. It was picked up by 11-year-old Hazel Grummitt—William's younger sister—who hurried after Blanche and said, "Here's your flower." Blanche took it, and reporters scribbled frantically in their notebooks as the two innocents smiled at each other.

Meanwhile, the avid search for Earl Pender continued. A month after he disappeared, his mother, Susie Zmich, identified the body of a man killed in a railway accident at Franklin Boulevard and West 25th as her fugitive son. But the police were skeptical; the body was mangled beyond easy recognition and Mrs. Zmich's motherly sorrow seemed a trifle perfunctory. Official disbelief proved to be a wise policy a month later, when, on November 7, word came from San Francisco that Earl had been captured by local police in a saloon at Howard and 3rd streets. When finally extradited back to Cleveland, Pender ruefully told the story of his capture. He had just signed on to a British freighter as a deckhand and was only 20 minutes away from sailing when he decided to go for "just one more little drink." He had run into a previous acquaintance from his strike-breaking years the day before and was anxious to see a familiar face before he went aboard the Canada- and London-bound ship. While leaving the bar with his friend, Edward Eeks, he was grabbed by two detectives whom the reward-hungry Eeks had alerted. The dangerous Pender surrendered without a struggle.

Earl likewise didn't struggle much at his trial on December 16, 1910. Realizing that the chief witness against him would be William Van Gelder, now in the full, eager tide of his I-was-misled-by-drink-and-bad-companions rehabilitation rhetoric, he pleaded guilty to second-degree murder and accepted a life sentence in the Ohio Penitentiary from Judge H. B. Chapman. But Pender was adamant about his actual, limited responsibility for the death of Clara Rayner. He admitted being with Van Gelder at Kamm's Corners on the fatal night, but he claimed he had not fired his revolver and that he had told William not to fire: "I never could do anything with Willie. I told him again and again never to shoot, but when he took a few drinks he lost his head. I did not know that Willie's bullets hit anybody until I read the papers the next morning."

Pender righteously insisted that his conscience was clear with regard to Mrs. Rayner's death, and he poured smoking hot scorn on the idea that he was a hardened "fiend" who had corrupted and misled an innocent, naive boy into murder and mayhem: "I didn't lead Willie . . . into this sort of thing, no matter what he says. I know a thing or two about his early life. Why, he was in this stick-up business before I ever met him. When he was a kid he stole $35 from a farmer to pay his mother's rent and then spent it to get drunk." In fact, Pender concluded, he had met Willie Van Gelder when the "innocent" adolescent held up Pender's father on a West Side street. Adding a nice family touch, Pender's father chimed in, insisting that Earl had always been a bad boy and that he wasn't at all surprised by his son's murder of an innocent woman.

In the end, however, Pender, like his erstwhile criminal companion, came to his senses and began playing to the newspaper gallery. As he left Cleveland for the Ohio Penitentiary on December 20, he delivered himself of an unctuous homily on drink that could have come from the pious lips of Willie Van Gelder himself: "What did it? That's easy. Whiskey. I am not a fool, and if I had been sober I don't have to tell you that I would never have been found in such a deal. Whiskey—let a man fuss with it long enough and it will get him."

As he left his Cuyahoga County jail cell, Pender laid down his guitar and said, "I hate to part with this. The guitar helped me to forget my troubles." Sheriff Hirstius was so moved by this remark that he let Pender play a few more musical selections before his final departure. When last heard of in 1922, Pender was still in a Columbus cell, and Willie Van Gelder had returned to the new life he had promised to make so much of. Clara Rayner sleeps still in her grave, surrounded by an urban sprawl unimagined by her or those who mourned her despicable murder.

Chapter 10

"TO GET A WOMAN OR ELSE"

The Sheila Ann Tuley Horror

Everyone there agreed it was probably the best 10 minutes of Harold Beach's life. When he left the Ohio Penitentiary death row in Columbus at 8 sharp on the night of February 2, 1948, he was walking briskly and clutched a large wooden crucifix in his hands. He was also praying, and the seven guards and seven witnesses could hear him mumbling his Act of Contrition as he was strapped into the electric chair: "Oh my God, I am heartily sorry for having offended Thee . . ." He finished the prayer and had begun a Hail Mary when warden Ralph Alvis turned and nodded to the executioner at 8:04 p.m. As Harold got to the end—". . . now, and at the hour of our death, Amen"—the first jolt of 1,950 volts hit, and he stiffened back in his seat. Forty seconds later the current was brought down to 500 volts, then jacked up again to 1,950. At 8:10 he was pronounced dead and removed from the chair to begin his last journey to an unmarked Columbus grave. The only mourner present was his mother, Evelyn, true to her promise that she would "stick by him" to the end. That end had now come, a fitting episode of brief, brutal violence to conclude, perhaps, the worst story in Cleveland history: the murder of Sheila Ann Tuley.

Harold Beach killed Sheila Ann Tuley, but Fate surely lent its own malign hand. It was the night of New Year's Day in 1948, and Sheila's father, Edward Tuley, 32, wanted a cigarette. He often sent Sheila out to the drugstore on such errands, so neither he, his 30-year-old wife, Elsie, nor their landlord, Joseph Moriarty, who lived with them in the modest frame house at 1333 East 124th Street, thought it inappropriate when Sheila left at 7:50 p.m. for the D. & N. Drugstore at East 125th and Superior Avenue. She put the list in her purse (three packs of Camels, a comic book, a sports

Mr. and Mrs. Edward J. Tuley.   Sheila Ann Tuley.

magazine, and tooth powder), pulled on her winter clothes (green coat, white woolen sweater, brown oxfords, pleated navy blue skirt, rubber boots), grabbed a pink parasol, and stepped outside. It was just starting to rain, but it was mild for January, and it was only two blocks to the drugstore, a trip the eight-year-old Sheila often made. But as she left for the short journey, there were two things her parents didn't know: the D. & N. Drugstore was closed, and they would never see Sheila alive again.

Sheila was expected home by 8 p.m. She was keen to listen to *The Aldrich Family*, her favorite radio program, and when she didn't come back, Edward Tuley donned a robe and began looking for her in the neighborhood streets. Not finding her, he called the police and returned to his search. Three hours went by as he frantically combed the wet streets, and he was about to give up when he saw police cars and a crowd in front of the house of C. James Endicott at 1318 East 124th Place, a block over from his own home. Edward pushed his way through the police and spectators to the porch, and a photographer's flashbulb went off. In its light Edward saw his daughter there. She was lying in a pool of her own blood, one leg folded under her, as the brilliant lights from a reflected Christmas tree cast a macabre glow on her body. Cleveland's most horrible murder mystery had begun.

The police weren't certain what had happened, and neither was anyone else. The Endicotts had been visiting family in Mentor all

day and had not returned home until
about 11:30 p.m. As they got out of their
car and walked to the porch, 15-year-old
James Endicott thought he saw a large rag
doll lying there. It wasn't a rag doll; it
was Sheila Ann. Cut seven times, with
deep, slit-like injuries, she was lying face
up with her head to the street. On the
three Christmas-wreathed porch windows were smeary blood stains, evidence
that the little girl had desperately sought
help at the Endicott house, where Beverly, her classmate at Rosedale Elementary School, lived. Although blood-
soaked, her clothes were not disarranged,
and even her babushka was still neatly in

Harold Beach.

place—in spite of the slit in it through which some sharp object had
fatally penetrated two and a half inches into her brain. Her purse
was at her side, still holding the five quarters and the list she had
left the house with four hours before. Even her bubble gum was
still in her mouth.

The police had a lot more questions than answers as they systematically searched the nearby streets and homes for evidence in
the hours that followed. At first they couldn't even agree what had
happened to Sheila. Coroner Samuel R. Gerber, roused from sleep
at 12:30 a.m. to examine the 47-inch, 50-pound corpse, quickly
pronounced the death a homicide, probably committed with a knife
or bayonet wielded by a short person, perhaps a juvenile. Some of
the Cleveland policemen working the case, struck by the fact that
Sheila's body was found a block away from home in the opposite
direction of her errand, theorized that she had been the victim of a
hit-skip driver, who left her body on a convenient porch. Detective
Lieutenant David E. Kerr, who initially had charge of Sheila's murder investigation, led the hit-skip camp, highlighting some broken
auto headlight glass and a damaged windshield wiper found on
Thompson Avenue, which connected East 124th Street and East
124th Place. Her bloody puncture wounds, Kerr and others argued,
might have come from the metal grill of the death car. Some even
thought Sheila's wounds might have resulted from a bicycle collision—her body penetrated by spokes or sharp basket wires—or

even an unfortunate encounter with a picket fence. One retired bluecoat even hypothesized that Sheila had been the unintended target of a young boy's bow-and-arrow set received as a Christmas present. The only thing the authorities agreed on was Gerber's conclusion that six of the wounds had been superficial, almost teasing injuries. It was the seventh slit, just under her right ear, that penetrated Sheila's brain and probably rendered her blind at the beginning of the two to three hours it took her to die on the Endicott porch.

Meanwhile, police concentrated on combing the area for physical evidence and witnesses, and rounding up every known psychopath, pervert, or suspicious person within a square mile. There turned out to be a lot of them, at least in the opinion of the many neighbors who turned them in. So many were rounded up for jailing and questioning by Sunday, January 4, that Lieutenant Kerr observed, "Everybody in the neighborhood lives next to someone who is queer. We are now at the point where psychopaths are calling us." But Kerr's collection of suspects proved surprisingly poor: although many of the men picked up had sexual offense records, all of them were able to prove alibis for the murder evening. And an alternative suspect pool of feeble-minded and retarded persons proved likewise innocent. Although some of them were even found with suspicious weapons, sober heads judged them utterly incapable of having planned or perpetrated Sheila's abduction and murder, much less escaped from the scene. Commenting on the horror of the crime and official frustration with the case, one detective said to *Plain Dealer* columnist Roelif Loveland, "This is about as bad as they come."

The paucity of genuine witnesses aggravated investigative difficulties. It was only 237 child-size steps from the Tuley home to the D. & N. Drugstore, and yet Sheila had somehow disappeared during her walk, probably within only a minute of leaving home. And the handful of persons on the neighborhood streets at the murder hour had seen no trace of her. Nor had any of them seen her walking the 215 steps between the Tuley and Endicott homes. One of the potential witnesses was Parmer Austin, 12, who was walking his dog just before 8 p.m. and had passed the Tuley home several times without seeing Sheila. Another was Henry Markam. He, too, had left home about 7:50 p.m. for the D. & N. drugstore but he, too, did not see Sheila. Markam did see a "tough-looking" man in a leather jacket, but he turned out to be perfectly innocent after

Cleveland police spent a great deal of trouble running him down. By Monday morning, January 5, when Sheila was buried in Calvary Cemetery, all the police had to show for their efforts was a list of more than 600 suspects or potential witnesses examined, and a Cleveland populace alarmed by newspaper headlines that screamed of 627 psychopaths and "1,100 perverts" running wild in Cleveland streets. Adding to the civic din was highly public handwringing over Cleveland's poor street-lighting and the lack of institutions in which to lock up the kind of psychopath who had made Sheila Tuley his victim. Excited by the specter of drooling, predatory perverts roaming Forest City streets, some neighborhoods began to organize nightly patrols by fathers to ward off potential killers. One such watchman was Regis McAuley of East 147th Street, father of five and *News* sportswriter (and future confirmation sponsor of the author), who told newsmen: "We feel the mere presence of several men strolling through an area will discourage anyone with evil intent from entering this neighborhood."

By Wednesday, January 7, almost a week after Sheila's murder, the crux of the investigation's puzzle was clear. By that time almost everyone agreed with Gerber's diagnosis that someone, probably a juvenile or a short-statured male, had stalked Sheila, dragged her into a secluded area, stabbed her, and fled (leaving Sheila to stagger, bleeding, to the porch), or that the killer carried her body to the Endicott porch and left it there. But where had he accosted her, where had he stabbed her, and why was she found so far away from her original destination? The preliminary theory was that she had been abducted at the corner of East 124th Street and Thompson Avenue, which was really just a rat-infested alley running west to East 124th Place. But after talking to her neighbors, police discovered that Sheila and her friends had been in the habit of taking a shortcut to Superior Avenue that led them east behind some houses, past the back of the Ambassador movie theater on the left, and then north to Superior and East 125th Street. But neither evidence nor eyewitnesses placed Sheila on either path on the fatal night. True, a meticulous Cleveland patrolman, Hugh Corrigan, had found a quarter on the pavement of Thompson Avenue, but what it meant wasn't clear at the time, and the manhunt ground on. Some voices were already adding Sheila's murder to the list of 250 unsolved homicides in Cleveland since 1930.

One of the nastier episodes in the Tuley tragedy developed on Thursday, January 8. By now the police had already disproved several "confessions" to the Tuley murder, so it was with undisguised enthusiasm that Lieutenant Kerr announced the next day the arrest of the "best suspect we have had yet." The unidentified man was 41 years old, a friend of the family, had even babysat for Sheila and her brother Edward, and—better yet—could not satisfactorily account for his whereabouts on the night of January 1. When police found a suspiciously stained knife in his toolbox and witnesses who saw him drinking in several bars near the murder area at the critical time, the match in the case seemed almost too good to be true.

Which it was: The "friend of the family" turned out to be Joseph Moriarty, the resident owner of the Tuley two-family house, upon whom the police had, perhaps inevitably, turned their suspicions. But three days of interrogation and a successful lie detector test later, Moriarty walked out of Central Police station a free, if bitterly angry man. He admitted he had not been physically harmed, but he was understandably enraged at the drift his interrogation had taken:

> I want to say that the police didn't have the slightest business in bringing me in as a suspect. I was insulted by questions about personal matters. . . . Apparently some police officers have read books on abnormal sex psychology and I was accused of having abnormal sexual tendencies, which of course my service in the Army would deny, and which I now deny. I was never punched around by the police but what they did to me I most certainly call the "third degree."

Moriarty vented his severest scorn on Lieutenant Kerr, whom he characterized as "an actor, strictly ham."

Notwithstanding Moriarty's unfortunate experience, the irony of the Tuley investigation was that the police did almost everything right. They searched the neighborhood from top to bottom, including sewers, basements, and roofs. They interviewed nearly 1,000 people, following up every clue, rumor, and hint, no matter how remote. But the world being the inexplicable place it is, the break in the Tuley case came without warning and out of nowhere on Sunday, January 10. Maybe it was the reward of $7,000 posted for the capture and conviction of Sheila's killer, $5,000 of it offered by the *Press* on January 11. Or maybe it was just two guys trying to be public-spirited citizens, doing their bit in Cleveland's greatest

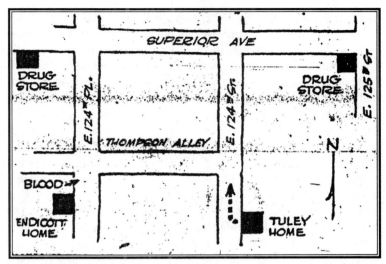

Map of Sheila's death route.

manhunt ever. Whatever the case, at 2:30 p.m. Sunday afternoon Inspector Michael Blackwell got a call from a friend, James T. Cassidy of 1846 Taylor Road. One of Cassidy's roomers, Dwight Bible, 22, had asked Cassidy to call the police and tell them about one of Bible's bowling acquaintances, Harold A. Beach Jr. Beach, according to Bible, was a "bad actor," lived near Sheila's home, had once served time for a sex offense, and had disappeared from Cleveland the day after her murder. Indeed, Bible had joked several times after Beach didn't show up to bowl on January 4 that "maybe he's the guy the police are looking for." But then he heard about the reward and remembered some comments Beach had made about little girls. Cassidy now retailed the information to Blackwell, and it was all the inspector needed to hear: he called Lieutenant Kerr, and a flying squad was on its way to the Beach home at 1508 Lakeview, just a few blocks from Sheila Ann Tuley's home.

Harold Beach Jr. was not at home, but his father and stepmother were, and they told Kerr that they hadn't seen 22-year-old Harold since the evening of January 2, when he had left the house, saying he was going roller skating. Harold's father told Kerr that Harold Jr. had probably gone to live with his mother, Evelyn Beach Kimball, in Baltimore. No one in Cleveland had her address, but the next morning Kerr called the Napanoch Reformatory in Ulster County, New York, where Harold had served a five-year term between 1942 and 1947 for molesting an 11-year-old boy whom he had threatened to kill unless the child submitted to his desires. Reformatory officials furnished the information that Evelyn Kimball's last known residence was 2225 Callow Avenue in Baltimore. Several hours later Baltimore police, led by Lieutenant George G. Bryan and Captain Henry J. Kriss, grabbed Beach as he was changing a tire at a gas station in downtown Baltimore. He had gotten a job there on January 3, the day of his arrival, and had already decided to leave for Florida when he was picked up. After questioning Beach for several hours, Bryan called Kerr and said, "This guy is lying and he's plenty hot." An hour later Beach confessed to the murder of Sheila Ann Tuley, and just minutes after that Kerr and his men returned to 1508 Lakeview Avenue, where they found a suitable four-inch paring knife in a kitchen drawer and a raincoat with a bloody pocket hanging in the basement. Arraigned the next morning in a Baltimore court, Beach waived extradition and was on his way to Cleveland minutes after that.

However it came about, the Sheila Ann Tuley case was one of Coroner Gerber's finest hours and did much to cement his reputation as a canny medico-legal analyst. As Beach recounted repeatedly, without any display of regret or emotion, Sheila's murder had happened in much the fashion theorized by Gerber. Accosting her within 60 seconds after she left home, Beach had lured her into Thompson Avenue, asking "Do you want a quarter?" Sheila followed him west, almost to East 124th Place, when Beach halted and told her to follow him through a gap in the fence behind the garage of Nicholas Pinno's house at 1314 East 124th Place. Stepping through the gap, Beach handed her the quarter, pushed her down, and tried to force her to—in the words of the court record— sodomize him. She resisted, so Beach brought out the knife he had in his pocket and began prodding her in the back with it. Then, as Harold put it:

> "I just lost my head. She started yelling and I'd done time before. ... She began to cry. I got frightened and stabbed her in the back. She was bent over and I jabbed at her. She started to yell. I stabbed her in the head. She kept on screaming and I kept on stabbing. Maybe six or seven times. I was scared. But I didn't

think I'd hurt her very much. I knew I was doing wrong when I stabbed the girl."

Beach had then fled to his home, washed off his bloody knife, and hung his raincoat in the basement. Almost four hours later, about the time Sheila's body was found on the Endicott porch, Beach returned to the gap in the fence on Thompson Avenue to find her gone. He didn't know she was dead until he saw the next morning's *Plain Dealer*, and he immediately decided to flee to Baltimore. He told reporters when he was brought to Cleveland that he had never doubted that he would get caught: "They couldn't help but get me. My fingerprints were all over the boards on the fence."

Harold A. Beach Jr. was exactly the kind of perpetrator most authorities had imagined in this horrible case, and the details of his life were unsurprising to those who perceived him as either a satanic killer or a brutalized victim of society. His father had left when Harold, the unwanted child of a forced marriage, was five months old. He subsequently was shunted between indifferent grandparents and various institutions for the precociously delinquent. Released from prison in 1947 after serving his term for the molestation conviction, he was paroled to his father in Cleveland. A loner without social skills, and sensitive about his short stature of just over five feet, he was known by co-workers and neighbors as a subnormally intelligent loser who constantly verbalized his obsessive fantasies of sexual conquest of women—especially young girls. Treated as the social leper that he was, he hung around area drugstores, consuming innumerable Cokes, ranting about his imaginary sexual exploits, and working at a variety of casual jobs, including a stint as an usher at the Ambassador Theater. The public portrait that emerged in the weeks after his arrest was of a repellent pariah whom nobody had ever wanted and who had at last reacted to his tormented isolation like an enraged animal. When asked why he had taken his knife with him that night, he told interrogators that he was determined "to get a woman or else."

Harold Beach got as fair a trial as could have been expected. He signed two lengthy confessions before his indictment on first-degree murder charges on January 15. (Indeed, Beach was so prodigal with his confidences that one reporter asked him, "Is there anybody in this town you haven't confessed to?") The previous afternoon he had willingly accompanied police to the Thompson

Avenue site, where he cooperatively reenacted the murder. And the police had all the physical evidence they needed, even without Beach's cooperation: they had the knife, whose point fit perfectly into the wounds on the corpse of Sheila Ann, hastily exhumed by Gerber's order on January 15. They also had Beach's green raincoat, the pocket of which was still covered with dried blood matching that of Sheila Ann Tuley.

Harold's much-anticipated trial opened on February 24, 1948, Judge Samuel H. Silbert presiding, Frank T. Cullitan and Victor De Marco prosecuting, and Jesse W. Woods and Walter Booth defending. Much to his credit, Silbert tried from the outset to prevent the sensational trial from becoming a "Roman holiday" (the very phrase, interestingly, with which the Supreme Court would later overturn Sam Sheppard's 1954 conviction). There had already been unseemly goings-on in the media whirl around Beach, and he had been showcased by his captors in public scenes of televised hysteria, complete with shouting newsmen, in both Cleveland and Pittsburgh. Silbert was determined to stop these shenanigans, and he disappointed Cleveland radio stations when he refused to allow their microphones in his courtroom. The betting line on Cleveland streets as the trial opened was 2–1 that Harold would end up in Lima State Hospital for the Criminally Insane.

Court-appointed defense lawyers Woods and Booth did their best, but Clarence Darrow in his prime could probably not have saved Harold A. Beach. A confessed "pervert killer," he continually shocked spectators by his demeanor, frequently described by Cleveland newspaper reporters as "unemotional," "sulky," and "smirking." Determined attempts to render his confessions to Baltimore and Cleveland police inadmissible were steadily overruled by Judge Silbert, despite the facts that Beach had not been encouraged to get a lawyer (these were pre-Miranda days), and his mother had been denied access to him in the hours after his arrest. And, given his inappropriate behavior, the last thing Woods and Booth could afford to do was to put their client on the stand. Nor could they stop the melodramatic presentation of the prosecution, which insisted that the jury of five men and seven women personally examine Sheila's bloody clothes, the murder knife, and the gruesome morgue photos.

With the facts against them, Woods and Booth strove desperately to construct an insanity defense. But X-rays of Beach's head taken at Huron Road Hospital failed to support claims of a brain injury suffered when Harold's mother, Evelyn, fell down a flight of stairs atop him when he was 15 days old. And while the prosecution didn't challenge tests indicating Beach had a mental age of 11 and an emotional maturity of considerably less, the defense had to concede that Harold Beach, by his own repeated admission, had known the difference between right and wrong when he stabbed Sheila Ann Tuley. Woods and Booth's insanity defense ultimately turned into a disastrous, slippery slope in which they progressively conceded that Beach wasn't insane, he wasn't brain-damaged, and he wasn't retarded. That left them with the claim of an "irresistible impulse," an invalid defense under Ohio law and one the jury wouldn't buy in any case. It was a hopeless cause, and Walter Booth admitted to reporters, "We're grasping at straws."

There were enough fireworks to satisfy the 80-odd trial buffs in attendance every day. After the preliminary skirmishes over the confessions, Cullitan vowed there "would be no holds barred and no quarter given"—and he was as good as his word. Evelyn Beach Kimball, Beach's distraught mother and the only relative who stuck by him in his extremity, had to be removed from court when, goaded by Cullitan's relentless cross-examination, she screamed, "You're a liar! I'll go, but he's lying terrible!" But before she left the stand, she painted a lurid portrait of a very sick boy who set fires in closets and even on his dinner plate at a young age. Sickening excerpts from the transcript of his trial for molesting the 11-year-old boy in New York were read aloud, including the death threats he used to impose his will. No fewer than five psychiatrists and one psychologist were enlisted to tutor the jury on Beach's mental condition: four of them termed him sane, while Dr. Marguerite Hertz argued that his Rorschach test results indicated otherwise. Dr. Harry Lipson, who claimed Beach had murdered Sheila while temporarily insane, was effectively ridiculed by Cullitan as "Ten Second Lipson." Summing up the state's case, Victor De Marco slammed Beach's paring knife violently into the arm of his chair and pleaded for the electrocution of Harold A. Beach:

> "Let us think of Sheila Ann, that beautiful, lovable little angel watching us from up in heaven where she surely must be now. . . . Why, with all that force I cannot drive [the knife] into this wood one-sixteenth of an inch! Can you imagine the suffering

and pain of that little child, clawing at the window, crying 'Help me! Help me, please!'"

By the time De Marco finished his oration, the jury and spectators were openly weeping and sobbing aloud. Judge Silbert had already had to clear the court several times because of repeated booing and hissing by spectators during the presentation of Beach's defense.

Walter Booth knew when he was licked. Rising to make his final plea, he turned to his client and made the following statement:

> "It now becomes my duty to do the last thing I can to stand in the way of burning this boy, Harold Beach, in the electric chair. Harold, you have had a fair trial. I am going to do something without precedent, to my knowledge, in a courtroom. I am going to ask this jury for a verdict of guilty of murder in the first degree. I do think your verdict should include recommendation of mercy. I don't want you to find him guilty of second degree murder. His mind proves he should be put away for life."

Booth finished his plea to the stunned jury with a bitter reflection that some others should have been named in Beach's murder indictment: the parents who didn't want him, the institutions that failed him, and even Edward Tuley, who should not have sent his little daughter out on dark, unsafe streets to get his cigarettes on the evening of New Year's Day.

The jury members weren't the only stunned persons in the courtroom. Jesse Woods followed his co-counsel's speech with an acrid disavowal, insisting that Booth's decision to seek a first-degree murder conviction was done without his consent and demanding that the jury find Beach guilty of second-degree murder instead. "I'm surprised at what he's doing," complained Woods. "He didn't consult me. Booth is playing right into the state's hands." Begging for the jury's mercy, Woods summed up Beach's failed life in one pathetic sentence: "He needed love and he didn't have it."

To virtually the surprise of no one, the jury went out at 5:50 p.m. on March 11 and returned with a verdict of first-degree murder without a recommendation of mercy at 8:57, after only 182 minutes of actual deliberation. It only took four ballots, and there was unanimity about Harold's guilt from the start. Two female jurors voted for mercy on the second ballot, only one on the third, and all voted for the electric chair on the fourth. When summoned to hear his fate, Beach answered the judge's query with a toneless, "No, I haven't anything to say." It was an interesting contrast to the boasting words he had uttered to sheriff's deputies only minutes before: "I'll be around East 105th Street and Euclid Avenue in 30 years eating pork chops."

Beach's inappropriate levity had returned to its wonted form by March 16, when Judge Silbert sentenced him to the electric chair. Returning from court, Beach bragged, "I'm still laughin', ain't I? Nothing is over until you are in the ground. I looked the judge right square in the eye when he came to that part about the electric chair."

Evelyn Beach Kimball and Jesse Woods stuck by the doomed Harold until the end. Evelyn visited him at the Ohio Penitentiary death house as often as possible, and Woods took Beach's hopeless legal appeal up to the Ohio Supreme Court. When the latter court refused to overturn the verdict on October 22, 1948, Beach at last began to prepare for death, converting to the Catholic Church and praying daily. After the final court ruling, even Woods gave up, telling *Cleveland News* reporter Howard Beaufait:

> I have an obligation to society. Beach is as dangerous as a leopard. I would not want to be responsible for setting him at large again . . . It is his emotional machinery that has gone haywire. He cannot control or censor his impulses. It was inevitable that he would commit a serious crime sooner or later. He would do so again if freed.

And so Harold Beach went to his fate on a winter day in 1949. The Tuley family moved out of the neighborhood, and Edward and Elsie divorced soon after the trial. The day after Beach was electrocuted, the *Press* paid its $5,000 reward to Dwight Bible and James T. Cassidy for the tip that led to Beach's capture. And Sheila Ann Tuley sleeps in Calvary Cemetery, but the questions raised by her death are with us still. How should society deal with damaged individuals like Howard A. Beach and the evil that they do? The question was well put by two participants in the spirited public conversation that ensued in the wake of Sheila Ann's murder. In a letter to the *Press*, Arthur J. Koch of Standard Avenue articulated the case for society's protective vengeance:

I always said the law stinks and I'll say it over and over. Why?
Because it's too easy on these butchers that roam the streets. I
say make the law so stern that for rape, molesting a woman or
man, give the skunk who did it the electric chair the next day.
Not life, so they can come out in ten years and do it again. . . .
Make it death and the quicker the better.

Most Clevelanders of that day or ours would have agreed with
Koch. But let William F. McDermott, perhaps the most eloquent
writer in the history of Cleveland journalism, have the last word in
this tortured debate. Writing the day after Beach was captured,
McDermott was shocked by his crime—and even more appalled by
the society that produced its perpetrator:

> You cannot escape the feeling that the community, or the general
> organization of society, are not entirely without blame for such
> crimes. The investigation of this particularly wanton and
> hideous murder . . . brought to light the fact that more than 600
> psychopaths who ought to be hospitalized are walking the
> streets without surveillance. Presumably anyone of them is
> capable of the violent impulses that led to the knifing of the
> Tuley girl. We do not put the knife into their hands, but we give
> them the opportunity to use the knife. So long as society is
> unwilling, or unable, to provide institutional care for people
> whose mental illness is such that they are potentially dangerous
> to human life, society must accept responsibility for the
> tragedies that ensue.

Chapter 11

REVENGE OF THE GRAYBEARDS

The Fabulous
Meach Brothers of Rochester

The story of the Meach brothers of Rochester is a tale so satis-
fying that it would be tempting to make it up. Fortunately and
astonishingly, it's all true and, as the expression goes, much, much
stranger than fiction. Before it was over it put two men in their
graves, two more back in prison, and made an unlikely hero out of
an old man. It doesn't take much of an ironist to realize that if the
story happened today, the good guys would probably end up in
prison, and the bad 'uns would successfully claim victim status and
the rewards of a million-dollar wrongful death lawsuit. So return
with me to an exotic locale in the thrilling days of yesteryear—
rural Lorain County in 1902—and exult in the wonderful tale of the
fabulous Meach brothers.

"Unlikely heroes" is a commonplace rubric that doesn't even
begin to describe Loren, John, and Jarvis Meach. Living on the 80-
acre farm they had inherited from their parents many years before,
the three elderly, heavily bearded bachelors had long thrived as
eccentric characters and much-talked-about recluses in the eyes of
their neighbors in rural Lorain County. Beginning as farmers,
drovers, and wool buyers in the years just after the Civil War, by
the turn of the century the Meach siblings had parlayed their agri-
cultural and mercantile profits into a fortune that was the subject of
considerable local envy and gossip. It was well known that Loren,
80, John, 74, and Jarvis, 68, were well-to-do; although rather reclusive in their personal relations, the three brothers had been generous with loans to their needy neighbors over the years, especially
in the hard times after the Panic of 1893. Indeed, it was said that
their quiet cash loans of as much as $25,000 to local banks during

WEDNESDAY, OCTOBER 15, 1902   Fair and warmer.   ONE CENT.

HE BAGGED
FOUR THUGS

From the *Cleveland Daily World*, October 15, 1902.

periods of financial embarrassment had saved those institutions from panic-caused collapse. Oddly enough, though, the Meach brothers didn't believe in banks much, and all their neighbors knew—or at least thought they knew—that the Meaches kept enormous amounts of cash, gold, and jewels in their house, much of it in an elaborate safe and the rest buried in secret locations on the farm. In other words, it was a crime scene waiting to happen, and in due course it did.

The story proper began on the early evening of October 14, 1902. At about 5:40 p.m. section superintendent O. E. Durkee of the Big Four railway saw six men get off at the Rochester switch and start walking down the road. He thought no more about it at the time, although he did notice that three of them were well dressed, whereas the other three were garbed more like "tramps." He returned to his work, and the three men disappeared into the evening.

An hour and a half later, John Meach, returning from an errand, ran into the six men just outside his house, just two miles out of Rochester. They were now wearing red or black handkerchiefs to hide their faces, and they grabbed him, beat, bound, and gagged him, and tied him to a tree. Leaving a man to guard him, the other five approached the house. As they got to the side door, Jarvis Meach, who had heard a suspicious noise, opened it up. Things happened very quickly after that. The Meaches' pet bulldog lunged for the men—and was instantly shot dead through the forehead. Hitting Jarvis on the head with a pistol butt, the men dragged him into the kitchen, beating him and kicking him for several minutes. Rendering him unconscious, they tied him up and stuck a gag in his mouth. Leaving two men to guard him, the other three went into Loren Meach's bedroom.

Loren, bedridden and senile, put up no resistance as the robbers gagged him and tied him up with torn sheets. They were in such a hurry that one of them, stumbling over Loren's trousers on the floor, merely kicked them under the bed—without checking them or finding the $3,500 in cash in the pockets. They then went into a little room off the bedroom, where the Meach brothers kept their fabled safe. Unpacking his kit of soap, nitroglycerin "soup," and super-hardened drill bits, one of them began preparing to blow the safe in a calm, professional manner.

It was at this juncture that the burglars committed their fatal blunder. As subsequently analyzed by Cleveland captain of detectives (and future legendary chief of police) Fred Kohler, the gang was an impromptu and uneasy mix of seasoned "peter men" (professional safe crackers or "cracksmen") and "yeggmen" (amateur local thugs recruited for their inside knowledge of the target). Not knowing their professional companions well and uneasy that they might be cheated out of the contents of the safe, the two yeggmen, who had been guarding the unconscious, bleeding Jarvis in the kitchen, left him in order to keep an eye on the safecrackers. Soon after they departed, Jarvis came to and managed to work his pocket knife out of his pants. Opening it with his teeth, he slowly sawed through the ropes around his hands and chest until they fell to the floor. . .

Thanks to the knowledge of their local helpers, the cracksmen who invaded the Meach homestead that night knew that the brothers kept a lot of money in the house. They also knew that the Meaches were aged and probably decrepit. What they obviously didn't know, or take seriously, was the fact that all of the Meach brothers were experienced in the use of firearms. Indeed, they were all known as crack shots, especially Jarvis, whose ability with a gun was later recalled by John Meach for a *Cleveland Press* reporter: "A dead shot. Yes, Jarvis can shoot. We can all shoot but Jarvis beats us all." So it wasn't really too surprising that Jarvis's first act after getting out of his upper ropes—his feet were still tied together—was to wriggle across the floor and pick up a double-barreled shotgun. Turning around, he began wriggling toward the door of Loren's bedroom . . . .

A minor irony later remarked upon was the fact that the shotgun—a favorite

Jarvis Meach.

Where the burglars were killed,
showing shotguns.

of Jarvis's known affectionately as "Old Bunty"—was loaded and
ready to fire. Just the previous day, Jay Schindler, a visiting neighbor, had asked Jarvis whether "Old Bunty" had been cleaned lately.
It had not, and when Schindler protested, Jarvis replied, "Well,
clean it if you like. I shan't." Which Schindler did, reloading it with
shot and setting fresh caps.

The enraged Jarvis caught up with his tormentors at an oppor-
tune moment. Hearing a noise from the kitchen, they were just
coming through the door when his first barrel fired. The charge hit
the man in front point blank in the chin, blasting most of his face
and killing him instantly. As he fell to the floor, the second barrel
fired, hitting the man behind him and turning the top of his head
into "very lattice-work," as a *Cleveland Leader* writer gleefully put
it. As the other three fled upstairs, leaving a trail of bloodstains,
Jarvis wriggled back to the kitchen for another gun.

Jarvis didn't have to look hard. Witnesses later did a firearms
census of the Meach home and discovered one or more weapons in
every one of its 15 rooms. Within moments he had his hands on
another beloved shotgun, this one called "Little Pet." By now he
had his feet untied, and rushing outside, he caught up with the three
remaining robbers just as they dropped to the ground from the second-floor roof. Jarvis blasted the first, hitting him in the hand and
leg as he fled toward a nearby orchard. He also hit the second,
putting 57 pieces of shot into his thigh. The third escaped unscathed

into the orchard, and as the exhausted, injured Jarvis began ringing a large outside bell to raise the alarm, he fainted dead away.

Jay Schindler, the erstwhile gun cleaner, was the first to arrive on the ghastly scene. When he asked the senile Loren what had happened, all the old man could say was "They're all dead! They're all dead!" In fact, Loren thought both of his brothers had been murdered, but matters became clearer when they found the bleeding Jarvis outside and John Meach appeared, having worked his way out of his bonds. His captor, too, had fled upon hearing the first roar of Jarvis's shotgun.

Within hours the hue and cry went out throughout Northeast Ohio, and posses of local farmers fanned out through the countryside, searching for the four fugitives. They soon found the first, bleeding by the orchard fence, where he had fainted from loss of blood. He identified himself as James Casey and willingly volunteered details of the one-sided gunfight but refused to say anything more. A second burglar, identified as William Davis, was caught by county deputies the next morning about 9:30 as he attempted to hide in the Wellington stockyards by the railroad tracks. Both Davis and Casey were taken to the Elyria jail, and the dead men were carted off to the morgue.

Jarvis Meach, much to his surprise, became the hero of the moment throughout the state of Ohio. Although he made little of his own heroics, his neighbors, newspaper editorialists, and lawmen were ecstatic at the blow against crime struck by the unlikely sexagenarian. Coroner G. E. French ruled both deaths justifiable homicide even before the bodies were cold on Wednesday, October 15, and police chief George Corner expressed an almost universal sentiment when he said, "I'd like to subscribe to a fund for a medal for the old man who did the shooting, for he's done more to discourage such outlawry in Ohio than all the convictions the police could secure in 10 years." Three days after the shootings, Park Foster, president of the Lorain County Banking Company, opened a drive to purchase a gold medal and a fancy new shotgun for Jarvis Meach. A similar effort was conducted in Cleveland, with contributions collected by the Hough Avenue Savings Bank.

One of the dead burglars remained unidentified, his body unclaimed and buried in a potter's field. The other turned out to be one Frank Granville, alias Frank C. Scanlon, an experienced cracksman known to police between Chicago and New York City.

After Cleveland detective Fred Kohler identified Scanlon in the Elyria morgue, he broke the news to Scanlon's wife. She provided perhaps the oddest performance in the Meach saga. When first shown the picture of the dead burglar, she became hysterical, screamed "Oh, Frank! Frank! How could you do it? How could you bring this disgrace upon me!" and fainted dead away. There followed a peculiar scene, recalled later by Fred Kohler:

> When she revived [there] came the strangest part of the performance. She sat up, picked up the picture, looked at it, and began to laugh. I thought for a moment she had lost her mind, until she crumpled the picture up, threw it to the floor, and continuing laughing, said, "How did you enjoy the little tragedy, captain? I'm a pretty clever actress, am I not? That man is not Frank Granville, is not my husband. I fooled you nicely, didn't I?"

Mrs. Granville alias Scanlon didn't fool anyone for long. The police eventually found some tell-tale red and black handkerchiefs in the couple's home at 185 Berlin Street, not to mention enough nitroglycerin "soup" in the basement to blow the entire block to smithereens. And Mrs. Granville's unabashed grief was convincing, indeed, when she finally saw what was left of her husband at the Elyria morgue and shrieked, "My God, Frank! My God, my God! It's him! It's his hair! My God, Frank, I didn't think I should live to see this. Oh, my poor baby! Oh, to think of the dirty brute who did it, when he was so good to me!"

After a stimulant restored the chastened Mrs. Granville, she took Frank's body away for burial in Cleveland's Woodland Cemetery.

The two captured burglars were eventually tried and convicted for their part in the Meach business. James Casey, known to newspaper readers as the "gentlemanly burglar," turned out to be a hardened criminal known as "Slick Tommy" McHearn. Owing perhaps to his documented college education, his December 1902 jury spared him the rigors of a life sentence for his crimes. Davis fared likewise, and widespread rumors that the gang's confederates were planning to storm the Elyria jail and liberate their comrades proved to be false. (They were reputed to be remnants of the infamous Lowry gang of "Blinky Morgan" and the "Seven Lowry Sisters of Sin"—see the author's chapter on Morgan in *They Died Crawling* for more details on this fascinating clan of criminals.)

Casey's trial, at least, provided some unintended moments of

The four Lorain County robbers.

hilarity to counterbalance the tragedy of the October events. Attorney Jay P. Dawley, who had frequently defended members of the Lowry gang, tried to defend his client with an aggressive cross-examination of the prosecution witnesses. Putting crusty John Meach on the stand, he triggered the following dialogue:

> Dawley: You were pretty badly frightened?
> Meach: Nary a bit. I was jest as cool as a cucumber, and nary a bit of goose-flesh came up on me.
> Dawley: What did the men say to you?
> Meach: They said: "You're the tall, blankety-blank one and we want you. Don't you argue it a bit."
> Dawley: Then what did you do?
> Meach: Well, I didn't argue none.
> Dawley: Did you have any money?
> Meach: You bet, an' them fellers wasn't 'cute enough to get it. I laid on it.

Injuring his client's case further, Dawley asked John Meach what kind of dog the burglars had shot to death at the door of the Meach homestead: "The best dog man ever had. He was faithful, kind, and loved us. He never got nothin' but his feed an' he was killed by 'em damned scoundrels."

Plunging on, Dawley finally asked John why he was sure that the men he found on the floor of the house were dead. He replied, "They acted like they was dead."

Loren and Jarvis died within a few months of their most exciting night, Jarvis's decline accelerated by the injuries and shock of the events. John Meach continued on at the old homestead until he finally passed away in July of 1905. Not surprisingly, the news of his imminent death brought a horde of expectant relatives, all hoping he would reveal the location of the fabled Meach riches. He did not, expiring in silence and, no doubt, with grim satisfaction. All eyes at once turned to the safe in the room off Loren's bedroom, but its cracking, as Casey, Granville et al. had found, proved troublesome. After several failed attempts, an expert from the Diebold Safe Company of Cleveland was brought in, and the tumblers eventually yielded to his manipulations. The rusty door, with traces of burglar's soap applied by Casey, opened to reveal packets and billfolds stuffed with cash, much dating back to the Civil War. The total was about $70,000. No trace was found of the enormous caches of gold and jewels reputed to be buried at unknown spots on the 80 Meach acres. The proceeds of the Meach estate went to the children of two deceased sisters of the dead brothers.

Perhaps more importantly for readers unconcerned with the heirs' inheritance, the safe also yielded the secret of the Meach brothers' peculiar lifestyle. A yellowed covenant, signed years before by the brothers, revealed that they had made a secret pact after their parents died never to marry—as they had promised their mother—and to live together on the farm. This vow they kept for all the remaining years of their lives, hardly ever permitting a female even to venture onto the Meach property. Their reclusive, laconic ways had only been aggravated by the terrible events of October 14, 1902, and Jarvis and John then swore a second oath that they would never tell anyone where they kept their money and valuables. They all took the secret to their graves.

As for cynical souls who are inclined to dismiss the Meaches as miserly, misogynist cranks, well, let this inspiring story end with this revealing anecdote from the files of the *Cleveland Press*. When asked whether he and his brothers hated women, John Meach left the room and returned with an old photograph, saying:

> Think much of women folks? Here is a little woman, bless her dear heart, we think a good deal of. It's mother. She's been dead and gone 28 years, and because of her, us boys stuck together. She wanted us near her and we wanted to be with her.

When asked if that was why they never married, John replied, "I guess; and when she died we were too old."

Chapter 12

"WITH DEMONS YOU'RE DEALING"

Dr. Chapin's Date with Death

It is one of life's unjust ironies that most murderers seem far more interesting than their victims. This rueful contrast is no less true in Cleveland than anywhere else. Sam Sheppard is far more vividly recalled than his unfortunate wife—and it's not just because he outlived her by 16 years. No one in Lakewood remembers much about publisher Dan Kaber, except that he was atrociously murdered by his good wife, Eva, with lots of friendly help from her mother and daughter. Connoisseurs of Cleveland gangsterdom can reel off the names of criminal luminaries like "Jiggs" Losteiner, "Shondor" Birns, Danny ("the Irishman") Greene, or John ("the Sheik") Leonard Whitfield—but who remembers the names of the men they put in the graveyard? Well has Shakespeare said, "The evil that men do lives after them / The good is oft interred with their bones."

A clear exception to this unhappy rule was Harry Lorenzo Chapin. Like a figure sprung from glamorous fiction, he fascinated Clevelanders of the World War I decade with his outré persona, his luxurious lifestyle, and his unconventional literary output. True, his heyday didn't last long, and his end was undeniably untimely, unenviable, shabby, and violent. But for all that, Harry Chapin had a good run, was a far more interesting man than his killer, and managed to leave everyone talking about him after he was gone.

The Chapin case began at 4:20 p.m. on Thursday, November 8, 1917. Hotel inspector Winifred Leonard was checking the rooms on the third floor of the Colonial Hotel, located on Prospect Avenue at East 4th, adjacent to the Colonial Arcade. Pushing open the unlocked door of Room 309, she entered the room and almost stumbled over a body lying on the floor. It was a middle-aged man, he was wedged in between a chair and table near the front window

Harry Lorenzo Chapin, M.D..   Mrs. H. L. Chapin.

looking out on Prospect, and he was moaning and moving his lips as if trying to speak. There was a hotel towel wrapped around his head, but it did little to staunch the flow of blood that had already heavily soaked the carpet.

The Chapin case might have been solved a bit sooner if those first involved had acted a bit more sensibly. Leonard called David Mills, the hotel's assistant manager, and Mills called the hotel physician, Dr. Royce C. Frye. By the time Frye got to Room 309, the man on the floor was clearly dead, so Dr. Frye called Cuyahoga County coroner P. J. Byrne. Byrne called the Cleveland police before he got to the Colonial, but it was at least 7:05 p.m.—at least three hours after the murder was committed—before detectives Joseph Sweeney, James Hogan, and John Toner walked into Room 309. With them was Byrne's medical examiner, Dr. P. A. Jacobs, who looked at the corpse and exclaimed, "Why that's Doc Chapin! You must know him!"

There were few sophisticated Clevelanders who did not know, or at least know of Dr. Harry Lorenzo Chapin. Born in 1872 in Berlin Heights, Ohio, to a family of means, Harry Chapin dreamed from his earliest days of an adventurous life that would take him to exotic lands and storied sights. After attending Cleveland schools, Harry obtained a degree from Oberlin College, followed by medical studies at Western Reserve University. Taking his M. D. degree at the turn of the century, he embarked on a worldwide quest to see

all of the Seven Wonders of the Ancient World. He eventually succeeded—but only at a terrible price. Ignoring advice that he wear
protective eyeglasses when crossing the desert to see the reputed
site of the Hanging Gardens of Babylon, Chapin suffered severe
eye injuries caused by sandstorms and was totally blind by the time
he got to the Taj Mahal in India.

Lesser men might have given up. But Harry Chapin was made of
stern stuff, and he refused to let blindness alter his plans. He
resumed his travels and began to churn out volumes of poetry,
plays, and nonfiction, much of it based on his profound knowledge
of the mythology and cultures of the places he visited. He was
already making a name for himself as the literary "blind doctor"
when in 1905 he met Mrs. Anna Fries, the young widow of San-
dusky lumberman and ship owner Valentine Fries. Over the next
two years, Chapin courted Anna with all the force of his erudite
charm, and they were married on Thanksgiving Day, 1907. It was
a true love match; while Harry didn't hesitate to admit, in his self-
effacing way, that he reveled in the freedom afforded him by his
new wife's money, he was telling the truth when he described Anna
as "the idol of my soul and the object of my affections." Together,
the newlyweds returned to Harry's globe-trotting ways, and the
next decade sent them over 30,000 miles of land and water and
resulted in a flood of books like *The History of the Bible*, *Paradise
Regained*, *The Adoption*, and *Mythology: Poetry and Prose*. The
basis of their collaboration, of course, was that Anna could see, and
Harry could write, or as Anna put it, "I was the body and the doctor was the mind." The pace and content of their lifestyle changed
little after Harry's eyesight was partially restored in 1911, the
result of a daring operation by Dr. Arnold Knapp. Harry and Anna
continued their intellectual collaboration, and Harry also began to
acquire a reputation as an inventor of beauty products, as well as
explosives and other devices with military applications. By 1917
he was also, no doubt in his copious free time, writing photoplays
for the new-fangled motion-picture medium. Part of each year was
spent in travel, and the other part in residence at either the Hotel
Euclid or Colonial Hotel. By 1917, the Chapins had changed their
digs to the Hotel Hollenden on Superior Avenue at East 6th.

As his death disclosed, there was a dark side to Harry Chapin
that most people, even his friends, did not know about. Sometime
in his adult life, probably since his marriage, Harry had become a

drug addict, consuming ever larger amounts of the cocaine and morphine that his wife's ample fortune afforded. And if he didn't advertise it openly to his friends, he more than subtly hinted about his plight in such published poems as "Subtle Morpheus":

> Relief You can borrow
> For Pain and for sorrow,
> But the lender expects to be paid.
> And with legal tender
> You'll pay to this lender
> A debt you've unknowingly made.
> Divine is the feeling
> As o'er you come stealing
> The soft, subtle hands of relief.
> With demons you're dealing,
> And to them appealing
> For more of the food of your grief.
> Relief they will send you
> For a while they will mend you,
> But they poison the wound as they sew.
> You employ their assistance
> Until the will's no resistance,
> And the structure of habit will grow."

Although she retained a proper reticence about it after his murder, Anna clearly knew about her husband's habit and tried to get him to end his dependency. By the fall of 1917, she thought she had succeeded: Harry promised her that he was quitting and that he would break his ties with that "awful man from Chicago" whose visits the fearful Anna knew were connected with Harry's acquisition of narcotics. That, at least, is what Anna Chapin comfortingly believed when the telephone rang in the Chapins' Hollenden suite early on the afternoon of November 8. Chapin took the call and told Anna he had to go out to a meeting with someone "at the bank." She suspected it was with the "man from Chicago," but Harry reassured her. His private secretary, Elmer Reis, who probably knew exactly what was going on, begged to go with Chapin, but Harry refused, saying it was a "personal matter" and departed. No one except his murderer would remember seeing him after that until he turned up as a corpse on the floor of the Colonial Hotel.

The police on the scene there set to work immediately on the available evidence. Chapin's body was removed to the morgue after Coroner Byrne certified that Chapin had been killed by a massive blow to the back of his skull. Although the skin was not broken, the force of the blow had been great enough to drive seven pieces of broken skull into the brain, suggesting that the murder weapon, either a pipe or window-sash weight, had been wrapped in some kind of padding. No one paid attention to acting police chief Frank W. Smith's notion that Chapin's injuries were caused by an accidental fall. Although Chapin still had $165 in cash and some expensive rings on his person when found, his tie was cut in two and his valuable diamond tiepin was missing. Secretary Elmer Reis told the police he thought that the doctor was missing at least $10,000 worth of diamonds, watches, and other jewelry when he was found. Also found in Chapin's pockets were several envelopes containing small amounts of cocaine.

The physical evidence found in Room 309 didn't make much sense to detectives Sweeney, Toner, and Hogan. There was an empty black valise on the floor and a bag on the dresser containing apples and bananas. Underneath the bed linen they found a .32 Herrington & Richardson blue-steel revolver, serial number 315034, loaded but unfired. There was no trace of the probable murder weapon, and the carpet was littered with numerous cigar and cigarette butts.

John F. Haggerty and his incriminating signatures.

More dogged, if undramatic, sleuthing soon turned up more useful clues. In a wastebasket, Detective Sweeney found fragments of a package claim slip. Working for hours, he painstakingly reconstructed the pieces and discovered it was a claim for a package sent via the American Express Company from Chicago to Cleveland the previous day. The consignor's name was illegible, but the consignee's name was finally deciphered as "J. Haggerty." A trip downtown to the American Express office soon produced the package, which, when opened, was found to be full of waste paper, scrap iron, pencil stubs, and rags. Why, Detective Sweeney wondered, would someone send a package like this, much less insure it for $100?

The next clue found furnished the missing context. In the bathroom of Room 309 Sweeney noticed little bits of paper at the bottom of the toilet bowl. Remembering, one suspects, Gilbert and Sullivan's dictum that "the policeman's lot is not a happy one," Sweeney gingerly fished the sodden fragments out and began the long, tedious process of putting them together. When finally assembled on the following day, they formed a complete telegram containing the cryptic message: "Have 10 Shares Of 200 Percent Stuff Are You Ready."

Everything suddenly fell into place. The police knew that Doctor Chapin was a dope addict and that he had been meeting regularly with a man named John F. Haggerty, the "bad man from Chicago" feared by Anna Chapin and Elmer Reis. When further inquiries revealed that Haggerty had long been suspected of wholesale trafficking in narcotics, the whole thing clicked. Sweeney put it together like this: Haggerty had lured Chapin to Room 309 with a promise to sell him cocaine (the "200 Percent Stuff"). When Chapin got there, Haggerty had tried to sell him the package receipt in lieu of the actual drugs, promising him that they were all in the package itself. When Chapin refused or, perhaps, tried to grab the receipt, Haggerty picked up the sash weight he had brought in the black valise and hit Chapin a fatal blow.

Sweeney's theory was supported by the eyewitness testimony of Colonial Hotel employees. The man who had registered for Room 309 at 8 a.m. on the murder day had signed in as "A. N. Zemeen" of Philadelphia, but his description matched police data on John Haggerty perfectly. Howard Ford, a hotel steward, had been trying to sleep in the room across the hall from 309 at about 3:50 p.m. when he heard the voices of two men arguing there. He shouted, "For God's sake, if you want to fight, go outside!" and the noise diminished. About the same time, hotel maid Anna McDonald arrived at Room 309 with two towels that had been requested by telephone. The last piece of the puzzle fell into place when the murder weapon, a heavy iron window-sash weight, was found the day after the murder under a pile of debris in an alley behind the May Company. It was still wrapped in one of the towels Anna McDonald had taken to Room 309.

By the time the inquest opened at 10 a.m. on Monday, November 12, Dr. Chapin's funeral mass at St. John's Cathedral was almost over. Msgr. T. C. Reilly's eulogy dwelt, to no one's surprise, on the deceased's spiritual aspirations, rather than the lurid manner of his death. As soon as the funeral was over, Chapin's body, in a heavy bronze casket, was transported to Milan, Ohio, for interment in a mausoleum. Almost simultaneously, Assistant Chief of Police Thomas H. Mahoney swore out a warrant for John Haggerty's arrest on a murder charge, and Detective Joseph Sweeney left for Toledo to pick up the trail of the missing homicide suspect.

Sweeney's initial luck was not good. None of the conductors or porters on the railway lines running from Cleveland to Chicago could remember a man fitting Haggerty's description on any of the trains westbound from Cleveland on the murder evening. And when Sweeney arrived in Chicago, he was disappointed to find that Haggerty had been registered at the Hotel Dearborn from November 2 through November 9—which meant that he couldn't have been in Cleveland on November 8. Or could he? The dogged Sweeney insisted on interviewing the maids at the Dearborn and found that they remembered the man in Haggerty's suite. They disliked him because they daily had to clean up all of the cigarette and cigar ends he carelessly scattered on the rug. But two of the maids recalled how surprised they had been when they found no such debris to remove on the day before Haggerty checked out. That day, of course, was the murder day, and this discovery lent credence to the theory that Haggerty had come to Cleveland on the night of November 7, killed Chapin on the afternoon of November 8, and returned by train to Chicago in time to check out of the Dearborn on the 9th.

Another piece of evidence against Haggerty materialized when Sweeney followed up his Dearborn inquiries with a visit to James E. Callahan, Haggerty's personal attorney in Chicago. Callahan had no idea where his client was, and he told Sweeney he doubted Haggerty even knew he was sought by the police. But Sweeney was pleasantly startled, upon arriving at Callahan's office, to see the name on the door of one of his fellow attorneys: A. N. Zeman. The mysterious killer in Room 309, it seems, had simply borrowed the name of Callahan's colleague, and both the Chicago and Cleveland police were now certain that Haggerty was the man they wanted.

It took a while to find him, although by now the Feds were conducting their own assiduous search for the elusive drug peddler. The Cleveland police department flooded the Midwest with flyers containing his description, but nothing more developed for several

Where Dr. Chapin was slain.

months. But before he left Chicago, Sweeney had met a salesman who told him that Haggerty might be an oil-stock broker going by the name of Harvey. He promised to notify Sweeney if he ever saw the man again, if Sweeney would keep his name out of the investigation. The salesman was as good as his word: In late March a telephone call to Sweeney informed him that Haggerty was shacked up with a strawberry blonde in a Kansas City hotel. Early the next morning, the Kansas City police surprised Haggerty in his bed, and he was on his way back to Cleveland with Detective Toner by the beginning of April. Before entering a dank cell at the county jail he spoke with jaunty confidence to Cleveland reporters: "I'm not worried. I was not in Cleveland on November 8, had not been for a year before that and haven't been since. . . . I did not know I was accused of the crime until I was arrested in Kansas City. I won't say where I was on November 8 until I talk to an attorney."

Indeed, so cocky was the returning drug dealer that he asked for a public defender, saying, "I don't want to work to pay him after I get out."

Haggerty's confidence eroded significantly during the next two months, which he spent in the slammer. He was in a far more tractable mood when questioned in the last week of May and unpleasantly astonished at the evidence Sweeney had compiled against him. Cleveland's best handwriting expert, Dr. Henry Jenkins, was ready to testify that the handwriting on the package receipt, the package itself, the registrations at the Colonial Hotel and Hotel Dearborn, and several bail bonds signed by Haggerty in

1915 all belonged to the same person. Eyewitnesses could place him in Cleveland on Tuesday and Wednesday of the murder week. His alibi for November 8 was likely to be nullified by the testimony of the Dearborn maids who noted his slovenly habits with smoking products. His resistance to Sweeney's suggestion that he cop a plea to second-degree murder collapsed utterly when his interrogators pulled out their ace card: an eyewitness who had seen Haggerty in Cleveland only minutes after the murder—worse yet, that eyewitness turned out to be none other than Detective Joseph Sweeney. Known to his peers as "Camera Eye" Sweeney, the detective had almost run into Haggerty as the fleeing killer crossed Public Square on his way to the Union Station (located on the lake shore between West 6th and 9th) to catch the 5:45 p.m. to Toledo and Chicago. Sweeney hadn't even been aware of Chapin's murder at the time, but his steel-trap memory noted an already familiar face, and things snapped into final focus when he looked at Haggerty's mug shot several days later.

Haggerty knew when he was licked. On Monday, June 3, the day before his trial before Judge Manuel Levine was set to open, he signed a confession. In it he admitted that he had invited Chapin to Room 309 with the intention of selling him the receipt for the fake package of drugs. But Chapin, who had been previously burned by Haggerty, refused to go along with the idea, and they argued with increasing vehemence. Finally, about 4 p.m., Chapin slugged Haggerty, and when Haggerty hit him back, the good doctor fell and hit his head on the radiator, fatally injuring himself. Then Haggerty lost his head: "In the excitement I became panic-stricken. I lost my head and took his watch, trying to make it appear he had been killed by someone trying to rob him. I now realize that there I made my big mistake. I should have gone straight to the police and told them about it. Then I would never have to face such a serious charge."

Haggerty denied killing Chapin with the sash weight, claiming that Chapin's skull had shattered on the unusually thin radiator. And he got quite huffy on the subject of his public character: "I also want to say that I am not a man with a criminal record, as I have been painted. I have never before been convicted of any crime." [This was an outright lie, as he had pleaded nolo contendere to a mail fraud charge in 1915 and paid a fine in Federal Court.] "I was arrested only once, and then on the technical charge of suspicion."

Perhaps sensitive to the image of a solidly built 28-year-old hitting a blind man, Haggerty added, "I want to say that in spite of his dark spectacles Dr. Chapin could see. He was not blind."

Haggerty's story was serviceable enough for purposes of defense, but it certainly wasn't the truth. Although he never added to his statement, it is likely that when he lured Chapin to Room 309 with the promise of a phony drug package, he was running a con game not only on the good doctor but on the Chicago drug ring from whom he got the drugs he peddled. His denial that he brought the sash weight up to the room with him—it was proved conclusively that it didn't come from the Colonial Hotel—was pathetic, as was his denial that the unused gun under the bed linen belonged to him.

On June 4, 1918, John F. Haggerty pleaded guilty to second-degree murder, and Judge Levine sentenced him to a life term in the Ohio Penitentiary. Haggerty proved to be a model prisoner, however, and only 11 years later he walked out of prison a free man. But not for long. Some months after his release, examiner F. M. Hoopengarner of the state auditor's office discovered a $2,500 shortage in the Ohio state prison accounts. It turned out that model prisoner John Haggerty, entrusted with state-owned materials while working as a trusty at the Roseville prison brick plant, had been illegally selling materials to private contractors and putting the proceeds in a secret Zanesville, Ohio, bank account. The day he was released he went to the bank, got his money out, bought an automobile, and disappeared. Once again, the word went out to find his nemesis: Joe Sweeney.

It took some time for the detective to catch up with the elusive Haggerty. By the time Sweeney renewed their acquaintance he had become Detective Inspector Sweeney, and John Haggerty was serving a prison term at the Joliet prison in Illinois. But Sweeney had a long memory and had not lost his ability to bide his time. Sweeney had Haggerty picked up the day he walked out of Joliet, and the unlucky drug peddler resumed his interrupted life term in the Ohio pen—this time for good.

Chapter 13

"THEY OUGHT TO GIVE HIM THE WHOLE WORKS"

The Ruth Steese Murder

When the subject is first-degree murder, how much evidence is enough? Both opponents and supporters of capital punishment have long disputed what kind of evidence should be sufficient to support a death verdict. Many people believe the only worthy evidence when a person's life is at stake is the record of things seen: eyewitness testimony that places a murderer on the spot and caught in the commission of his evil act. That was the supreme argument for years—before DNA evidence was discovered—in the Marilyn Sheppard murder mystery. How could Sam face the death penalty on mere circumstantial evidence alone, his supporters argued? Some of it might be coincidental, and some of it might have been faked to frame him by the truly guilty party. The debate remains unsettled and probably always will be, seeing as murderers generally don't encourage audiences to their ultimate acts. But the question is a good way to frame one of Cleveland's most horrible and bizarre murder cases: the 1932 Steese murder mystery.

Everyone can agree on at least one fact in the case: Ruth Elizabeth Gilmore Steese didn't deserve to die. Attractive, personable, and kindly, she was the kind of woman men are lucky to have as a wife or sister, and women are lucky to have as a best friend. Born in 1906 and reared by her happy family in Glenville, vivacious Ruth Gilmore was well educated at Case Western Reserve University before she went to work for Ohio Bell Telephone following her 1926 graduation. She soon switched to a bookkeeping job at the Society for the Blind, where she worked for the next six years, creating a reputation as a solid, generous co-worker and someone who liked to help other people. Called "Betty" by her many friends, Ruth married her college sweetheart, Herbert Steese, in 1930, and the young couple began to plan for a happy future of family and career success. It was the Depression, of course, so there were setbacks along the way, as when Herbert lost his job as a draftsman,

Ruth Steese.

and they had to move in with Ruth's parents in East Cleveland for a while. But things were looking up as the last days of 1932 went by: Ruth's job was steady, Herbert had work at the Pocahontas Oil Company in East Cleveland, and they were making plans to move into their own house. Indeed, things were looking so good that Herbert had just given Ruth a piano for Christmas, and the two of them were planning to host a New Year's party when Ruth got home from her job on Friday night, December 30.

Ruth Steese never made that party. It is still not known exactly how and why, or even where she died that day. Two years of investigation, many suspects, several trials, and the execution of a man in the electric chair didn't settle those questions at all—even if justice was probably done. But we can be certain that she didn't spend the evening as she had planned. When the hour came for Ruth and Herbert to celebrate with their family and friends, she was already dead in the Cuyahoga County Morgue: shot, assaulted, blindfolded, and left to die by an unknown hand on a remote suburban road.

Ruth's last day was a typical one. She did the Society's banking at several Cleveland banks every Thursday, always accompanied by a Cleveland police escort because of the large sums she carried. But December 30 was a Friday, the Society's payday, and Ruth was off alone to make a Society deposit of $1,398.13 and to cash her own check. Characteristically, she offered to cash some other employee checks, and her boss, Violet Warriner, offered Ruth the use of her maroon Hudson since it was raining heavily. The grateful bookkeeper left the Society building at 2275 East 55th Street about 1 p.m. It was only several blocks to the Cleveland Trust branch at East 57th and Euclid Avenue, but Ruth was also planning to stop downtown at the Guardian Trust bank for more transactions and perhaps a spot of lunch at the R. C. Sandwich Shop on Euclid.

Ruth arrived at the Cleveland Trust branch at 1:10 and concluded her business by wishing Samuel Stewart, the teller, a happy new year. She had $191.75 in cash from the Society paychecks in an envelope and another $5.19 in cash and bills in her pockets and billfolds. She waved good-bye and walked toward her car, parked on East 57th. It was still raining heavily, and she probably couldn't see the interior of the Hudson because it was fogged up. She opened the car door . . . and she was never seen alive again except by her killer.

Joseph Novak was a small contractor, not much employed at the end of 1932. Which is why he was out rabbit hunting near Chardon instead of on a job or at his home on East 147th Street in Cleveland that same Friday afternoon. Some time after 12 p.m. he got into his car and began to drive into the city. Near the top of Gates Mills Boulevard and Old Mill Road he stopped for a few minutes, waiting for someone he had previously arranged to meet there. When his party didn't show up, he got back into his car and continued on Gates Mills Boulevard to Shaker Boulevard. Rounding the curve past Brainard, he bore west toward Richmond Road. As he drew nearer to the light there, he noticed a maroon Hudson, license plate number 27050, apparently stuck in the mud about 1,500 feet east of Richmond. Oddly, it was facing east in the westbound-only lane, and its front wheels were mired in the marshy tree lawn beyond the 10-inch curb. Thinking someone was in trouble, Novak stopped his car and got out. Walking to the Hudson, he could see a brown coat through the backseat window, and he opened the right back door. As he did so, blood trickled out. Looking inside, he saw a woman slumped forward on the back seat, her head and body half hidden by a piece of cardboard and an automobile robe. Looking closer, he saw that there was a silk scarf tied around the woman's throat, and a cloth blindfold around her eyes; her hands were tied behind her back, and there was a bullet hole in her forehead. Her pink underwear was on the floor of the car, and her death was so recent that her body was still warm to the touch. So was the hood of the Hudson, indicating whoever had murdered the woman had just left.

Beachwood Village was a different place in 1932 than today, and there was no dwelling in sight within at least half a mile. Novak stepped into the north lane of Shaker Boulevard and tried to flag down cars in the rain. The first car was driven by a physician, who said he had an emergency and couldn't stop. The man in the next car said he would carry the news to Pepper Pike authorities—but did not. Finally, Louise and Jack Hayden of Shaker Heights stopped, and they assured Novak they would notify the police. Within minutes the crime scene was swarming with police from Pepper Pike, Beachwood, Shaker Heights, and Cleveland. The Hudson's license plate was traced to Violet Warriner, who immediately screamed, "Oh, it's Ruth, I know it's her!" The body was then removed to the county morgue by Coroner A. J. Pearse and soon after identified by Ruth's brother Alan.

The police made as much as they could of the meager evidence. Coroner Pearse was able to tell them that someone had shot Ruth in the head at very close range with a .38 caliber revolver of unknown make. The bullet, which killed her within seconds, entered just above the left temple and exited just behind the right ear, ending up in the car upholstery. Someone had also begun to rape her but had not consummated the attempt; whoever it was had tied a cloth blindfold around her eyes and pulled her scarf tight around her throat, but not tight enough to strangle her. The twine used to bind her hands was thick hemp, and the cheesecloth fabric covering her eyes was the type used by chauffeurs to polish cars. But there were no fingerprints inside the car and no footprints in the rain-soaked mud of Shaker Boulevard. More specifically, the police wondered where and when Ruth Steese had been murdered. Was her killer hiding in the car when she came out of the bank? Did he kill her there or somewhere along the 11-mile route to the death scene? Was his motive robbery or rape—or both? The $191.75 in cash Ruth had been carrying was gone, but her expensive rings were left on her fingers and the rape attempt left unfinished. Had he intended to kill her, or was it a spur-of-the-moment act, committed when he thought she might be able to identify him later? And how had he escaped from the remote Beachwood area? The only thing authorities seemed smugly certain about was that the slayer was a white man. The idea for this crime, Cleveland detective Alfred C. Jones opined to reporters, could "have occurred only to a white man. Racial and even national characteristics show in criminal methods as well as in lawful pursuits of life."

What seemed the biggest break in the case came the next morning. William Hodgmann, a 20-year-old Chesterland resident, contacted the Cleveland police after reading about the Steese murder in the *Plain Dealer*. Brought into Central Police Station on Payne,

Hodgmann gave officials what seemed a critical eyewitness account. Hodgmann told them he had been driving from home to pick up his father in Parma Heights on the afternoon of the murder. Just after 1:30, he had stopped his Model T Ford truck at the top of Gates Mills Boulevard and asked a man there—who turned out to be Joseph Novak—whether he could drive the truck on Shaker Boulevard. Novak assured him he could, and Hodgmann went on his way. As he approached Richmond at about 1:45, he saw the Hudson stuck in the mud and a man standing next to it. Hodgmann slowed down to see if he could help, and said, "Is something wrong?" but the man shook his head and waved him on. When he had driven about a hundred yards, Hodgmann turned around and took another good look at him. The man he saw, he told the police, was about six feet tall, between 160 and 200 pounds, had a black pompadour hairstyle, slicked back, and a mouth of flashing, pearly white teeth. He was wearing a windbreaker, leather puttees, and breeches and was putting on a visored cap when Hodgmann turned around. It was the kind of cap used by gas-station attendants, and, coupled with the cheesecloth polishing rag, it pointed police suspicions toward a service-station attendant. Soon, squads of detectives and police were scouring Cleveland for a filling-station man who fit Hodgmann's description. Their efforts were redoubled during the following week when several other witnesses came forward with complementary evidence. One was Clarence Jackson, a 16-year-old messenger boy from Beachwood. He, too, had seen the visor-capped man just before 2 p.m., walking northwest through the muddy field at the corner of Richmond and Shaker Boulevard. The other was Lina Hudson, a woman who had seen a man of the suspect's description getting on a bus at Richmond and Mayfield Roads about 3 p.m. Hudson remembered the man vividly because he was so polite to her, his leather puttees and shoes were so muddy, and because he had to leave the bus momentarily at Green Road to change a $20 bill for his bus fare. And there were two women, Wilhelmina Steard and Eva Nollet, who remembered almost being hit by the maroon Hudson as it suddenly backed into Euclid Avenue from East 57th at 1:15 on Friday afternoon. Both of them remembered that there had been a man driving Ruth's car.

The police, led by Detective Inspector Cornelius W. Cody, did their best with these clues, but the case was already badly stalled by the time Ruth Steese was buried on January 3, 1933. Authorities had plenty of suspects and witnesses, but they couldn't seem to make the facts match up. Among those hauled in by the dragnet were a bloodstained man with a criminal record, who spent his time in county jail sobbing, "Oh my God!"; a 19-year-old youth from Geneva, Ohio, who spent some very unpleasant hours explaining away some bloody clothes he took to a dry cleaner; an unemployed bootlegger's associate seen on a Mayfield Road bus the afternoon of the murder; a man who disappeared after quarreling with his suspicious wife; and a 14-year-old delinquent who insisted to skeptical detectives that he had been the driver of the death car. All of them and more were taken down to Central Police Station and then released after William Hodgmann looked at them, one by one, and said, "Nope, it's not him." After several months of this, the police had given Hodgmann a lot of rides and taken him to a lot of meals, movies, and lineups—but were nowhere nearer to finding Ruth Steese's killer.

No one could have guessed, of course, that the killer would deliver himself into police hands. But that was exactly what happened in a bizarre skein of events that might have been strictly comical if placed in a less tragic tale. On February 19, 1933, just seven weeks after the Steese murder, 36-year-old Peter D. Treadway called the Cleveland police. An attendant at the Vacuum Oil filling station at East 21st Street and Prospect Avenue, Treadway told police that he had been robbed at gunpoint that morning at 11 a.m. The robber had taken $40, and Treadway came to the Central Police Station to file a report and to look at mug shots. After looking through several hundred, he finally picked out the Bertillon picture of a small-time Pittsburgh hoodlum named Benny Zeck. Zeck had only been arrested in Cleveland once on a suspected gambling beef, and Cleveland police were surprised to hear that he had become a stickup artist. And, as there was no trace of Zeck in Cleveland, they decided to let the matter rest. But Peter Treadway had now brought himself to their attention, and their curiosity about him would have ample opportunity to mature and flourish.

Peter Treadway.

Five months later, Peter Treadway erupted back into public

Benny Zeck, Peter Treadway,
and sketches of events.

notice in dramatic fashion. About 9 a.m. on the morning of July 23,
Treadway, bleeding heavily from a leg wound, crawled up the steps
of the Mayfield Heights police station on Mayfield Road. His story
was that he had been returning from Pennsylvania in his car with
$800 at about 7 that morning when he was abducted at gunpoint
while waiting for the traffic light at Carnegie Avenue and East
22nd. A duo of robbers had forced him to drive east to Shaker
Boulevard and then onto Gates Mills Boulevard. There, at a remote
spot, they robbed him and told him to keep driving. When he saw
a car coming, he suddenly hit the brakes, hoping he could seek aid
from the occupants of the other vehicle. At this point the robber
chief, none other than Benny Zeck, shot Treadway, but he managed
to deflect Benny's aim from his head toward his leg. Taking Treadway to a remote spot near Mayfield Road, his assailants beat him
further and left him for dead in the road. Oozing blood, Treadway
regained his car and drove it to within a few blocks of the station,
crawling the last few feet on his hands and knees.

It was quite a story, and Treadway made the most of its virtues.
It explained away, for example, the alleged $800 he had been
bringing from Pennsylvania—money that was needed that very

same day to cover a shortage in his accounts at the Vacuum Oil Company. Although no one knew it at the time, Treadway had been cooking the books there for some months, and his dramatic story of a holdup relieved him of considerable financial pressure. Better yet, the modus operandi of his assailants was eerily familiar, and the police, as he knew they would, seized upon its value at once: it was almost exactly like the Steese killing. The perpetrators had accosted him in daylight, forced him to drive almost exactly the same route probably driven by Ruth's killer, and then shot and left him for dead. The police hardly needed Treadway's hint that maybe Zeck was the Steese killer, and they lost no time in bringing the hapless Benny back from Pittsburgh.

Treadway had probably already made a fatal mistake in bringing himself to the attention of the police. If Zeck didn't turn out to be the man they sought, their attention might well turn to the unsavory Treadway, and if he had been smarter he would have realized the risk he was taking. Peter, in fact, was just the kind of man the police were profiling at this point as the likely Steese killer: an ex-con with a record of violence and robbery. Born on a Kansas farm in 1896, Treadway had run away to be a bellhop in a Kansas City hotel at the age of 14. The next year he was convicted of larceny and served a two-year term. No sooner was he released than he was arrested, convicted, and sentenced to a 15-to-20-year term for robbery. Convincing prison authorities he was going straight, he was paroled to enter the navy in 1917. He got out in 1919 and went to Philadelphia, where he dabbled in prizefighting and private detective work. Arrested for murder, he fled to Virginia with a girl with the delightful name of Boots Rogers—until they were apprehended, and he went off to the Pennsylvania penitentiary for a 20-to-life term. But Treadway was still a pretty ingratiating fellow, and he managed to wheedle a parole in time to show up in Cleveland in 1931. Here, he worked in a speakeasy on East 55th, where he met a girl named Margaret. Margaret didn't like his job, so he got a job at the Vacuum filling station about the time he married her in 1932. He was already stealing from his employers and probably committing a few small-time robberies, but as far as anyone knew he was keeping his nose clean—cleaner than Benny Zeck's, anyway.

Treadway's luck held for a bit longer. Although William Hodgmann accompanied the police when they brought Treadway to Pittsburgh in the summer of 1933 to confront Zeck, Hodgmann failed to notice anything familiar about the genial man with whom he chatted during the trip back to Cleveland. Indeed, *Cleveland Press* writer Ben Williamson later gleefully recalled the following alleged dialogue between Hodgmann and Treadway over sandwiches and beer: "Funny," said Hodgmann, "about that fellow I saw that killed Mrs. Steese. But I'll know him the minute I see him." Peter Treadway looked up, swallowed some more beer, put the glass down and said, quite deliberately, "It's a shame they can't hang the murder of this girl on this Zeck. If they ever catch the guy that killed her they ought to give him the whole works."

To the disappointment of Cleveland police, William Hodgmann didn't think Benny Zeck was the man he saw by the maroon Hudson. But they were determined to get Zeck on something, and despite the fact that he had a solid Pittsburgh alibi for the morning of July 23, Zeck was convicted of robbing and shooting Treadway and given a 10-to-24-year term in the Ohio Penitentiary. Screaming that he was innocent, Benny was led away, and the police returned to turning over the ice-cold leads in the Ruth Steese murder.

The conviction of Benny Zeck, ironically, was the worst thing that could have happened to Peter Treadway. Zeck's attorney, Leo J. Rattay, was a smart, determined lawyer, and he knew his client was innocent. He decided to do something about Peter Treadway. Hiring a private detective, H. Clay Folger, Rattay began to look into Treadway's criminal background and his current activities. Neither of them would bear much scrutiny, and Rattay gradually, over a period of months, began to put together clues about Treadway's violent past, and his current financial machinations, aided by compromising disclosures obtained from his fellow workers and friends. Interesting little details began to swell Rattay's Treadway dossier, details like his frantic juggling of the filling station accounts, his purchase of several revolvers, and the fact that he kept his bank account at the East 57th Street Cleveland Trust branch. Ultimately, as the autumn of 1933 wore on, he managed to persuade the Cleveland police, especially Detective Bernard Wolf, to share his interest in Peter Treadway.

The break Rattay and Folger were waiting for came on December 6, 1933. Discovering that Treadway was about to visit a filling station across the street from Central Police Station on Payne Avenue to make good on a bad check, Folger and Wolf were waiting, unobserved, when Treadway showed up. While Treadway was

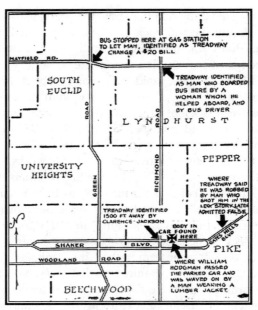

Treadway's steps traced in
Steese murder trial.

inside the station, Folger found a .38 revolver hidden in Peter's car.
That was a parole violation, for starters, and within minutes he was
under arrest and being grilled by Cleveland detectives.

Peter Treadway had a difficult time of it over the next few days.
No one except perhaps his attorney believed his later story that he
was beaten and burned with a cigarette by detectives Wolf, Emil
Musil, and Orly May. But he was questioned almost nonstop for
several days and nights, moved repeatedly from room to room, and
deprived of sleep—the standard "third degree" methods of the day.
He eventually admitted that he had made up the robbery stories
about Zeck and shot himself in the leg—but he was adamant that
he had nothing to do with the Steese murder. Indicted on a first-
degree murder charge, he did little to enhance his credibility when,
accompanied by three other prisoners, he escaped from the county
jail on February 24, 1934, via a rope made of blankets. Stealing a
car, he drove to Chicago, where he acquired a pistol and headed
west. Ten days later he was captured while trying to rob a filling
station in Hannibal, Missouri, and brought back for trial in April.

Waiving a jury trial, Treadway decided to put his fate in the hands of three common pleas judges: John P. Dempsey, Alva Corlett, and Walter McMahon. Prosecuted by John J. Mahon and James P. Hart, he was vigorously defended by Henry Du Laurence.

Peter Treadway's path to the electric chair was strewn with mainly circumstantial evidence. As prosecutors Hart and Mahon argued, the cheesecloth and twine were consistent with materials Treadway had access to at the station. The visored cap, the breeches, the windbreaker, and the puttees seen by at least four of the witnesses were identical to the components of his Vacuum Oil Company uniform. The gun found in his car on December 6 was the same gun he had used to shoot himself on July 23, and similar to the gun used on Ruth Steese. He had been absent from work on the murder afternoon, and Ralph Petre, his co-worker, testified that a revolver Peter kept at the station was missing that day and that Treadway's puttees, breeches, and shoes were muddy when he came in at 6 p.m. Petre and another worker testified that Treadway had telephoned them five days after the killing and begged them "if the dicks come around there on this Steese case, please don't mention anything about me having a gun." Still another co-worker testified that he had seen Peter cleaning a revolver in the filling station on December 31.

Although no one actually saw Peter Treadway shoot Ruth Steese, the state's witnesses hurt him badly by supporting the circumstantial evidence in the case. Surprisingly, William Hodgmann, the state's star witness, couldn't swear positively that Peter was the man he saw by the Hudson, only that he resembled him in some ways. (Perhaps young Hodgmann was feeling aggrieved with his erstwhile police friends; his sour explanation for failing to recognize Treadway on the trip from Pittsburgh was an angry "I never expected to see that man riding in a car with me.") But young Clarence Jackson remained sure that it was Peter, garbed in puttees, breeches, and windbreaker, that he saw walking through the muddy field about 1,200 feet away from him, despite Du Laurence's angry insistence that Jackson could not have seen anyone clearly at that distance. And both the bus driver and Lina Hudson remembered Peter as the polite, muddy man with the $20 bill who had to get off at Green Road to get change. Ruth Steese had been carrying some $20 bills in the money envelope taken from her, jeered Prosecutor Hart, and just how many men with muddy shoes, puttees, breeches, a windbreaker, and a $20 bill could have been walking on Shaker, Richmond, and Mayfield that winter afternoon?

Treadway was a lousy witness for himself, and his wife, Margaret, was worse. He claimed that he had left his Detroit Avenue apartment at 2 p.m. on December 30 and gone downtown to bowl and shop for shoes. The clerk at the Cort Shoe Store on East 4th Street did remember Peter—but she couldn't remember what time of day he came in. And his tale that he had been splashed with the incriminating mud seen by Ralph Petre while working on the carburetor on the left side of his car was mockingly destroyed by Prosecutor Hart's correction that the model Treadway drove had its carburetor on the right (curb) side. Loyal Margaret Treadway did her best for her man, although spectators described her as "twitchy, nervous" and "apparently on the verge of an emotional outbreak." Judge Dempsey's decision would later state that "her demeanor and method of testifying clearly demonstrates to the court that she was only doing what she considered her duty in assisting her husband." Which was a politely judicial way of saying that she was lying when she said Peter was with her until 2 p.m. on the afternoon of December 30.

After four days of argument, evidence, and witnesses, judges Dempsey, McMahon, and Corlett returned a unanimous verdict of guilty after only 55 minutes of deliberation. As Margaret Treadway slumped and sobbed, Dempsey stated that Treadway's version of events was "improbable and unbelievable," his charges of police torture "entirely without foundation," and that the evidence showed no one but Peter D. Treadway could have murdered Ruth Steese. Almost at the same moment the Treadway verdict came in, Herbert Steese was married to Dorothy La Verne Shaver at Fairmount Presbyterian Church in Cleveland Heights. The timing of Steese's nuptials was but a bizarre coincidence, and the happy couple left immediately for a honeymoon in New York City. Meanwhile, the unlucky Benny Zeck's troubles were beginning all over again. Released from the Ohio Penitentiary after Treadway's confession that the robbery-shooting was a hoax, Zeck accidentally struck and killed an elderly woman with his car on the way back to his Pittsburgh home.

Convicted of a murder perpetrated in the course of a robbery (the charge didn't include the attempted rape, but Judge Dempsey brought it up in his opinion anyway), Peter was sentenced to death on April 14, 1934. Just a few days later a Miss Mildred Johnstone came forward to support Peter's shoe store alibi. Swearing an affidavit, Mildred asserted that Peter was the man she had seen coming out of the Cort Shoe Store on East 4th at 2:30 p.m. on the murder day. Treadway's three judges refused to admit Johnstone's testimony as evidence, stating that it was "unsusceptible of belief." Mrs. Johnstone, for her part, failed to show up at two hearings about the matter, and the appeals process ground forward without her.

Treadway's appeal was turned down by three successive courts, including the Ohio Supreme Court, for a total of 13 judges. One by one the three stays of execution granted him ran out. On the last week of May 1935, he submitted to lie detector tests administered by a professor at Ohio State University. The tests proved "not conclusive," and he began to prepare for death. On the evening of June 1 he ate a last meal of steak and potatoes and then walked calmly at 8:16 p.m. from his Ohio Penitentiary death-row cell to the electric chair, accompanied by prison chaplain Rev. J. Alfred Sullivan. Dressed neatly in a dark shirt with blue tie and matching socks, he was saying a silent prayer to the Blessed Virgin Mary when the first jolt of 1,750 volts hit him, and he was pronounced dead at 8:21:30. After a public viewing at a West Side funeral home that was mobbed by the curious, he was buried out of St. Malachi's Church and interred in Calvary Cemetery. His last words to the public were a reiteration of his unwaveringly maintained innocence and a hope for his stepson, Margaret's child by a previous marriage: "I did not kill that woman. I was not there. I did not do that murder. . . . I'm innocent and God knows I am. [I hope] the guilty parties are caught. Maybe my wife could sue the state then and get enough money to educate my boy."

To Margaret herself, he wrote: "I am glad that I am going to meet my maker with a clear conscience and a blameless soul. I have told them everything I know and they don't believe the truth."

Such was Peter Treadway's pious hogwash for posterity. It's surprising how many such cold-blooded killers go to their deaths insisting they didn't do it, and Treadway's hot-seat disavowals were not unusual. Nor, really, was his crime: murder and robbery are not terribly imaginative or uncommon acts, and he had already tried his hand at both before encountering Ruth Steese. What was exceptional about Treadway's awful crime—and remains so—was his bizarre and relentless need to reenact his original crime for the benefit of a police audience. No one would ever have connected him with the Steese killing if he hadn't come to the police with his weird story of having been the victim of a similar crime. Why he did it doesn't much matter, and how he did it is of minor concern. What lingers and tantalizes is the question of why he so wanted to be caught and worked so hard to make it happen.

Chapter 14

THE CASE OF THE CARELESS KILLER

The Mentor Marsh Murder

It's the little things that count in life. If you're lucky, you have parents who tell you that—although you'll probably ignore it until you've learned it the hard way. It's all those little maxims, those simple rules of common sense like "Neatness counts," "You reap what you sow," and "Clean up your own mess." Rudyard Kipling called these everyday laws "the Gods of the Copybook Headings," and you don't have to be a poet-laureate genius to discover that they are ignored at great peril. If you don't believe it, consider the case of Henry Burns. Back in 1923 he became the central figure in a terrific Lake County homicide known to rapt contemporaries as the "Mentor Marsh Murder." Poor Henry didn't even do his dirty deed in the aforesaid marsh, but he certainly paid a dear price for not cleaning up his own mess. Not that Lake County lawmen did such a great job, either, in bringing hapless Henry to justice, as shall be seen in The Case of the Careless Killer.

It began early on October 25, an overcast day, just before dawn on Blackbrook Road in the so-called "B. & O." woods near the Mentor Marsh, about six miles from Painesville, a wetlands area and the site of the first Lake County settlement in 1797. Two women sitting in a car on the road, where they had come to go looking for chestnuts, saw a man come out of the woods with a basket in his hands. He immediately attracted their notice: His face was ashen, he was acting in a highly furtive manner, and before they said anything, he stammered, "There are no nuts in those woods, I might as well stop hunting." He then got into an automobile parked nearby and drove off. Suspicious, the women jotted down his license plate number: 453 465.

No sooner had the man left than two more men, dentists D. C.

Murdered Woman and Husband Who is Held.

Cornell and W. R. Beattie, excitedly came out of the trees. While hunting in a narrow lane in the woods just minutes before, they had come upon a large patch of blood on the ground. Seconds later they found a woman's blue felt hat, a pair of nose glasses, and an unexploded .22 caliber cartridge on the ground. All the items were soaked with blood. After talking with the women, the two men contacted the county sheriff's office in Painesville.

Sheriff's deputies Edward ("Big Ed") Rasmussen and Edward Graves, Lake County prosecutor Ralph M. Ostrander, and other lawmen were on the scene within the hour, and their further searches disclosed an increasingly ominous trail of evidence. A bloody stocking and a black oxford shoe led them just off the road to a trampled mass of grass and bushes, as if a body had been dragged over the area. More bloody pieces of clothing, including a fur coat and a blue skirt, finally led them to a pile of leaves and dirt at the bottom of a small ravine. Poking with sticks through two feet of debris, they soon uncovered the body of a dead white woman.

The corpse lay on its side, the limbs cramped as though someone had used force to cram the body into the shallow grave. The knees and one elbow were sticking out, the nose was broken, the right ear pulped, and the face beaten almost beyond recognition. What at first appeared to be bullet holes in the face and arms turned out to be wounds inflicted with a hard-edged object, like a screwdriver or the muzzle of a revolver. Except for a slip tied around the

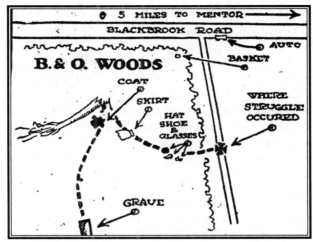

Map of murder scene.

upper part of the body, the other oxford shoe, and another sock, the body was nude. Everything was clotted and matted with blood, which trailed away in splotches 175 feet to the road. Also found in the grass nearby was some jewelry, including a watch that had stopped at 3:12. An autopsy performed that afternoon revealed that the victim had been buried while still alive.

The Lake County authorities didn't know the identity of the victim, but a quick call to Inspector Stephen Murphy of the Cleveland police revealed that the license-plate number jotted down by the suspicious women was registered to a Henry D. Burns of 4152 Lorain Avenue. Roadblocks were set up at the Cleveland borders, and a squad sent to his home found him gone. But the thirty-something Burns was well known to West Side patrolmen, and he was picked up on Wednesday afternoon at the peanut and popcorn stand he ran on West 25th Street, just across from the West Side Market. Shown the bloody clothing and jewelry, he identified them as belonging to his 35-year-old wife, Hazel, and expressed no surprise, indeed virtually no reaction at all, when told she had been found beaten to death in a Lake County grave. All he would say was that he had last seen her Tuesday afternoon at his stand and that he had assumed she was visiting friends or relatives. When asked why his hands were bandaged and why he had bought new shoes, he gave evasive answers. He was arrested and booked on suspicion of murder.

Taken to Painesville, Henry was thrown into a cell and subjected to an interrogation that could fairly be called brutal and would probably be unimaginable to readers of today, conversant as they are with prisoners' rights and Miranda warnings. Treated as guilty from the start, Henry was put through a nonstop third-degree "sweating" that lasted 56 hours and left him cowering like a lunatic in his cell, whimpering over and over again, "I didn't do it! I didn't do it! As God is my witness, I didn't do it!" Much of the interrogation, conducted by Rasmussen and other deputies, consisted of pushing grisly morgue photographs of his dead wife in his face and screaming at the exhausted, traumatized suspect:

> Look at it! See how she was beaten before she was crammed into the grave. Don't turn away, Burns—look at the picture! Did you do it? What did you do with the gun? Where did you put your old clothes? What became of the shovel you used to dig the grave? Look at that picture [a photograph of Henry at the time of his arrest, taken by a *Cleveland News* photographer]. Look at the terror in your eyes. Look at the tell tale bandage on your hand. The picture shows you as you are—a fiend and a murderer. What did you do for her? How did you repay the love she gave you? You killed her in cold blood, beat her into unconsciousness, crammed her while she still breathed into that shallow grave and trampled the leaves and earth over her to hide your crime.

Try as they might, Rasmussen and his crew could not break Henry, even after they took him to see the remains of his dead wife in the morgue and pasted up more gory photographs of her in his cell. When he tried to sleep, the deputies would shout at him, sing loudly, and stamp their feet. After more than two days of this severe regime, they finally let him collapse into an exhausted sleep, convinced he was so broken that even a full confession would not stand up in court. But even in this wretched state, he still insisted, "I didn't do it! I wish I was where she is now! I didn't do it! And if I did I hope God strikes me dead this instant!" Sheriff Ora Spink finally drew the line when numerous visitors to the jail begged for a peek at the infamous suspect, insisting piously, "He has suffered enough. I am not going to have him exhibited like an animal in a cage. He has not been proved guilty, and until he is the law presumes him to be innocent."

Not that the questionable interrogation methods of the Lake County authorities were the only reason for holding Henry D.

Burns on a Murder One rap. By the time the one-week anniversary of Hazel Burns's unearthing rolled around on November 1, Rasmussen and his men, now joined by Lake County sheriff Spink, thought they had more than enough circumstantial evidence to send Henry D. Burns to the electric chair. It didn't even matter that their investigation mirrored the almost comical ineptitude displayed by Hazel Burns's killer. Whoever it was had sloppily left tons of evidence lying around, and virtually none of it was found by the Lake County police officials who looked for it. Indeed, Henry's captors were so careless that they failed to search his pockets during his first week of incarceration, overlooking a jackknife and two shotgun shells he kept on his person.

The police did have a bloody raincoat button found in Hazel's shallow grave, but no raincoat to go with it. That turned up over the weekend, found by four boys playing in a Painesville dump four miles from the murder scene. On Monday night, William T. Hunter, one of an estimated 15,000 gawkers who had come to view the scene ballyhooed by the newspapers as the "Mentor Marsh Murder," was poking around in Hazel's grave with a stick. He apparently was more patient than the police, because he eventually fished an ancient and clay-encrusted pistol out of the water-and-debris-filled hole. It was a Smith & Herrington .32 caliber weapon, and it had two unfired, bloodstained cartridges still in it, both of them nicked but unexploded by the hammer. The condition of the gun and bullets accorded perfectly with the police theory that the killer had beaten Hazel to death in a frenzy after his gun misfired. A red-stained ax also turned up that week, along with Henry's hunting license and some personal photographs, including one of Hazel that someone had left in the murder area. Also found was a bloodstained handkerchief and a bloody scrap of paper with eight names on it, five of them belonging to women whom police were trying to link to Hazel and Henry in constructing a jealousy motive for the murder. So when the police finally got around to looking at Henry's car in Cleveland—five days after his arrest—they were not unduly astonished to find that it was liberally decorated with bloodstains, about a hundred of them, many of them featuring clear fingerprints, splotched and smeared on the doors, the fenders, the steering wheel, and the seats.

And that was just the evidence left at the murder scene and at the suspect's Cleveland home. When the police got to Henry's Mentor summer cottage, they found a bloody flashlight in a cupboard and

From the *Cleveland News*, October 31, 1922.

some buttons in a wood stove, strongly suggesting that someone
had recently burned some clothes there. The icing on the cake was
the discovery of a 50-count box of .32 cartridges in a drawer, minus
the one found by the hunters and the two unexploded ones in the
pistol—there were exactly 47 left. The only thing not found that
week was a cache of $2,700 in cash that Henry insisted he had hid-
den beneath a rug under a piano in his Lorain Avenue home. (It
never did turn up, suggesting that it was part of a bogus burglary
cover story Henry held in reserve).

A plethora of witnesses streamed forward to link Henry with the
copious physical evidence. To no one's surprise, the background to
Hazel's demise was a marriage that had gone terribly toxic. Henry
Burns (born Bruno Bubraski) had been married twice before he
wed Hazel; his first wife died, and his second union ended in
divorce. Hazel had first been married at the age of 14 to a man who
beat her and then found seeming happiness with Henry in 1920. It
didn't last long: within a year their angry quarrels were an epic to

their friends and relatives, and by June of 1922 Henry was living alone at the Mentor cottage while Hazel stayed at the Lorain Avenue flat above a bakery store. She continued to work at her husband's West 25th popcorn stand and occasionally visited him in Mentor. She told her friends, however, that she was in fear of her life from Henry.

Matters apparently came to a head on the weekend previous to Hazel's murder. Hazel came up to Henry's Mentor home on Sunday with some friends, including Mr. and Mrs. Joseph Damato. Both Joseph and his wife heard Hazel and Henry in angry argument Sunday over a local married woman with whom Hazel accused Henry of unseemly consorting. At the climax of the bickering, Joseph saw Henry reach under a pillow, where Joseph knew he kept a pistol. Even as Joe started to say, "I wouldn't do anything I'd regret later," Henry's hand came up empty. Enraged, he accused Hazel of stealing his gun, and she refused to give it back. The next morning she stomped off to the "other woman's" house and exchanged angry words with her despite the woman's protestations that her "friendship" with Henry (apparently Henry had a lot of "friendships" with young, attractive women) was innocent. There was more marital discord during the day, but that evening Hazel gave the pistol back to Henry and left with Mrs. Damato for Cleveland in her own automobile. As Henry drove into Cleveland that night with Joseph Damato, he confided that he had been "scared to death" that Hazel would kill him with the rusty pistol.

That was the last time anyone saw Hazel Burns alive. Lots of people saw Henry at his West Side stand on Tuesday, October 24, and some neighbors living near the Burns house at 4152 Lorain Avenue saw him come home there about 11 p.m. that night. An hour later, these same neighbors saw Henry and a woman get into his car. A minute later, the woman went back in the house and returned wearing a fur coat looking much like the one found near Hazel's shallow grave 36 hours later, minus the heavy coating of blood. The police also talked with considerable profit to Harry Meyers and Dr. William Marsh. Meyers ran a shoe store at 3070 West 25th Street, and he told police how Henry had rushed into his shop on Wednesday afternoon and bought a pair of new shoes. He refused to let Meyers repair his old ones and would not tell police what he had done with them. Dr. Marsh was the man who had treated Henry's badly bruised and cut hands on Wednesday morning, shortly after

Henry fled from the two women on the Blackbrook Road. Henry had told Dr. Marsh that he hurt himself by falling out of a chestnut tree while nutting, but his wounds were consistent with what might be expected if he had beaten Hazel with the very same bloody pistol that police now had in their possession as evidence. Strands of hair found on the gun matched strands taken from Hazel's corpse when it was exhumed from her Zanesville grave in early November. By that time Deputy Sheriff Rasmussen managed to turn up no fewer than four witnesses who had seen Henry in the woods with a shovel 10 days before the murder, giving credence to the theory that he had planned the murder and dug Hazel's grave in advance. That would make it first-degree murder, and that could send him to the electric chair. It looked bad for Henry D. Burns.

It didn't look much better for him when his trial finally opened on February 26, 1923, before Judge A. G. Reynolds in Painesville. By now the police thought they had firmly established motive, means, and opportunity, despite the fact that it was an almost entirely circumstantial case. They knew the Burns marriage was rancid, they could establish that Hazel had feared her husband, and they knew Henry was looking for a way to end his marriage without losing his presumably substantial wealth. They had the probable murder weapon, and they had witnesses who could tie Henry to it and place him at the murder scene. Not to mention the incredible amount of bloody evidence he—if he was the so-careless killer—had left so generously scattered over the murder area. It looked open and shut: Henry had driven Hazel to the death scene about 3 a.m. Wednesday morning and tried to shoot her just off Blackbrook Road. When his gun misfired thrice, he began to beat her in a frenzy with both the blunt handle and sharp muzzle of his pistol, smashing her face and skull again and again as he half carried, half dragged her toward the shallow grave he had dug in the B. &. O. woods. Burying her while she was still alive but unconscious, he hastily covered her with leaves and left to burn his bloody clothes at his Mentor cottage. His plan to clean up the murder scene later at his convenience had been aborted by the presence of the women and hunters in the area.

If Henry was scared by the case against him he didn't show it. When he came to court on February 26, he was easily, as the *Cleveland Press* noted, "the best dressed man in court." Walking to his seat, he adjusted his tie, peeled off yellow buckskin gloves, and

Sketch of Burns's third-degree grilling.

rearranged his new, natty brown suit. Although he showed no interest in the proceedings going on around him, he was sure to wear a new, impressive outfit on every day that followed. As he blandly explained it, "Well, I always liked clothes and I had them. I couldn't wear them lounging around the jail and this is my chance." Meanwhile, he just looked bored, often staring out the windows as his lawyers, P. L. A. Leighley and Harry T. Nolan, labored on his behalf in the intensive process of jury selection.

It looked to be a marathon ordeal. As spectators in the packed courtroom (there was only room for 70 people, most of them a standing-room-only crowd of females avid to see the notorious "wife killer") looked on during the trial's first week, Leighley and Nolan wrangled with Prosecutor Ralph M. Ostrander through three venires of over 100 persons. By the time court recessed on Friday, only 11 tentative jurors were seated, and both sides still had preemptive challenges left. Prosecutor Ostrander told reporters that at this rate the trial would drag into April.

It didn't. On Monday morning, March 5, at 11:30, defense attorney Leighley stood before Judge Reynolds and stated that his client had agreed to plead guilty to second-degree murder. Prosecutor Ostrander accepted the plea bargain, dropping the first-degree charges, and Judge Reynolds immediately sentenced Burns to life in prison, with the additional provisos that he spend two days a

month in solitary confinement and three days a week at hard labor.
Henry showed no emotion whatsoever and when asked if he had
anything to say, muttered, "Not a word, your honor." As Judge
Reynolds imposed the sentence, he told Burns:

> In all my experience as a lawyer and a judge I have never had
> before me a case like this with which you are charged. It is the
> most brutal crime I have ever known and you have pleaded
> guilty. I do not know what was passing through your mind, nor
> do I know what your eyes saw on the night of the murder. You
> will have a long time to reflect as you are a comparatively young
> man. Your eyes and God's alone saw that crime committed, but
> it is my painful duty to sentence you in accordance with the
> degree of guilt to which you pleaded. The court trusts nothing
> like this will ever occur before us again.

Reynolds was at least partially wrong. Five years later to the day,
Lake County resident Velma West pleaded guilty in the same
courthouse to the second-degree murder of her husband, Edward;
it would be difficult to say whether Edward's hammer-slaying was
more or less brutal than the taking-off of Hazel Burns. [The Velma
West murder saga is recounted at length in the pages of the author's
The Maniac in the Bushes.]

Prosecutor Ostrander, sensitive to public outcry at the plea bargain, took great pains to justify the unexpected verdict. Citing the
jury-selection ordeal, he noted the probable length of the trial and
its expected cost to the Lake County taxpayers, an estimated sum
of $10,000. And there was also the problem of the seemingly over-
whelming evidence. Virtually all of it was circumstantial, and the
prevailing wisdom was that juries were reluctant to convict on its
merits alone, which is why all the prospective jurors were asked if
they opposed the death penalty and were willing to convict on
purely circumstantial evidence. Ostrander knew that Burns's
lawyers were preparing to construct a sympathetic portrait of their
dapper, seemingly meek-mannered client, a strategy already under
way when they asked prospective jurors: "Would you be preju-
diced against Burns if it was shown he came from Poland at the age
of 16 and has paid his own way ever since?"

As the *Cleveland Press* suspected, the prosecution was going to
have an uphill battle to "convince the jury that Burns is a super-
brute, the kind of a man who could beat his wife into unconscious-

ness, bury her alive, and leave her to die in the shallow grave that he had dug for her." The man they saw in court looked like what he said he was: a well-dressed, self-made man who ran a popcorn stand in downtown Cleveland.

The crucial decision in the trial, actually, was made by Henry Burns himself. Even before jury selection was completed, he talked to his lawyers on Friday afternoon and told them he was guilty. He gave them a more elaborate confession on Saturday, and they told him to think over a plea bargain until Monday. He agreed to it then, and after some initial resistance from Ostrander, the deal was cut. The public was, quite naturally, disappointed: the plea bargain meant that the gory details were never going to come out, and the ensuing slew of newspaper articles explaining the sanctity of lawyer-client confidences didn't appease public curiosity a whit.

Nor did Henry Burns's long-anticipated "confession," which he made to Sheriff Spink and Deputy Rasmussen as he was taken to Cleveland, manacled between them on the 7:55 a.m. interurban, on March 8 for his one-way train ride to the Ohio Penitentiary. Printed in full on the front page of that day's *Cleveland News*, Burns's self-serving, whiny statement was a tissue of bold lies intermingled with a few verifiable facts. In his version, uncontested by his dead spouse, he had taken Hazel out to the Mentor cottage on Tuesday night at her request. On the way back, she feigned illness and had him pull over to the side of Blackbrook Road in the B. & O. woods. The next thing he knew, he felt his own pistol in his side and heard the hammer snap three times. He threw himself out of the car and screamed, "Hazel, Hazel! Where are you!?" She was right beside him, and he heard the hammer snap once again in vain. They struggled for the gun as he wrestled with her through the woods, and he finally started hitting her with the pistol in self-defense. He beat her until she was unconscious and stopped resisting, then sat awhile, exhausted, on the running board of his car. "Sometime later I came to my senses and self-preservation was my first instinct" was how he termed his next moves, and most would also characterize them as extraordinarily serendipitous. Henry claimed in his statement that he just happened to find a shovel nearby and that he just happened to stumble upon a half-dug hole in the ground, into which he hastily crammed Hazel's beaten body and covered it with leaves. He then motored to Mentor, where he burned his blood-saturated clothing and threw the bloody flashlight in a cupboard. He returned about dawn to clean up the scene, thinking he could pass himself off as a chestnut gatherer. He lost his nerve when he met the curious women, and he returned to Cleveland, planning to clean up his bloody car at his convenience.

Henry's story was a farrago of clumsy, grotesque falsehoods. The testimony of Mr. and Mrs. Damato indicated that Henry, not Hazel, brought the murder weapon to the scene. The blood on the outside of his car indicated that the fatal beating occurred no more than 10 feet away from it, contradicting the extensive struggle area claimed by Henry. And the character of the grave itself indicated that Henry had dug it with some care, probably in advance.

The only lingering loose thread in the Hazel Burns homicide, known still to most Lake County murder buffs as the "Mentor Marsh Murder," is the question of whether Henry Burns actually committed first- or second-degree murder. Although most theorists agree that he lured Hazel to the B. & O. woods with the intention of shooting her, some argue that her death was unpremeditated—therefore second-degree homicide—because Henry's original intention was to shoot her, and the vicious, frenzied beating only evolved when the gun unexpectedly malfunctioned. Of such fine legal distinctions is the law composed and only Henry Burns, long since gone, ever knew what really happened and why during that awful night in the woods. As he put it plaintively to reporters at the end of his trial, "People wouldn't believe it, no matter what I said."

Chapter 15

THE SCOVILL AVENUE MYSTERY

The Murder of Sonny Hoenig

Kidnapping in Cleveland has been mercifully rare. In spite of the well-publicized cases of Beverly Potts, Tiffany Papesh, and Amy Mihaljevic, it has been an uncommon crime in Forest City annals, occurring far less frequently than, say, double homicide, infanticide, or outright child murder. One of its cruel ironies, though, has been the obscure character of its rare targets. Few would have heard of the victims or their families but for these hideous crimes; as a corollary to their relative anonymity, it remains difficult, indeed impossible, to assign clear motives to their unknown abductors. Such was the case with Cleveland's first kidnap victim, Alexander "Sonny" Hoenig, whose terrible death in 1907 riveted the attention of Clevelanders for a fortnight and cast a revealing searchlight on its barbaric police methods and on the character of one of its most interesting immigrant populations.

Called "Sonny" by his doting parents, Alex Hoenig was an endearing child. Three years and four months old in April of 1907, the blond-haired, blue-eyed Sonny was sweetly dispositioned, blessed with enchanting good looks, and a favorite among adults and children alike in the teeming Jewish neighborhood in the lower Woodland Avenue area, where Sonny's family lived at 2822 Scovill Avenue. While his father, David Hoenig, ran the family grocery attached to the house and mother Anna kept house and spelled David at the counter, Alex was most often to be found playing outside his home with his sisters Dora, 10, and Yetta, 7, and the other neighborhood children. Taller and brighter than average for his age, Sonny was also an unusually tractable child, noted for his soft manners, his obedience—he never fussed about his bedtime—and his streetwise caution. He never talked to strangers, he would not cross the street alone, and he knew his parents' address and telephone number by heart. "I am Sonny Hoenig," was his frequent introduction to one and all. He was the adored only son of his sixty-year-old father and a mother past childbearing age.

Alex ("Sonny") Hoenig.

The evening of Monday, April 29, came and wore away like any other mild spring night. David Hoenig was busy with customers in his store, Anna was occupied with domestic tasks, and Sonny was playing with his friends at the corner of Scovill Avenue and East 28th Street. About 8 p.m., he and another area boy, "Jonesy" Brown, 10, were running along the Scovill curb with a neighborhood Newfoundland dog, when Sonny stumbled and started crying. At that moment, Mrs. Benjamin Vinegar happened along the street and, misinterpreting the situation, cuffed Jonesy with her newspaper, screaming, "What's wrong with you?" Grabbing Sonny by the hand, Mrs. Vinegar hauled him into the Hoenig parlor, advising Anna Hoenig, "What do you mean by letting Alex play on the street? He will get hurt." Anna laughed, and mildly disagreed with the well-intentioned busybody. She gave Sonny a glass of milk, and then both Mrs. Vinegar and the boy returned to their respective activities on the street. He returned to his tricycle and Jonesy at the corner, and they played for several minutes, until Jonesy left to talk to his mother. When he returned three minutes later, Sonny's tricycle was still there, but Sonny was gone. No one except his murderer ever saw him alive again.

At about 8:15 p.m., Anna Hoenig asked Dora to fetch Sonny from outside; it was his normal bedtime, and he liked to be readied for bed by his father. Dora went outside and looked up and down Scovill—no Sonny. She returned and informed Anna, and Anna searched outside for several minutes before returning to get David and both girls. Within the hour the whole neighborhood was frantically searching for Sonny, who had disappeared as quickly and completely as if the earth had swallowed him up.

Although David Hoenig called the police within the hour, they didn't show up until midnight. Sonny was still not to be found, and within another 12 hours virtually all of Cleveland's policemen and

Sketch of murder neighborhood.

thousands of its citizens were combing the streets, train stations, and docks for a trace of the vanished Sonny. The police, especially Chief Fred Kohler, boasted confidently of soon cracking the case, and promising clues began to pour into Central Police Station on Champlain Street. Talking tearfully to police, David Hoenig was most suspicious of a man who often hung around his store, trying to ingratiate himself with local children, especially Sonny, with gifts of candy. He was William Schwartz, a 28-year-old alcoholic and unemployed plumber, and he was scooped into police custody for a prolonged period of third-degree "sweating" that lasted, intermittently, for the next two weeks. Kohler's men put more faith, however, in the clues furnished by Mrs. H. J. Goodman, the owner of a shop at Central Avenue and East 30th Street. She told detectives that she had seen a man running on Central Avenue at East 38th Street, just about the time Sonny disappeared. The man was 20 to 25 years old, stocky, 5'8", wearing a worn, dark suit and slouch hat—and he was carrying a small boy who looked like Sonny. Mrs. Goodman also claimed that she had seen the man talking to a young servant girl, Rose Srulovitais. Rose stoutly denied even seeing such a man, much less talking to him. Fred Schneider, a conductor on a Scovill Avenue streetcar, told a similar tale of seeing a blonde woman with a child on his car at about the same time but could only say that the two got off at East 55th. Someone else reported that he had seen a man carrying a child, wrapped head to

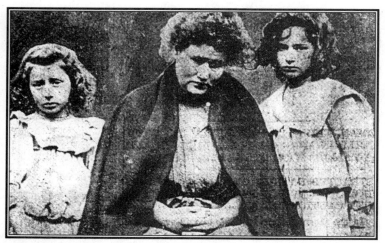

Mother and sisters of the murdered child.

foot in a shawl, on another streetcar. Still another tale came of someone seeing a boy who looked like Sonny having his locks shorn in a downtown Cleveland barbershop. None of these stories aided the police much, and 24 hours after Sonny vanished, hundreds of posters with his picture and a description in English, Yiddish, and Italian began to go up on shop windows and telephone poles all over Cleveland.

With no trace of Sonny or his abductors, the biggest question for the police was a simple one: motive. "Why should anybody steal the boy?" asked Chief Kohler, and most Clevelanders could only echo his puzzled query. No ransom note was ever received by the police or the Hoenig family, and no ransom demand would have made sense. David Hoenig was a poor man in a poor neighborhood: burned out of his business by a fire in Detroit, he had arrived in Cleveland two years before to try and make it in the milk business. He had recently gotten out of that line, blaming the strictures of the new Cleveland health code, and was attempting to support his family as a general grocer. His whole business, he estimated, was worth only $100, and he already owed more than that in liens against him stemming from lawsuits. The abduction of this harmless child made no sense to anyone, and police spokesmen and pundits could only mutter vaguely about the possibility of a "moral pervert" in speculating about the probable perpetrator.

Meanwhile, the police continued to predict a break in the case, made a lot of noise in the neighborhood, and unmercifully "sweated" the most available, if not likely, suspects. A squad of detectives under the command of Sergeant James Doran systematically—or so they had the public believe—tore apart the Hoenig household and yard, digging up the cellar and grounds, searching in the walls, and even examining the mephitic depths of the numerous neighborhood outhouses. Such labors produced nothing, nor did the third-degree sessions with William Schwartz and Sonny's devastated parents. Chief Kohler, like many of his predecessors and successors, claimed to have eliminated the uncivil excesses of the "third degree" process, but a later statement by Anna Hoenig told a different tale about the man who reveled in the title given to him by Lincoln Steffens, of "best police chief" in America:

> After I had given my testimony [at the inquest] I was taken into another room, where I was confronted by three men. One of them was Chief Kohler . . . . Some of the things said to me were: "You know very well that you have known other men and that Alex was not your husband's baby. . . . Now, as a matter of fact, Mrs. Hoenig, wouldn't you rather have a tall, handsome, well-built man than an ugly-looking little fellow like your husband?" . . . One of them said he would [prove his charges of Mrs. Hoenig's alleged adultery], that the man who knew all of the circumstances was on the outside and that he would be brought in to face me. The man left the room and I waited. Presently he returned and said that he was not there at that time.

David Hoenig related a similarly nightmarish ordeal at the hands of Kohler's finest, recalling that the chief took the lead in browbeating the grief-stricken father: "You know very well that you murdered your boy to collect money from your people through sympathy. Now, Hoenig, you know you were jealous of your wife, that you murdered your boy because you knew he was not yours, because you know you are too ugly a man to have so handsome a child."

To which David Hoenig could only reply, "My God! Are you not human? Have you no children? Wouldn't I give all I have for my boy?"

With no breaks appearing in the case, the *Cleveland News* offered a $500 reward on Thursday, May 2, for the safe return of

Sonny Hoenig; an additional $500 was offered for the arrest and conviction of his presumed abductors. Meanwhile, the police looked into stories that a Bedford farmer to whom David Hoenig owed $125 had sworn vengeance and that Anna Hoenig had recently had harsh words with an Italian peddler over some rotten bananas. These leads led to an unpleasant hour for the Bedford farmer and some minor, fleeting public hysteria about a reputed "Black Hand" plot against the Hoenigs. But the search ground fruitlessly on.

The expected break finally came on Friday, May 3—but it only widened and deepened the tragic mystery. About 9:20 a.m., Mrs. Mathilde Leopold, a charwoman at the butcher shop/residence owned by Benjamin Z. Cohen two doors west of the Hoenig home, went to the backyard to dispose of some refuse in barrels kept there for the purpose. Lifting up the lid of one, she saw a pair of little shoes sticking out of some broken crockery.

Then she saw that there were legs attached to the shoes. Mathilde screamed and ran to one of Cohen's assistants, 19-year-old Reuben Dvorkin, who went to the barrel and pulled out the stiff, dirty corpse of Alexander "Sonny" Hoenig. Sonny was clad only in his underwear, black stockings, and shoes; his blue velveteen pants and green shirtwaist were found next to the barrel. Within minutes a crowd of about 500 women and children, many of them weeping, thronged the congested area, obliterating whatever physical evidence the police might have found, including the barrel, which was knocked to pieces.

Although an initial examination suggested the boy had been drowned—his shoes and stockings were soaking wet—the postmortem conducted at the county morgue by Coroner Thomas A. Burke, Dr. O. T. Schultz, and Dr. W. J. Hewitt eventually concluded that Sonny had met death by asphyxiation. There was a lot of sawdust in his hair and stockings, and, more importantly, enough in his trachea and lungs to indicate that he had choked to death on it. Bruises on his body, especially his neck, implied that death had come after a struggle with his captors. There was undigested corned beef, apple, and milk in his stomach, apparently consumed after he disappeared on Monday night, as his mother, Anna, kept him on a strict kosher diet. The condition of the corpse suggested that Alex had not been dead for more than 36 hours, implying a time of death no sooner than Wednesday night. More oddly, the

Georgi Udolf and Reuben Dvorkin,
suspects in the Hoenig murder.

freshness of the cadaver, its stiffness, and the dampness of its lower
extremities led the doctors and some of the investigating police to
conclude that it had been kept in an icebox or similarly cold place
for several days.

The police didn't have to look hard for such a place. Just inside
the back door of Cohen's store, only a few yards from the death
barrel, was a large icebox that Cohen used to refrigerate the meat
he sold. There were similar iceboxes at the Hoenig store and other
shops around the block, and police began taking careful samples of
the sawdust used in such stores for insulating iceboxes and soaking
up animal blood. Their initial theory in the wake of the discovery
of Alex's body was that he had been kidnapped and then murdered
at some nearby but unknown location. Fearing discovery as police
continued their house-by-house search throughout the first week,
the killer or killers had removed the body from its refrigerated
locale on Thursday night and furtively dumped it in one of Benjamin Cohen's waste barrels. A blind alley off East 29th Street led
to a point only two houses away from Cohen's backyard, and a
man's footprints were seen in the mud on both sides of the broken
fences that permitted access to the barrel area. (The footprints were
part of the evidence helpfully destroyed by the crowds of curious
gawkers who flooded the murder site throughout the long weekend
after Sonny's body was found.)

The police also didn't have to look hard for additional suspects, although they were still cheerfully sweating Sonny's parents and William Schwartz. Several hours after Sonny was found, the police took away Benjamin Cohen and his two assistants, Reuben Dvorkin and Georgi Udolf, on suspicion of murder. For the next 10 days each of them was subjected to a brutal regimen of arrest, interrogation, release, followed by arrest, interrogation, release, in a harsh pattern that Reuben Dvorkin bitterly recalled a month later: "The police got me in a room and one man said, 'If you didn't kill the boy, say that you know who killed him. Say it, say it! Say that you were insane when the deed was committed, that you didn't know what you were doing. Crazy men are never punished in this country. For a short time you will be in an asylum. Only say that you killed him. I will protect you.'"

At one point in one of his interrogations at the 8th District station a rope was brought into the room, and Dvorkin was told he was going to be hanged on the spot if he didn't confess.

Actually, Kohler and his men had nothing more than some equivocal circumstantial evidence against Cohen, Dvorkin, and Udolf. Although the body was found on Cohen's property, no less an authority than Sergeant James Doran could attest that the body had not been in the barrel when Doran searched it on Thursday afternoon. The normally bustling activity in the crowded backyard area made it unlikely, in fact, that the body could have been placed there until after 11 the previous night. And for all the supposed certainty of the police that the dead Sonny had been kept frozen in Cohen's ice chest, there was no evidence to prove it. (Apparently Doran and his men had not searched any of the neighborhood ice chests prior to finding Sonny's corpse.) Nor was there any evidence to accuse either Udolf or Dvorkin of spiriting Sonny away on Monday night; although both lived in a room above the suspect ice chest, both of them had good alibis for Monday night. There was no specific motive to connect them with Sonny's murder, other than the happy thought that either of them might be the "degenerate" sought by the police.

Other reasons for thinking the police were on the wrong trail became public knowledge in the week that followed the discovery of the body. Jonesy Brown, the last one to see Sonny alive, was finally located and told a story of seeing two strangers in the blind back alley near where Sonny was playing about 8 p.m. on Monday. One of them had a flat nose and a dark gray hat; the other was a black man. The two men yelled at Sonny and Jonesy and told them to scram. Sol Lindner, age 8, of 2839 Scovill Avenue, backed up Jonesy's memory with his own recollection of the flat-nosed man in the alley. And on May 8, Sam Spero, a neighborhood contractor, came forward with a story that he had seen two men like those in Jonesy Brown's description near the alley at 11:50 p.m. the night before the body was discovered—and the black man was carrying a bushel basket!

The Spero and Brown disclosures opened a flood of intriguing if ultimately useless reminiscence. A barber on Central Avenue told Kohler's detectives about a customer who came in for a shave the night after Sonny vanished; he told the barber, "We'll get that Jew ---- Hoenig yet. They'll find that boy right around in the neighborhood." Mrs. Joseph Heffler, whose bedroom window was only six feet away from the death barrel, told of hearing a strange noise outside at 2 a.m., just seven hours before Sonny's body turned up, "I heard a sound like a moan, which frightened me. But I could see nothing wrong." Adolph Kial, who owned a shop on East 49th, told police that a man came there at 8 a.m. on Friday—an hour before the body was actually discovered—and told him to take his poster of Sonny down from the window because the body had been found in a barrel near his home. Better yet was the fortune-teller who told David Hoenig's sister-in-law that Sonny was being held in the attic of an unknown building on Woodland Avenue but would be returned on Thursday night—as he in fact was.

Meanwhile, the inevitable processes of the tragedy inexorably ground on. Sonny Hoenig was buried on Sunday afternoon in a small pine coffin at the Jewish cemetery on Lansing Avenue. The event was attended by as many as 10,000 persons, most of them simply curious or morbid, and the funeral ended in a disgraceful mob scene as the crowd trampled flowers, shrubbery, and even some children in its eagerness to gorge on the grief of the Hoenig family. They weren't disappointed: Anna Hoenig fainted several times during the service, and both David Hoenig and his aged mother threw themselves across the open coffin at the graveside in hysterical grief, the father crying, "The blood of my innocent child! Where is the murderer? Is there no justice for my boy?" Rabbi S. Margolies, who presided over the service, cited the text of Deuteronomy, chapter 21, as an injunction to anyone in the crowd with knowledge of the murder to come forward. Manuel Levine,

Cleveland police prosecutor and Mayor Tom Johnson's liaison to the Jewish community, also spoke, assuring the crowd that everything possible was being done to bring Sonny's unknown murderers to justice.

Chief Fred Kohler, with his usual bad timing, picked that same day to announce his mature theory about Sonny's death. When first informed of Kohler's statement, David Hoenig looked around the cemetery and said, "This is hardly a place for jesting." Assured that it was no joke, he responded, "My God! Can he be in his right mind? Why do they call him the 'best' chief?"

Kohler's much-mocked hypothesis was that Sonny's death had been an unfortunate accident, whose tragedy was compounded by panic on the part of whoever had discovered the body. Kohler warmed to his theme in the May 6 *Plain Dealer*: "Prompted by his childish curiosity, that boy wandered into one of the iceboxes in the rear of the butcher shops . . . A moment later someone, unaware that the child was inside, swung shut the heavy door and locked it. Frightened, the boy began to cry. His sobs were too weak to penetrate the thick walls of the refrigerator. In despair, he threw himself face downward on the floor, heaped with sawdust. As he gulped in his despair particles of sawdust found their way into his mouth and down into his bronchia. They choked him . . . The next morning someone opened the door to find "Sonny" Hoenig . . . stretched out on the floor of the icebox, stark in death."

Whoever that someone was—and Kohler clearly believed it was Cohen, Udolf, or Dvorkin—had decided to hide the corpse, for fear of being blamed for Sonny's death. It had lain in a freezer for about three days before its discoverer had spirited it to Cohen's trash barrel late Thursday night. Kohler concluded his startling explanation by promising an arrest of the guilty party soon. Noting that it was illegal to put a corpse near meat or vegetables, he stated that the suspect "will be booked for a violation of the health ordinance."

David Hoenig wasn't the only one who thought Kohler had lost his mind. Butcher Cohen had a reputable eyewitness, the all-seeing Mrs. Vinegar, who was willing to testify that Sonny Hoenig was decidedly not in the Cohen icebox when she stopped off to buy a steak just minutes after dragging Sonny back to his mother. The unkosher food in Sonny's stomach clearly suggested that some stranger had fed him before he ended up in anyone's refrigerator. Coroner Burke and the autopsy doctors insisted that Sonny had been alive until Wednesday, May 1, and that the marks on his body indicated that he had suffocated while struggling with someone stronger than he was. Nor did Kohler's bizarre theory explain why Sonny was nearly nude when his corpse was found. Burke's inquest, which opened on May 6, ratified his conclusion that Sonny Hoenig had been murdered by an unknown person or persons, much to the displeasure of Chief Kohler. The final nail was pounded into the chief's hypothesis by Harry Adelstein of the Hebrew Relief Association. The day after the funeral, using a young boy so similar to Sonny that he had already been repeatedly mistaken for the missing child, Adelstein tested Kohler's theory by locking the boy in several neighborhood ice boxes. The child's screams from inside each refrigerator could easily be heard out on the street. Defending himself with his usual vigor, Kohler continued to insist that Sonny's death was accidental, an arrest was imminent, and that the Hoenig case was a top police priority. He reiterated his belief that the events of the boy's death, the concealment of the corpse, and his return had all taken place within 100 feet of the Hoenig home. Turning a more ruffled, if less public face to his subordinates, Kohler promised them that if they "failed to round up the murderer that every man jack would go back to a beat and patrolman's pay." Neither event came to pass.

The Sonny Hoenig mystery disappeared as a public and media obsession about the middle of May. After two weeks of perfectly frightful treatment at the hands of the police, Sonny's parents, Benjamin Cohen, Georgi Udolf, and Reuben Dvorkin were released for good. William Schwartz, the ne'er-do-well plumber, was arrested and jailed, but not for murder; he was thrown into a cell to sober up, after showing up too drunk to testify—twice—at Sonny's inquest. Nor were butcher Benjamin Cohen's problems quite ended: in late June he was indicted for arson. It seems the authorities suspected him of burning down a grocery store he owned at Scovill Avenue and East 31st Street for the insurance money. By that time, Sonny's parents and Reuben Dvorkin had gone to the newspapers with their charges of police brutality and extortion. Mayor Tom Johnson, after reading Anna Hoenig's statement—and aware that feelings in the Jewish community were running high about the methods Kohler's men had employed—called the chief on the carpet and announced an end to third-degree procedures in Cleveland. Kohler, for his part, "positively and absolutely" denied any wrongdoing on the part of his staff—and promised it wouldn't happen again. But judging from the treatment meted out to Christina Lipscomb the following year—a story chronicled elsewhere in these pages—Kohler's men did not alter their technique a whit.

There were two false confessions to Sonny's murder. One came from a man in the Bowling Green city jail in the week after Sonny's body was found; the confessor's motive for claiming guilt was unclear, but his story was easily disproved, as was the story of 17-year-old Alva Cohen, a boastful juvenile delinquent who told Cleveland police in November 1909 that he had murdered Sonny. Alva, it seems, fancied himself the "Jesse James of Cleveland," and he eventually admitted to authorities that he made the story up to impress his youthful fellow gang members.

More than 90 years have gone by since sunny Sonny Hoenig met death at a cruel killer's hands. David Hoenig soon moved away from his house of bad memories, and the vibrant Jewish neighborhood on whose sidewalks Sonny played is no more, replaced by the impersonal and pompous architecture of Cuyahoga Community College. But his blood still cries out from the earth for justice, no less so than on that sad Sunday when Rabbi Margolies pled for the man with guilty knowledge to come forward.

Chapter 16

"JUMP, BOYS, IT'S A CRASH!"

The Doodlebug Deathtrip

People of the modern age like to look back condescendingly at the medieval "Age of Faith"—but its mundane credulities were as nothing compared to the naive confidence we denizens of the 20th century place in the infrastructure of technological systems that make the realities of contemporary life possible. Every day most of us step into machines—airplanes, trains, and automobiles—and let them take us whither we will, secure in the certainty that they will get us there safely and uneventfully. Most of us don't comprehend how these complex machines and systems work, but our confidence in them and the human beings that run them remains generally secure. After all, 999,999 times out of a million, nothing goes wrong, so why shouldn't we persist in our childlike faith in things we don't understand?

This is a story about that one millionth time, when everything that was supposed to work didn't, and the common sense and good judgment that usually prevent our complex world from dissolving into murderous chaos failed. It failed in 1876, when Amasa Stone's pigheaded arrogance placed a defective railroad bridge over Ashtabula Creek. It failed in 1895, when a trolley conductor took Car No. 42 over the edge of an open swivel-bridge on Cleveland's Central Viaduct. It failed in 1916, when safety officials for the waterworks tunnel project ignored the warning signs of explosive methane gas in intake crib No. 5, 128 feet below Lake Erie. It failed in 1929, when an unthinking Cleveland Clinic employee hung an exposed electric light bulb right next to sheets of flammable nitro-cellulose X-ray film in a basement record room. And this is the now-forgotten but still terrible story of how it failed in Cuyahoga Falls on July 31, 1940: the fiery tale of the Doodlebug Inferno.

From the *Cleveland News*, August 1, 1940

Why it was called a "Doodlebug" remains an elusive question. "Doodlebug" is the slang name given to several species of insects, including a variety of dung beetle. Perhaps it was the shape: although the general outline of the gas-electric vehicle resembled an old-fashioned trolley car, the appearance of its long, bulging gas-line tanks carried underneath suggested the swollen shape of a bug's larvae. Or maybe it was the hybrid, mongrel nature of the self-powered car, which drove itself over the rails with an engine powered by the gasoline it carried below. By 1940 the word was an accepted term in railroad jargon, and users of the one-car commuter service that ran the 12 miles between Hudson and Akron used the term affectionately to describe the train that took them daily to their jobs and homes, and to other trains linking Northeast Ohio to the rest of the nation. Whatever the reason, it wasn't what anyone would call a fair match when the Doodlebug hit the Pennsylvania Railroad FC-4 freight train at 6 p.m. on the dot that last day of July 1940.

Carrying 46 passengers and crew, plus its several hundred gallons of gasoline fuel, the Doodlebug probably weighed 122,000 pounds when it collided with the FC-4. Or rather, the FC-4 collided with it: with 73 loaded freight cars, the FC-4 outmatched the Doodlebug by several million pounds, not to mention its superior momentum. When they collided almost exactly at the Front Street crossing in Cuyahoga Falls, the bulk and force of the FC-4 told immediately. Cleaving the metal-plate skin of the Doodlebug "like a melon" (as one eyewitness described it), the lead locomotive of the FC-4 "telescoped" its way into the crowded Doodlebug, smashing its way through seats, poles, partitions, windows, and human beings as it ploughed relentlessly forward. Forcing the Doodlebug backward down the screeching rails, the FC-4, its own brakes screaming, didn't come to a stop until it had pushed the punctured car five hundred feet north of the point of impact. Even as the two trains shuddered to a stop, still locked in their lethal embrace, the gasoline tanks under the Doodlebug exploded and drenched both trains in a hot torrent of burning gasoline. Before the gaze of horrified eyewitnesses, the crushed Doodlebug and its human freight began to burn up in pillars of flame that reached out 25 feet from either side of the double wreck and as high into the air. How had this happened?

It certainly shouldn't have, everyone later agreed. When the Doodlebug left Hudson at 5:49 on its regular run to Akron, its route and orders were clear. Engineer Thomas L. Murtaugh had a copy of them, as did conductor Harry B. Shaffer, and their import should have been unequivocal to these experienced railroad men: "Engine 4454—running extra—Arlington to Hudson—to meet No. 3380, gas-engine 4648 at Switch 1, Silver Lake."

What it meant in normal English was that the Doodlebug (Engine 4648) had a "meet" order with Engine 4454 (FC-4) at the number 1 switch at Silver Lake, several miles north of Cuyahoga Falls. The section of the Pennsylvania Railroad used by both trains was a one-track line, so it was a matter of routine for the southbound Doodlebug to lay over ("meet") on a rail siding at Silver Lake while any northbound train passed it. The Doodlebug could then proceed south, but only after it called Hudson for permission to proceed onto the next "block" or section of track south of Silver Lake. Block operator O. L. Rickey had personally given the "meet" orders to Murtaugh and Shaffer at Hudson, and the crew of the FC-4 was given identical orders at Arlington sometime after 5 p.m.

To this day nobody knows why it happened. Engineer Murtaugh brought the Doodlebug to the number 1 switch at Silver Lake right

on schedule. But then, instead of switching to the siding and calling Rickey to get block permission, he just kept right on going.
Murtaugh himself would not remember the accident, so why he
kept the Doodlebug going south remains a mystery. Neither conductor Harry B. Shaffer, brakeman A. L. Bailiff, nor baggage man
Charles Bilderback, all familiar with the run, said anything, and
Shaffer later recalled that he was too busy taking tickets from the
passengers and checking them off his list to notice anything
unusual. But just before 6 p.m., he happened to glance at his watch
and looked up to see . . . the outskirts of Cuyahoga Falls instead of
the expected view of the Silver Lake siding. As he told it later from
his hospital bed: "I jumped up to go up front and find out from
Murtaugh why we had passed the siding. Just as I got to my feet, I
looked out and saw the locomotive of the freight train rounding the
curve ahead, coming toward us. I knew we were going to hit. We
were going 50 to 55 miles an hour. I ran back into the baggage
compartment and yelled, 'We're going to hit! Jump!' Then I
jumped."

Shaffer wasn't the only one who saw the disaster coming. As the
lead locomotive of the FC-4 pulled out of the curve just south of
the Front Street crossing, engineer O. M. Lodge and fireman E. N.
Reynolds suddenly saw the Doodlebug coming at them. Jamming
the brakes, Reynolds watched in shock as his train cleaved the
Doodlebug's front and began driving it up the track. Simultaneously, Lodge and Reynolds heard the explosion of the Doodlebug's
tanks. Seconds later they were covered with a shower of burning
gasoline that spread over the first two dozen cars of the FC-4.
Stumbling out of their cab and frantically smothering the burning
fuel on their skin, they ran toward the flaming Doodlebug.

Wesley Payne probably had the best view of the wreck. Sitting
in his '35 Buick at the Front Street crossing gate, he was watching
the Doodlebug go by. He didn't see the freight train until it hit the
Doodlebug, and he watched in stupefaction as they collided with a
terrific crash, burst into showering flames, and started moving
northward on the track. Within seconds, Payne's car was covered
with burning gasoline. Jumping out, he began running for the
nearby Cuyahoga River along with other bystanders, some of
whom were on fire. Stumbling down a ravine, Payne injured his
left knee and was later stitched up at St. Thomas Hospital. His verdict on the wreck echoed that of everyone else who saw it: "I

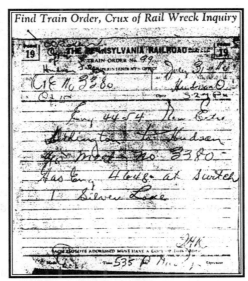

Find Train Order, Crux of Rail Wreck Inquiry

Copy of order for the missed
layover at Silver Lake.

served in the World War and fought in active battles in France but
the confusion and turmoil that followed the explosion was more
horrible and ghastly than anything I saw in the war."

What Payne remembered about the horrific scene agreed with
the accounts of all who saw the aftermath of the crash. The initial
impact of the locomotive and the freight had smashed virtually
everything inside the Doodlebug, mixing broken seats, windows,
and other debris in a veritable salad of metal ruin. At the same time,
it had thrown almost all of the passengers forward toward what was
left of the front of the car. (Actually, the "front" was the back, as
the dual-control setup of the Doodlebug allowed it to run forward
or backward without turning around; it had been traveling "backward" when it hit the FC-4.) They were probably all dead when the
first rescuers arrived. Those who came to help remembered that the
most macabre aspect of the horrible scene was its unearthly, eerie
quiet—there was not a cry, moan, or scream to be heard, only the
sound of flames licking hungrily at the Doodlebug wreckage. Witnesses could see the passengers inside, many of them either
crammed up against the windows or sticking out through the windows like ripped-open sacks of laundry. And it was just as well they

all seemed to be dead because it took some time to get the 43 bodies out. The weight of the collision had warped and bent the sides of the Doodlebug so forcefully that it took crews working with acetylene torches many hours before they could extricate all of the bodies. Not that there was much left of them: although some corpses were thrown clear of the train, many were charred and burned beyond recognition. Jewelry, dental work, and pieces of clothing would eventually identify all the victims.

Miraculously, there were three survivors of the wreck. One was engineer Murtaugh, who apparently saw the FC-4 coming and dived out of the driver's cab before the crash. He fractured his skull and sustained other, minor injuries but survived, unable to understand or recall why he had driven the Doodlebug to its deadly end. Delirious, he was taken to the hospital, where he repeatedly moaned, "Get me out of here, I've got to get back to work." Another who escaped the inferno was conductor Harry Shaffer, who ran back through the baggage compartment, shouting "Jump, boys, it's a crash!" At least that's what Tod E. Wonn, age 24, remembered him saying, even as he watched Shaffer hurtle out the side door. Wonn, a Pennsylvania Railroad section hand, was riding as a "deadhead" passenger, that is, free of charge. Sitting in the baggage area, Wonn didn't even have time to wake his friend, Bruce Kelly, who was sleeping beside him. The trains had already collided when he jumped, and his clothes were on fire when he hit the ground. Rolling through the brush, Wonn managed to extinguish the flames. Stumbling, covered with blood and in shock, Wonn wandered into a filling station run by Fred Eckman near the Front Street crossing. Crying "My buddy, oh my buddy!" Wonn refused to let Eckman's wife, Molly, attend to his wounds, and he ran out of the station and back to the railroad tracks, searching vainly for his dead roommate, Bruce. But Wonn came out of the wreck in better shape than conductor Shaffer, who lost his right hand and foot, probably when the Doodlebug was pushed over them by the FC-4 freight.

Local safety forces and many civilians performed well in the emergency. Within minutes, area policemen and sheriff's deputies were drawn to the scene by the sound of the crash and early reports on local radio stations. One of them was L. P. Seller, Cuyahoga Falls fire chief: "I was there two minutes after the wreck and the Doodlebug was already a furnace. I heard no screams and realized everyone inside was dead. Some victims were hanging partly out of the windows and they were on fire. Some were pushed out by the force of the freight still pushing and they littered the tracks on either side. They were all shattered, bleeding, and burnt. The interior looked as though a tornado hit it."

Especially heroic and grisly was the work of the men who brought the bodies out. Working for hours to cut them out of the twisted metal, they endured sights and sensations rarely seen outside a devastated battlefield. And their work wasn't made any easier by the behavior of the many ghouls who soon showed up to gawk at the wreckage. Before the day was finished, as many as 20,000 people would converge on the scene, significantly hampering the work of safety forces, who repeatedly had to drive the crowds back with force. Perhaps the person who best kept her cool and rendered useful service that day was Molly Eckman, who tried to help the dazed Tod Wonn when he stumbled into her husband's station. Living only 80 feet from the point of impact, Molly had been washing dishes when she heard the familiar tootle of the Doodlebug and looked up to see the passengers at the windows looking back at her. Seconds later, she heard the crash, and the next thing she saw was the Doodlebug going by in the opposite direction. As soon as she saw it burst into flames, Molly ran to her linen closet and got all the towels she could carry. "I knew they would need bandages," she later explained. Heading toward the tracks, she could feel the heat as the burning gasoline did its pitiless work. Another who acted well was the Reverend Joseph Butler, an assistant priest at St. John's Cathedral in Cleveland. Visiting friends in Cuyahoga Falls, he heard sirens and went to the scene of the crash. Standing by the ruined car and performing his creed's rite for any Catholic dead who might have been on board, he offered conditional absolution as each of the bodies was brought out of the wreckage.

It only took firemen about 15 minutes to get the flames out when they finally arrived on the scene about 20 minutes after the crash. There were some anxious moments, particularly for the FC-4 crew, as they watched the burning gasoline moving toward the fully loaded petroleum tank cars of the 73-car train. But engineer Lodge and fireman Reynolds, ignoring their own burns, stayed on the scene and helped direct the efforts of firemen to contain the danger to the freight train. Oddly, considering the fate of the Doodlebug,

Wreck Death of 43 Ruled Accidental by Coroner

Crew of Motored Coach Is Blamed, but No Criminal Action Is Anticipated

From the *Cleveland Press*, August 2, 1940

the collateral damage from the accident was minor. Although the railroad ties were partially burned for a length of 500 feet, the rails themselves held firm, and the single-track line was returned to normal service by the following morning.

Summit County coroner R. E. Amos and his aides dealt with the aftermath of the tragedy in methodical, professional fashion. Supervising the long hours of bringing out the dead, Amos had workers stack pocketbooks, glasses, briefcases, and burned clothing carefully, so as to aid in identification of the bodies. Moving briskly, Amos got the inquest under way the next morning. As engineer Murtaugh and conductor Shaffer were too badly injured to testify, the evidence available to the panel was limited and secondary. But Amos managed to file a report the very next day, finding that the crash had occurred because Murtaugh and Shaffer had disobeyed their written orders. It would appear that Amos, for lack of any better testimony, relied on the views of F. W. Krick, Pennsylvania Railroad division superintendent, who stated: "Apparently, both the engine man and conductor on [the Doodlebug] had proper orders to wait at the Silver Lake siding and let the freight train pass. But apparently both of them had a mental lapse at the same time."

After conferring with Summit County prosecutor Alva R. Russell, Amos ruled that Murtaugh and Shaffer could not be prosecuted, as the wreck involved "no specific violation of any statute."

The entire matter was just a case of mass "accidental death." Additional probes by Pennsylvania Railroad officials, the Ohio Public Utilities Commission, and the Interstate Commerce Commission added nothing significant to the solution of the Doodlebug puzzle.

Conductor Shaffer blamed the whole thing on Murtaugh's oversight, and Murtaugh himself couldn't remember a thing. But Murtaugh's wife defended him stoutly to newspaper reporters, saying: "I am certain that when he took the Doodle-Bug on that main line he was doing it under orders. I know him well enough to be sure that if he had had orders to stop at a siding he would have stopped. I am certain that if he was able to defend himself from these charges he would say that he had no such orders . . ."

Unfortunately for Murtaugh, Shaffer's duplicate copy of his orders was found in the wreck, confirming the theory that he had, for unknown reasons, ignored his orders. But both Murtaugh and Shaffer had other defenders during the firestorm of recrimination that ensued from the Doodlebug wreck. Speaking for the Brotherhood of Railway Trainmen on August 5, legislative representative George A. Fox blamed the accident on the Pennsylvania Railroad's cost-cutting practices. Stating that there had previously been three signalman stationed on the 12-mile Hudson-Akron line, Fox declared that the accident would not have happened if the Pennsylvania Railroad had not eliminated the signalmen jobs as an economizing measure: "We can't agree that this crew with long experience on the line could have made a mistake in such explicit procedure. We have been in constant dispute with the railroad to assign operators to the signal stations. We've maintained that it's not the business of an engineer or a conductor to do the work of an operator. . . . Whenever a safety measure is required costing money, the railroads invariably resist installing it and they come around to it only because the trainmen's organizations put pressure on them."

And that was that. The mess was cleaned up, the dead were eulogized and buried, and Doodlebug service was soon restored to the Akron-Hudson line. Ironically, the train made its last run on July 31, 1951, exactly 11 years to the day after the Cuyahoga Falls catastrophe. Today, virtually no one remembers either the Doodlebug or the fiery tragedy that took 43 lives. So let the last words go to Dr. Charles D. De Gruchy, an eyewitness, who uttered the most eloquent account of the horror:

I was on my way home to Silver Lake when the crossing lights caused me to stop my car. The Doodle came sailing along and I thought nothing about it until I happened to turn my head and saw the freight bearing down from the other direction. . . . The flasher light was going—there was no screeching of brakes [Author's note: most witnesses heard the brakes screech]—there was no warning signal from either train. The locomotive just seemed to disappear into the Doodler . . . there was a crash—a terrific explosion and a shower of splotches of flames like maple leaves falling in the autumn breeze. Glass fell like hail—or like someone threw a bucketful of buckshot. . . . I went back to the train where a few people had gathered. I saw the bodies packed around the nose of that locomotive right to the roof. The steam and flames shot out all around them. They looked like sardines sprinkled with the debris of the coach. It was as silent inside that car as a church sanctuary.

Chapter 17

"ALL WILL HAVE GONE TO DECAY"

The Billy Whitla Story

Cleveland has had more than its share of big-time crime. The "Sugar Wars" of the 1930s and the violent acts of legendary criminals like "Jiggs" Losteiner, "Blinky" Morgan, "Big Jim" Morton, and Shondor Birns bear comparison with the legendary criminality of such storied cities as Chicago, Detroit, and New York. But in at least one category it has, mercifully, lagged behind: kidnapping for ransom. Yes, there have been famous cases of vanished youngsters in the Forest City area—Beverly Potts, "Sonny" Hoenig, and Amy Mihaljevic spring to mind—but their unhappy fates came at the hands of sick perverts rather than greedy extortionists. True, there have been many threats, especially back in the '30s, when the pressure of economic want and the example of the Lindbergh case tempted some to make mercenary threats against the children of wealthy Clevelanders. But nothing came of such bluffs, not counting, of course, the tragic kidnapping of Julie Kravitz and his wife by the deranged Michael Levine in 1979. But there was a time, many years ago, when a child kidnapping made Cleveland the focus of national headlines and a thousand rumors, and the scene of a thrilling denouement. It was March 1909, and it seemed like everyone in the world was looking for Billy Whitla in the streets and dwellings of downtown Cleveland.

The Whitla case began exactly at 9:20 a.m. on Thursday, March 18, in Room 2 at the East Ward elementary school in Sharon, Pennsylvania. William ("Billy") Whitla, eight years old, had just gone to the blackboard with a piece of chalk to inscribe the "Motto of the Day," a common exercise in schools of the era. Suddenly, there came a knock at the door, and in stepped Wesley Sloss, the school janitor. Speaking to Billy's teacher, Anna Lewis, he told Anna that

William ("Billy") Whitla and his parents.

there was a man outside with a buggy and a note from Billy's father asking that the boy be brought to his father's office at once. Helping Billy on with his coat, Lewis talked briefly to the stranger, who had a dark complexion, stubby mustache, dark hair, and a dark suit. Everything seemed all right to Lewis; such parental requests were not unusual, and the man was well-spoken and respectably dressed. Saying good-bye to Billy, Lewis laughingly joked, "I hope they don't want to kidnap you, Billy." And as she watched the man hoist Billy up into the horse-drawn buggy, Lewis got one last look at what millions of Americans would soon recognize as a description of winsome Billy Whitla: "a blue-eyed, fair-haired, handsome little fellow of a very charming disposition—a favorite of all who know him. When he left he wore a cap, gray-check blouse suit, and a black sweater bound in red."

Three hours went by. When Billy failed to return home at the noon recess, his mother, Mrs. James Whitla, called Lewis at the school about 12:20 p.m. As soon as Lewis told her about the stranger's note, Billy's mother knew something was terribly wrong: her husband was out of town and would not have sent for his son. But Mrs. Whitla didn't remain in suspense for long; at 1 p.m. the mail came, and in it was a note that read: "We have your boy and no harm will come to him if you comply with our instructions. If you give this letter to the newspapers or divulge any of its contents, you will never see your boy again. We demand ten thousand dollars in $20, $10, and $5 bills. If you attempt to mark the money, or place counterfeit money, you will be sorry. Dead men tell no tales. Neither do dead boys. You may answer at the following addresses: *Cleveland Press, Youngstown Vindicator, Indianapolis News,* and *Pittsburgh Dispatch.* Answer: 'A. A. will do as you requested. J. P. W.'"

It was obvious from the outset why the kidnappers had targeted young Billy Whitla. Although his father, James P. Whitla, was only a moderately successful attorney and local politico, everyone in Sharon knew that adorable Billy, by all accounts an irresistibly winning boy, was the apple of his Uncle Frank's eye. Uncle Frank, who had married Mrs. Whitla's sister, was better known to Sharon and the world as Frank H. Buhl, an industrialist and founder of one of the companies that had been merged into the U. S. Steel Corporation several years earlier, and a multimillionaire of reputedly fabulous wealth. Residents of Sharon and surrounding towns had often seen Billy in the company of his Uncle Frank, and it was immediately assumed that Buhl would pay almost any price— much less a meager $10,000—to retrieve his beloved nephew from his unknown captors.

The hunt for Billy got under way immediately, directed by Buhl, who was soon joined at Billy's Sharon home by a shocked, angry James Whitla. Police, volunteers, and state militia began scouring the area around Sharon by late afternoon, and by evening the first clues were began to trickle in. Shortly after Billy left the school, a classmate had seen him alight from the buggy and mail a letter at the corner of Sharpsville and Hull Streets. The Sharon police, led by Chief Martin Crain, correctly concluded it was his own ransom note, as it had been addressed in his handwriting. More eyewitnesses had later seen the rig going north to Clark Avenue over the bridge to Superior Street and heading west out of town. Sometime before noon, the buggy was again spotted by several farmers as it headed west toward Warren through the towns of Brookfield and Howland Hills.

The first real break in the case came late Thursday afternoon, when Frank Peck, a Warren livery man, reported finding a horse and buggy abandoned on Market Street. It matched the description of the kidnapper's getaway vehicle, and that clue soon led to a livery man in Sharon, who identified the rig as one he had rented to a man at 8 a.m. on Thursday morning. But while this confirmed police suspicions that Billy's abductor had fled west, they were unsure as to where the trail led after that. Given the four newspapers mentioned in the ransom note, it was likely he was headed for a big city—but which one?

Six major railroads intersected in the general Warren area, and it was possible that Billy and his captor were already hundreds of miles away. Meanwhile, as evidence of their concern, Sharon-area law-enforcement authorities rousted local Italian communities on the theory that the kidnapping was related to local "Black Hand" activity. Sharon residents did their part by almost lynching a terrified "drummer" who resembled the description of Billy's stocky, dark-complexioned, mustachioed abductor. Sharon patrolman Jay found it necessary to keep the bloody-minded mob at bay with his drawn pistol until he could get the salesman out of town on a train.

Meanwhile, over the loud objections of the police, James Whitla made it unequivocally clear that he wished to cooperate with Billy's kidnappers. Begging the police and newspaper reporters to stay out of the case, he publicly and repeatedly stated that his only concern was Billy's safety: "I don't want the kidnappers prosecuted. They may have the money. We will do as they wish. We will ask them no question. I want my boy, and he is all that I want. People tell me we should not meet the demands of the kidnappers. They say the kidnappers should be punished, because to pay the money and let them go would encourage crime. It's easy to talk that way about someone else's boy, but Billy is my boy. If it encourages crimes to get him back, I can't help it; everything they ask shall be done."

At the same time, James Whitla hired operatives of both the Pinkerton and Perkins private detective agencies and made it clear that their chief mission was to keep the police out of the affair as much as possible.

The pace of events picked up on Friday. That morning, James Whitla received a second ransom note. It read: "We have seen your advertisement and conclude you mean to play square. Be ready to act upon further instructions."

The brevity of the note was frustrating, particularly to Billy's mother, who by now was in a state of sleepless hysteria, punctuated by bouts of weeping and sobbing vows that she would never punish her darling Billy again. But the timing of the second note told the Whitlas and police far more than its text: it had to have come from Cleveland, because the *Cleveland Press* was the only one of the four papers that had printed the story on Thursday. Everyone immediately concluded that the kidnappers and Billy were holed up in Cleveland, and the focus of the Whitla case now moved there. Public and police interest was further stimulated when Frank Buhl arrived in Cleveland late Friday on the strength of a report that Billy had been seen in the lobby of the Hotel Euclid.

Alas, it was not true. The boy in the Hotel Euclid did look like Billy—and he had been kidnapped!—but it was only a shabby coincidence involving an ugly custody contest over the Billy look-alike. But by the time Buhl sorted out the confusion and left Cleveland, James Whitla had received yet a third letter. The kidnappers were ready to deal: "Take the 6:50 train to Youngstown and go to Ashtabula. Go to the Hotel Smith. There you will receive a letter addressed to A. C. White. You must leave Sharon alone and no one must accompany you at any stage of the journey."

The letter also told him to bring the $10,000 and, like previous notes, was accompanied by a short note in Billy's handwriting, evidence to the weary and frantic father that Billy was still alive: "Tell mama not to worry. I will be home with her tomorrow. I am in a house that has many trees around it. I am well now. Your loving son, Billy."

James Whitla tried hard to comply with the kidnappers' demands, but the contrary imperatives of police and reporters turned the ransom drop into a farce. He arrived in Ashtabula on time and went to the Hotel Smith on Saturday night, March 20, about 8:30 p.m. to get his letter. But by that time a hotel night clerk had inadvertently opened the missive addressed to "A. C. White" and had alerted Ashtabula police. James Whitla followed the instructions in the opened letter exactly and dropped off the package containing the $10,000 at Flatiron Park, a few blocks from the Ashtabula business district. Placing it underneath the butt-end of a cannon there, he returned to the Hotel Smith, where he had been promised Billy's return at 1 a.m. But by the time he left the money, the park was surrounded by local police and *Press* reporters, and their obvious presence deterred the kidnappers from making an appearance. Early the next morning Ashtabula mayor H. B. Cook and the police retrieved the unopened package of cash.

James Whitla was furious at the police and scared for the safety of his son. But he was persuaded by one of his hired detectives,

G. S. Ward of Philadelphia, to make an open newspaper appeal to the kidnappers, renewing his pledges of good faith. The notice read: "It was only by an unfortunate mistake that your affair with Mr. Whitla was not closed Saturday night . . . I give you my word that this is true . . . It was only by an unfortunate blunder that the Ashtabula police tried to effect your capture. The letter you sent to the hotel was opened at the desk by persons who had no authority to do so."

On Monday, March 22, Cleveland was in a state of anxious anticipation. By that evening, the Pennsylvania legislature had offered a reward of $15,000 for the apprehension and conviction of Billy's kidnappers, and thousands of Greater Clevelanders anxiously scanned the faces of mustachioed, stocky men and fair-haired boys in hopes of cashing in. There was a piece of sheet music celebrating "Billy-Boy: The Kidnapped Child" for sale in Cleveland shops, and a special life-size photograph of Billy was printed in all 200,000 copies of that afternoon's *Cleveland Press*. As if that weren't enough, the *Press* hired Pat Crowe to do commentary on the Whitla case. Crowe, a reformed criminal, had become famous a decade earlier when he kidnapped Eddie Cudahay, the son of a meatpacking magnate. Now an evangelist, ex-jailbird Crowe attempted to soothe public fears about Billy's fate, noting that he had publicly threatened to burn Eddie's eyes out with acid—but he hadn't really meant it, and Billy's captors probably didn't either. Only marginally more reprehensible was the entrepreneur who purchased the kidnapper's abandoned rig for $275 and now announced his attention to charge the public for a glimpse of the notorious horse and buggy.

Such intense levels of public enthusiasm and cupidity, of course, led to some unfortunate incidents. More than one stocky man in company with a light-haired boy was hauled in by police in Cleveland and other cities within a two-hundred-mile radius of Sharon. A potato farmer from Curwensville, Pennsylvania, traveling on a B. & O. passenger train with his young son was dragged off the train for a "sweating" in Altoona and underwent a similar ordeal in Cuyahoga Falls the next day before he convinced suspicious lawmen of his true identity. Demonstrating that Cleveland had become the cynosure of the Billy Whitla hunt, police chief Fred Kohler's men logged more than 3,500 telephone calls offering tips on Billy's whereabouts, supplementing the generous number of futile arrests

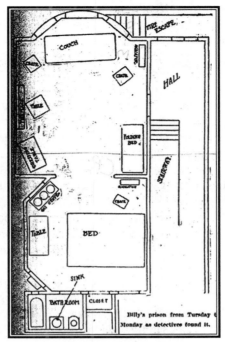

Diagram of hotel room where
Billy Whitla was held.

Cleveland's finest had already made in the case. By Monday evening, however, they had narrowed their efforts to an area bound by Superior Avenue, East 21st Street, Chester Avenue, and East 30th Street. The letter directing James Whitla to Ashtabula had been mailed from a postbox at Payne and 30th, and Kohler was convinced the kidnappers had their lair in that area.

After his experience in Ashtabula, James Whitla wasn't taking any chances. When he got another ransom letter on Monday he kept it to himself and followed its instructions exactly. Taking his $10,000 wrapped in newspapers in a valise, he eluded the police, took an Erie Railroad car to Cleveland and got off at East 55th. Going to a drugstore at 5602 St. Clair owned by Theo Urban, he asked for a letter held there for "William W. Williams."

Urban handed him the letter, which had just been delivered by a newsboy, that directed Whitla to drop his cash package off at a grocery store located at 1383 East 53rd Street. Whitla took it there, handed it over to Lena Hendrickson at the store counter, and, per his instructions, went to Parlor M of the Hollenden Hotel at East 6th and Superior Avenue to await the return of his son. Neither Hendrickson, Urban, or the newsboy had any comprehension of the real nature of the exchange in which they had participated.

About 8:15 that evening, a small, fair-haired boy wearing blue-tinted glasses got on a streetcar at Payne Avenue and East 30th Street. Pale, shaking, and obviously frightened, he refused to talk to curious passengers, conductor F. J. Logan, or the motorman, A. J. Meeker, muttering only that his name was "Jones." He had a note pinned on him stating that he was to be let off at the Hollenden, but conductor Logan decided it could wait until the trolley made its return trip from Public Square. As it went by, however, Ed Mahoney, 17, who was walking down Superior looked up and saw Billy at the window of the Payne Avenue car. Mahoney had seen the life-size photograph of Billy in that afternoon's *Press*, and he began running after the streetcar, hollering at Meeker to stop. By the time he caught up with it, it had returned to the Hollenden, and Mahoney and Thomas Ramsay, who had also recognized Billy, took him off the car and into the Hollenden. There he was grabbed by a man named Prince Hunley and hustled toward Parlor M.

The ensuing scene was sheer pandemonium. Someone said, "There's a boy here!"—the next moment Billy ran into his father's arms. As hundreds cheered and stomped with joy and more hundreds began to converge on the Hollenden, James Whitla tried to take his child to his room to rest. But the public was insistent, and he and Billy had to spend quite some time before well-wishers and newspaper photographers would leave them alone for a well-earned rest.

It was obvious from the moment he returned that Billy had been drugged, and it was some hours before his father and police could get any coherent details from the tired, dopey child. But the story he told, incredible and melodramatic as it was, made perfect sense and explained how Billy had seemingly vanished off the face of the earth after his captor took him to Warren. The man who took him had told Billy that there was a terrible smallpox outbreak in Sharon and that he was taking Billy to his father to prevent the police from putting him in a quarantined pest house. Unless Billy hid from the police, the man warned, he was likely to end up with smallpox and be horribly scarred for life. So when they arrived in Warren early that Thursday afternoon, Billy had obligingly hidden in a lumber-yard, while his abductor had his mustache removed. They had then taken a train to Ashtabula, switching there to an interurban car that brought them to downtown Cleveland late Thursday night. Taking Billy to a residential flat, his captor introduced him to a woman sporting a red-spotted face and a nurse's outfit. Her name was "Jones," the man said, and Billy was to call himself Jones, too, lest he be taken away to the infectious pest house. They told Billy that he was living in a special hospital with 300 patients like himself and 35 nurses in attendance.

Billy had stayed with the man and woman in the flat until Monday evening. The man was gone most of the time, and although the woman treated him kindly, she made him stay away from the windows and hide in a cupboard under the bathroom sink whenever there was a knock on the door. Finally, on Monday evening, the man who had taken him from school walked him down to East 30th Street and Payne and put him on the Hollenden-bound car. It was like something out of a dime novel and all of it perfectly true.

Unfortunately for his kidnappers, that wasn't all Billy remembered. Although he had been warned away from the windows, he remembered seeing a stone church and streetcars marked "Cedar" and "Chardon." And better yet, he remembered some of the signs he could see through the windows: "Hotel Thorpe" and "Sam Corso." That narrowed it down considerably: only three buildings in downtown Cleveland afforded a view of all these sights—and they were all residential structures on the south side of Prospect Avenue just west of East 21st Street. Describing his kidnapping room more precisely, Billy revealed that it contained an iron bed, a folding bed, a couch, stained glass in the upper third of its three front windows, and a tear in the ceiling.

That should have been enough for Chief Kohler's men, but it wasn't. Detectives George Moore and Joseph Bernard began searching the three suspect buildings at 8 a.m. on Tuesday, March 23, the morning after Billy was returned. By 9 a.m. they had worked their way through the first floor of the Granger Apartments, a residential hotel at 2022 Prospect Avenue. They knocked on the door of Room 2 on the second floor, and it was answered by an attractive, red-haired woman still in her nightgown. After she awakened her male companion, Moore and Bernard asked permission to search the room. Finding nothing, they departed. Some

Helen Boyle.

minutes later they finished searching the building and returned to Elizabeth Mills, the proprietress, asking if she had any suite matching the particulars of Billy's detailed description. "Why that's Room 2," replied Mills, and the stunned Moore and Bernard flew back up the stairs. But their prey had already vanished. Mills herself had seen the red-haired woman leave a minute before, saying she was going out to buy potatoes. Her male companion had apparently taken the hint and likewise departed. The only further information about the reclusive and now elusive couple that Mills could offer was that they called themselves "Mr. and Mrs. Walters" and that Mr. Walters had rented the flat on March 13. Detective John Shibley now took a very thorough look at the abandoned flat and soon discovered a bottle of ether-soaked candy and pieces of a nurse's uniform.

This was not model police work, and Chief Kohler soon demoted Moore and Bernard, although his public stance was that the Granger debacle was all James Whitla's fault for not cooperating fully with police. Meanwhile, unbeknownst to Kohler and his men, the red-haired woman was still in downtown Cleveland, engaged in a shopping spree at the Bailey's and May Company department stores. About noon, she and her male companion went to Patrick O'Reilly's saloon at 2158 Ontario Street and had a few drinks. They departed for more shopping that afternoon and returned about 5 p.m. for additional liquid refreshment. Pat O'Reilly became suspicious sometime during their second visit. He had a vague mem-

James Boyle.

ory of the man as a machinist he had known in Cleveland a few years before, and he was astonished at the number of crisp new bills and boastful remarks about money the couple was throwing about his modest saloon. O'Reilly made up his mind when the woman, somewhat in her cups, pulled up her skirt, grabbed her leg, and shouted, "This leg is worth $5,000." She then grabbed her other leg and said, "That is worth another $5,000." As soon as the couple left, O'Reilly grabbed his telephone and called Cleveland police.

For once luck was running the way of Kohler's men. O'Reilly called back about 10 that night to say that the couple had returned and were about to leave the bar. Detectives Frank Wood and Frank Shattuck were waiting for them when they left a few minutes later, and, after asking them a few questions, Shattuck told them to accompany him to Central Police Station on nearby Champlain Street. As they turned onto Champlain, the man broke away and began to run.

Seizing the woman firmly by the arm, Shattuck fired one shot into the air. And that was all it took: the fugitive stumbled on the tracks at the West 5th Street crossing and meekly surrendered to Detective Wood. Taken to cells, the couple refused to say anything until matron Louise Love discovered $9,850 in currency sewn into the inside of the woman's skirts. Shrieking and cursing, the woman finally broke down and said, "Well, you've got us. There'll be hell to pay in Sharon tomorrow. And I'm the frail little woman who planned it all."

It took some time to accurately identify Billy's kidnappers. The man refused to say anything, and the woman told a series of conflicting falsehoods up to the moment she entered the penitentiary. He was the less interesting of the two: a thirty-four-year-old plumber named Jimmy ("Lefty") Boyle, the black sheep of a respectable Sharon family, who had dabbled in his younger days with petty theft and assault and faced jail-breaking charges. He had disappeared from Sharon 10 years before and served for a time in the U. S. Army before he met Helen McDermott in an East St. Louis dive. Whether she then drew him into her web of evil or whether they were immoral peers is a question that was fiercely debated—but it is irrefutable that Jimmy's life became a lot more interesting after Helen came into it.

Her biography was like something out of the maudlin sheet music of the day: "Just Tell Them That You Saw Me" comes to mind. The daughter of William McDermott, a respectable Chicago fireman, Helen (née Anna) had received a good education, capped by some months of vocal training at a convent in Wisconsin. But upon her return to Chicago in 1906 at the age of 18, she took up with bad companions and began drinking in saloons, and William McDermott disowned her, which didn't matter to the already hardened Helen. Several months later she was living in Kansas City with a career felon named Frank Parker. Helen seems to have called herself "Mrs. Parker" at this time, and there is no doubt that she was running con games involving forgery and theft with Parker. But when Parker went to prison in 1907, Helen went to work as a maid. Well, sort of a maid. Her scheme was to steal employment references from genuine housemaids, insinuate herself into wealthy households, and then abscond with the valuables. H. C. Dyer, a St. Louis lawyer, had a typically bad experience with Helen: hired as "Clara Stratton" on a Thursday to do housework and care for his children, she vanished the following Monday with $6,000 in jewels.

It was probably about this time she met Jimmy Boyle, who defenders would later say was trying to go straight. If he was, his defenses were inadequate to overcome the charms of Helen McDermott: in 1908 they were arrested in Springfield, Illinois, for practicing the same forgery cons Helen had worked with Frank Parker. They managed to get out of that jam and soon turned up at the house of Jimmy's aged mother, Catherine, in Sharon, where

Jimmy introduced Helen to his family as his wife. Whether she really was has never been proven: a marriage certificate was never produced, and in Sharon Helen continued to receive letters sent to "Mrs. Frank Parker" from her erstwhile and imprisoned swain. In any event, she made a good and demure impression on Jimmy's family, and they breathed a sigh of relief that he had at last turned out so well. It is probable that Helen didn't try to impress her new in-laws with a performance she was famous for in St. Louis dives: when in her cups she would jump on a table, shouting "I'm an a actress, I'm a singer, and I'm a money-getter."

In the six weeks before her trial, Helen did her best to secure the goodwill of her captors. Jimmy stayed sullen and silent, but she turned on all the personal charm that had formerly gained her so many unhappily unsecured loans in her days as a soft con artist. Chief Kohler himself was obviously smitten with her, and a *Cleveland News* reporter waxed poetic in narrating the attractions of the jailbird siren: "She is slender and fair. Her hair flames. She is sunshine and tempest, fair skies and a withering sirocco. . . . But her beautiful golden hair shows no signs of age or trouble. It is a tremendous mass of bright hair, and all her own. Most of the curl is out of it now, but it is truly a 'crown of glory.' . . . One wonders how a woman of her apparent education and refinement was led to marry a man like Boyle, who does not bear the same evidence of gentle breeding . . ."

Alas, the newspaper happy talk ended abruptly when the Boyles were carted off to the Mercer, Pennsylvania, county jail at the end of that tumultuous March week. Billy Whitla had already returned to Sharon in an almost royal progress, with cheering crowds in the thousands thronging the Youngstown and Sharon railway stations to get a glimpse of him. Indeed, Billy seemed to be having so much fun that one little Youngstown boy was moved to comment enviously to a *Plain Dealer* reporter, "Gee, it must be great to be kidnapped." The same crowds also turned out for Helen and Jimmy, although their passage was punctuated by cries of "Lynch 'em" and "Shoot 'em."

Helen and Jimmy's separate trials, held six weeks later in Mercer, were the merest formality. The physical evidence itself (the nurse's costume, the ransom notes and telegrams, the ether-soaked candy used to dope Billy) was damning enough, and Billy proved a devastating witness against his former captors. It was thought that Helen might try to beat the rap by claiming she was coerced by her husband, a common defense in such cases. But Helen couldn't prove that they were married, and telegrams sent to her at the Granger in Cleveland tied her tightly to the kidnapping plot. Both Helen and Jimmy intimated frequently that there were others involved in their plot, hinting that prominent families were fearful of imminent exposure. But it was all hogwash: Jimmy never took the stand in his own defense, and he was quickly convicted on child-stealing charges in a two-day proceeding before Judge A. W. Williams. As soon as he was convicted, Helen's trial began, featuring the same witnesses and evidence used against Jimmy. Once again, Billy, the star witness, delighted spectators, so much so that Judge Williams threatened to clear the court, tut-tutting that the trial was "not a vaudeville show." The trial audience particularly enjoyed Billy's response to Prosecutor Gordon's question, "What becomes of people who don't tell the truth?" "They go to hell," said Billy to general applause. It was no wonder that Helen didn't take the stand either: her defense attorney, S. H. Miller, must have reasoned that it would be like trying to fight Little Lord Fauntleroy or Rebecca of Sunnybrook Farm in cross-examination. When the jury went out on May 8, they spent only a minute in finding Helen Boyle guilty of aiding and abetting child stealing.

No one ever credited her story that she herself had believed Billy Whitla was a fugitive from the smallpox pest house. And even if she had evaded the Mercer jury, Cuyahoga County prosecutor John Cline had child-stealing and blackmail indictments waiting for her, just in case.

On May 10, 1909, Judge Williams sentenced Jimmy Boyle to a life term and gave Helen 25 years. She made a half-hearted attempt to kill herself with a morphine overdose but soon settled down to working on her appeal. She turned down an offer of bail money to allow her to go on the vaudeville circuit in the interim, as did Billy's father, although the entrepreneur who wanted to put Billy on the stage generously offered to throw in a private tutor.

The years went by. Although they had their differences, Helen and Jimmy never turned on each other, continuing to correspond and visit when permitted, always ending their letters with the affectionate code words, "Isle of View" (meaning "I Love You"). After years of petitioning, Helen was pardoned and released from the Western Pennsylvania Penitentiary on June 25, 1919. Picked up by her loyal brother, William, at the prison gates, she said "I'm happy to be free," and disappeared into obscurity. Interviewed in 1925 in Chicago, she stated mournfully, "There is nothing even faintly romantic about crime. It makes you pay even after the law is through." But she was luckier than Jimmy Boyle, who died in the same western Pennsylvania prison on January 23, 1920, of pneumonia. His last recorded words were "I don't want to die."

Ironically, life wasn't much kinder to Billy Whitla. Following in his father's footsteps, he became a lawyer and practiced in the hometown he had made famous in 1909. Married to a woman named Eleanore Thorp and the father of two young daughters, he died unexpectedly of influenza-related pneumonia on December 28, 1932, just nine months after the kidnapping that eclipsed his own: the abduction and murder of Charles A. Lindbergh Jr.

Perhaps the only ones who benefited even in the short term from Billy Whitla's kidnapping were those who shared in the $15,000 reward. After much haggling, $5,000 went to Patrick O'Reilly, $6,900 to the Cleveland Police Pension Fund (Shattuck and Wood's share), $2,000 to Prince Hunley, and the remainder to other claimants. Twenty-three years later, Thomas Ramsay, one of the first to identify Billy, remembered that he got nothing but $5 from James Whitla and conceded, "I figured the lad was bound for Hotel Hollenden, anyway, and would have got there. I didn't see where I had a real claim."

Let us end with a last, lingering, even fond look at the seductive Helen Boyle. She had an uncanny effect on virtually all the men she met, and even Judge Williams, before sentencing her to 25 years, was heard to remark, "There are a lot of men here who would like to have married this woman." Maybe she was right when she protested, while in the Cleveland jail, to a *Plain Dealer* reporter, "I am not the vulgar person they have made me out to be." But she was hardly the injured, wifely ingenue, either, and there were many who thought the reason she and Jimmy hung around O'Reilly's saloon that night—a suspiciously foolish move in an otherwise well-contrived plot—was so that Helen could drink Jimmy blind and abscond with all the money. The dramatic aspects of the plot (the play-acting of the smallpox subterfuge, Jimmy's various disguises involving complexion and facial hair) also seemed far more indicative of a theatrical background (Helen had apparently toured in both vaudeville and light-opera companies before meeting Jimmy) than of the criminal imagination of a small-town plumber and petty felon. The inescapable conclusion after sifting through the evidence is that Helen McDermott Boyle was the mastermind behind Billy's abduction and that the jury went easy on her because she was an attractive—very attractive—woman. So let beguiling Anna Helen McDermott Parker Boyle supply the final epitaph, a doggerel rhyme on the Whitla case that she wrote from her Mercer County cell in March 1909:

> In the year two thousand nine,
> One hundred years from today,
> Little Billy, Jim and Helen
> All will have gone to decay.
> So what's the use?

Chapter 18

DEATH ON A DAVENPORT

The Assassination of William E. Potter

In the pre-Teflon era of the 1920s, you might say councilman William E. Potter was the Harry Houdini of Cleveland politics. Often criticized, frequently attacked, sued, and indicted, he roller-coasted through the Jazz Decade seemingly invulnerable to attack by his many enemies. Publicly pilloried by the Citizens' League in 1925 for conflict of interest (it seems Potter had sold building materials to no fewer than 32 clients who received favorable appeal rulings from his city zoning board), he belligerently scorned the charges, and Collinwood voters echoed his stance by returning him to the Cleveland city council for five consecutive terms. Indicted for taking an alleged $500 bribe to facilitate a city land purchase of a lot at East 113th Street and Gray Avenue, he was acquitted on April 17, 1929. Six months later, Potter and city clerk Fred W. Thomas were indicted on charges of having an illegal interest in the city's purchase of a lot intended for a playground at Coit Road and St. Clair Avenue. Almost simultaneously, Potter and Robert Bunowitz, a plumbing contractor and Potter associate, were indicted on charges of harboring Harmon G. Atwater, a real estate agent who had expedited the Coit Road–St. Clair deal and was now a fugitive from justice. But Bill Potter's luck held: On December 16, 1929, he was found not guilty of the harboring charge, while Bunowitz was convicted and sent to prison. (Adding insult to injury, Potter was named as a co-defendant in Bunowitz's divorce suit against his wife.) Exactly a week later, both Potter and Thomas were found not guilty in the playground case, and the 45-year-old Potter walked out of the Cuyahoga County courthouse still a free man. As if to underscore his political impunity, three other participants in the playground deal—Atwater, ex–Cleveland councilman Liston Schooley, and his son, Liston Schooley Jr.—were serving prison terms. William E. Potter, known as "Rarin' Bill" for his prodigiously loud and witty demagoguery in city council and on the hustings, was still the Harry Houdini of Cleveland politics.

Maybe his charmed life had to end—even Harry Houdini eventually took a punch he couldn't handle—and by late 1930 it looked

William ("Rarin' Bill") Potter.

as though such a fatal punch was headed Potter's way. Although he had not yet been convicted of anything criminal, his legal troubles had exacted severe personal and professional costs. Abandoned as a political pariah by the Cuyahoga County Republican machine in the 1929 elections, Potter lost the Collinwood seat he had held for 10 years. Burdened by immense legal fees stemming from his three criminal trials, Potter had also lost immense sums in 13 lawsuits stemming from his business as a building-supplies merchant and other financial activities. Although he was still dapper and optimistic in public, it was clear that Bill Potter was on his uppers as the grim Depression year of 1931 loomed: to friends he confessed he was "stone broke." By that time he could no longer make payments on his bank loans, and he, his wife Beatrice, and their two teenage daughters were living in half of a converted barn behind their former bijou Tudor residence at 1842 Rudwick Road. Worse than that, it looked as though public officials were putting together a legal trap even "Rarin' Bill" couldn't escape.

Infuriated by Potter's repeated acquittals, which had become the greatest stench in the public nostril since the four trials involving Judge William McGannon a decade before, Cuyahoga County prosecutor Ray T. Miller was determined to bring him to book. On January 15, 1931, Potter was indicted on perjury charges stemming from both of his 1929 trials. His erstwhile associate Bunowitz was singing to the grand jury, Atwater had already talked, and it was expected that the Schooleys would incriminate Potter in exchange for parole considerations. It looked like the end of the line for Bill Potter, and the word on the street was that he would either have to come clean or face some serious cell time at last. The moment of truth or consequences would come on February 9, when Potter's

880 Parkwood Drive: The fatal living room.

perjury trial opened in criminal court. The smart money was betting that he would talk and take some big names down with him.

It was a pity it had to end this way. For all of his alleged sins—none of which were ever proven in a court of law—Bill Potter was a man of parts, however misused and squandered during his tempestuous life. Brought up in a Catholic orphanage, Potter left at the age of eight to start his career as a newsboy on the tough street corners of Chicago. He would in later years tell a tearful tale of how he was almost adopted by a compassionate millionaire but fled back to the streets when the man's wife objected, a tale that may have more to do with Potter's perusal of *Wuthering Heights* than with his factual biography. Coming to Cleveland as a young man, he became a bricklayer and would later frequently reminisce about laying brick for the new county courthouse he came to know so well as a politician and defendant. Starting as city building inspector in Mayor Baehr's administration, Potter ran unsuccessfully for county commissioner and Cleveland councilman before winning the Collinwood seat in 1919. Never losing his common touch, the gum- and tobacco-chewing Potter soon became well known and beloved by many for his thundering tirades and populist sneers, denouncing his Citizen's League detractors as "professors" and vowing he would not publicly wear a plug hat even for the visiting Queen Marie of Romania. As with many successful politicians it was impossible to say where the sincerity stopped, and the con began. But even his enemies praised him as a man who told you what he thought of you without subterfuge or pretense. And everyone (well, everyone except maybe Robert Bunowitz) remarked on what a sentimental family man Potter was, citing his uxorious manner and doting attentions to his children.

No one knows exactly when or why Bill Potter died, but it's certain that the Potter murder case began at 5:05 p.m. on Sunday, February 8, 1931. Picking up the ringing telephone at the 8th Precinct station at East 80th and Superior Avenue, Lieutenant Stephen McNally heard an excited voice tell him that an apparent suicide's body had been found on a davenport in Suite 4 at 880 Parkwood Drive. Taking two patrolmen with him, McNally went to the two-story, 12-flat brick apartment building. Fred Laub, the building custodian, met them at Suite 4 and tried unsuccessfully to open it with a key. The four then trekked to the back porch, where they entered through the unlocked kitchen door.

Trial reenactment of the murder sequence.

Sure enough, when they got to the living room, there was a dead body on the davenport. It smelled bad, it was a fast-decomposing white man, and it was sprawled face down across the davenport with its legs hanging over the end onto the floor. It was Bill Potter, although the corpse was in such bad shape that even the policemen, who knew him, didn't recognize what was left of him. Cleveland's only genuine political murder case had begun.

There wasn't much evidence for the police to work with initially. After the body was clearly identified as Potter's, Coroner A. J. Pearse's autopsy disclosed that Potter had been badly beaten and fatally shot in the head. Authorities reconstructed the scene: Potter had been beaten around his head—his skull was fractured—before someone put a .38 caliber lead-jacketed slug through his right temple. The slug ranged downward before exiting behind his left ear and leaving enough blood to mat his hair to the davenport. The fatal bullet was found in the davenport upholstery, while another three slugs from a .32 caliber gun were found in the wall behind the davenport. At least one of the extra slugs had been fired at Potter, drilling his overcoat but not hitting his body. Pearse's estimate was that Potter had been dead for five days when he was found.

For its sheer volume of inexplicable circumstances, the Potter case remains in a class by itself. The behavior of almost everyone involved made little sense then or now. To begin with, Potter had lain dead and rotting for five days without anyone noticing that he was missing or doing much to find him. His own wife, Beatrice Potter, although worried about his absence by her own admission, had not mentioned that he was missing until the day her husband's body was discovered. City detectives, sent to her house on behalf of court authorities seeking the name of his defense lawyer in his impending trial, didn't find out he had been missing for about 120 hours until 4:30 p.m., only 35 minutes before the body was found. Potter's car, a Chevy sedan, was similarly overlooked. Parked on Parkwood Drive near the death flat, it had sat for three days with its lights on before Mrs. Laub, the custodian's wife, decided to do something about it. Finding an address on a package in the automobile, she called the Potter residence on Friday, February 6, and told Mrs. Potter about the abandoned car. Mrs. Potter sent someone to bring the car home—and did nothing further about the matter. Cleveland patrolman Norman Hagelin had also noticed the Chevy with its lights on Wednesday, February 4; determining that it was not stolen, he likewise did nothing further about the matter—an oversight that would cost him six months' worth of vacation days later. But Hagelin fared better than patrolman Harry G. Mizer. On Wednesday morning, February 4, Mizer, while serving as a school crossing guard, was approached by neighborhood resident Meyer Weisman. Weisman gave Mizer a .38 caliber revolver with a bloody handle that he said he had found on his Bryant Avenue lawn while on his way to work. Mizer took the weapon home and told no one about it, even after the newspapers announced that ex-councilman Potter had been shot and beaten with the handle of a .38 caliber revolver in a flat just a few yards away from where Weisman had spotted the bloody gun. Mizer, who, it developed, had also lied on his police application, was fired for his bizarre dereliction of duty.

Circumstances proved even weirder back at the fatal apartment. Custodian Laub's story was that he had rented Suite 4 on January 28 to a man identifying himself as "M. J. Markus," a grocery-chain representative. Laub remembered "Markus" as about 30, well dressed, "Jewish" in appearance, slender, 5'9" tall, 150 pounds, with black hair and a long, thin nose. Paying $20 down, "Markus" had left the remaining $45 monthly rental in Laub's mailbox several days later. Fred Laub had not seen Markus again, and no one had moved any furniture or belongings into the apartment. But Fred's wife, Margaret, had called the Illuminating Company in early February, identified herself as "Margaret Markus," and requested that the current be turned on in Suite 4. (Mrs. Laub's dogged assertion that she often performed this service for tenants was greeted with skepticism but never disproved.) Subsequently becoming concerned that a lamp had been burning in Suite 4 for four days, Margaret decided to do something about it on Sunday night, February 8. Finding the front door locked, she went to the rear and found it unlocked. Discovering the body, she called her husband and Suite 3 resident Charles Fate, and they called police after ascertaining the man on the davenport was dead.

Police interviews with neighborhood residents soon found witnesses a bit more perspicacious than the Laubs. Mrs. Joseph Berger, whose Bryant Avenue apartment window faced the rear of Suite 4, told police she had seen a man and woman at the kitchen window about 4 p.m. on February 3, the most probable murder day. The woman, blond and attractive, was about 27, dressed in black, and seemed, Mrs. Berger said, "to be very nervous." Berger didn't get a good look at the man, who eventually drew his companion away from the window and Mrs. Berger's inquisitive eyes.

Better yet, from the police point of view, was the witness found in Suite 2, the flat below the murder suite. Her name was Betty Gray (alias Mildred Scribano). A sometime prostitute of questionable antecedents, she lived there in unmarried bliss with Julius ("Gene") Redlick, an ex-convict, pimp, and robber with an impressive police record. Redlick remained reticent under ungentle police interrogation, but Betty Gray was eager to talk, and her statement blew the case wide open. Gray swore she had been sitting in her "sun parlor" on February 1 when a man fitting the description of Fred Laub's "Markus" had rung her doorbell. The man said he had forgotten his key, and she let him in the building. "Markus" apparently had not recognized her—but she had recognized him as Hyman ("Pittsburgh Hymie") Martin, a bootlegger, shakedown thug, and petty gangster known to her during her prior career of easy virtue in the Steel City. She had seen him again enter the building about 30 minutes later, this time with his own key. She also revealed that she had heard a "thud or sort of a scraping noise" between 7:15 and 7:30 on the evening of February 3, the most probable murder time. The talkative Gray was less forthcoming with Cleveland newspaper reporters, and was rewarded by them with the moniker of "Bashful Betty."

Betty's uncanny recognition was all the Cleveland police needed. They already knew Hymie Martin as a gaudily attired member of the criminal subculture of the East 105th vice district, and a flying squad led by Detective Bernard Wolf picked Martin up in Pittsburgh after tricking him into a rendezvous. (Martin thought he was helping some wanted felon hide from the police). Confronted with the Potter murder charge, the usually gregarious Martin clammed up and asked for his attorney, Samuel S. Rosenberg. Rosenberg began a habeas corpus motion, and Martin made it clear he would vigorously fight extradition to Cleveland. He knew he wasn't going to get much of a break in a city whose morning newspaper described him as "dressed in the approved racketeer style. He has a light gray hat with turn-down brim, a brown suit, a long blue chinchilla overcoat, a white scarf and highly polished pointed shoes."

Cleveland police countered Martin's maneuvers with two bold moves. First, they rushed an improbable but genuine surprise witness to Pittsburgh to confront Hymie, a 16-year-old schoolgirl by the name of Queen Esther Morgan, and a resident of Suite 1 at 880 Parkwood Drive. Morgan picked Martin out of a lineup as the man she had seen going into her apartment building twice between January 30 and February 3. Or so Cleveland police said: Martin stoutly maintained that Morgan had failed to identify him until clumsily prompted by anxious detectives. In the end their conflicting versions didn't matter at all. Impatient with looming legal technicalities, Detective Wolf and Sergeant James Hogan put Martin in a police car on the afternoon of February 18 and sped back to Cleveland with the virtually kidnapped gangster before Pittsburgh officials were aware of what was going on. As *Cleveland News* reporter Howard Beaufait later wrote, Wolf apparently reasoned that Pennsylvania officials weren't going to make a big fuss about losing an undesirable citizen wanted on the most notorious murder rap ever in a sister city.

Things just got progressively worse for Martin as he sat in a Cleveland jail cell. Betty Gray took a look at him and said, "That's the man I saw coming into the murder suite." And Fred Laub swore repeatedly that he was Markus, the man who had rented Suite 4. Speedily arraigned on a first-degree murder charge the day after he was kidnapped from Pittsburgh, Hymie, together with his legal counsel, William E. Minshall, began making plans for his trial on March 25, 1931.

It's hard to believe now, especially when surveying the way the Potter murder case was covered in Cleveland's three daily newspapers, how thin the case against Hymie Martin really was. Perhaps it was the hysteria created by the total of $21,000 in reward money offered for the conviction of Potter's killer. Or maybe it was just the undeniable sleaziness of Hymie Martin (possibly aggravated by the residual anti-Semitism suggested by his frequent characterization in the newspapers as "Jewish" looking). Aside from witnesses who placed him in the murder flat at times other than the probable murder hour of 7:30 p.m., Tuesday, February 3, there was little to connect him with the ugly demise of "Rarin' Bill." Certainly the known events of Potter's last day didn't tie him tightly to the flashily attired, relatively small-time Steel City hoodlum and whiskey runner. Kissing his wife good-bye in mid-morning, Potter had hung around City Hall most of the day, gassing with cronies like Fred Thomas and waiting in vain to see Safety Director Edwin Barry on some matter whose nature was never discovered. Leaving City Hall, Potter had next been seen at the restaurant of Larry Lanese's Euclid Village Tourist Home at 24049 Euclid Avenue. Meeting his brother-in-law James Hoffman there, Potter had asked Hoffman to accompany him to a "business meeting" that evening. Potter didn't say what the meeting was about, but Hoffman recalled that he seemed casual about it and unruffled by Hoffman's refusal to go with him. With 23 traffic lights between the restaurant and the death flat, it would have taken Potter at least 18 minutes to drive the miles to 880 Parkwood Drive. Police theorized that Potter, who had been lured to the flat rented by Martin, was murdered almost as soon as he arrived there, accounting for the noise Betty Gray had heard between 7:15 and 7:30 p.m.

Hymie Martin's first trial didn't disappoint those who expected sensational testimony and dramatic moments. The state, led by prosecutors Ray T. Miller and P. L. A. Leighley, charged that Potter's death had been the result of a deliberate plot by those who feared possible exposure in his upcoming trial. Ray T. Miller put it like this: "William Potter was put on the spot by some group of men who desired his death. This death was planned several days in advance, so that he was brought to the apartment with the intention that he be killed. The apartment was rented for that purpose. Hymie Martin procured the place. The evidence will show that Martin was hired by someone in Cleveland to help plan that killing. The man who desired Potter's death is known to Martin."

All of which may have been true—but the evidence Miller and Leighley presented proved no such things. The .38 revolver found by Weisman, still matted with Potter's hair and blood, made a grisly appearance, but no evidence or witness tied Martin to its possession or use at any time. Fred Laub placed Martin in the murder flat in late January but at no later time, much less the presumed murder night. Mrs. Joseph Berger testified that she saw a couple in the suite's kitchen window at about 6:30 p.m. on February 3—but she admitted that the man resembled Gene Redlick, not Hymie Martin. Queen Esther Morgan repeated her claims that she had seen Martin in the building—but not on February 3. And a number of witnesses provided alibis for Martin that placed him elsewhere than in Suite 4, Parkwood Drive on February 3. Pittsburgh hospital records showed that Martin had been at a Pittsburgh medical facility paying a hospital bill for his mother on January 28, the day he allegedly rented Laub's flat. Charles Stalker, a City Hall hanger-on, unconvincingly contradicted such claims, swearing that he had seen Martin and Potter together there in the early afternoon and that he had spoken to both of them. Cleveland traffic patrolman Andrew Bessick asserted that he had also seen the two, together with a third man, that afternoon near City Hall.

Mary ("Akron Mary") Outland.

The real bombshell at Martin's first trial was the appearance of his girlfriend, Mary Outland Woodfield, or "Akron Mary," as she was known to inquiring minds forever after. Contacted neither by police nor prosecutors, she called the Pittsburgh police on March 15, just 10 days before Hymie's trial opened and asked to be picked up. She wanted to testify in Hymie's behalf, saying, "My Hymie couldn't have murdered Potter because he was with me at that time." Seductively clad in such outfits as a black velvet dress, black felt turban, black pumps, and flesh-colored hose, she was a newspaperman's dream and a prosecutor's nightmare. (Her hot wardrobe was nicely contrasted by the *Plain Dealer* with Betty Gray's "light pongee tan dress, such as any hard-working salesgirl might wear.") And her testimony at Hymie's trial was the best he could have hoped for, wrung from the frequently sobbing woman by an aggressive prosecutor. Her story, maintained intact under ferocious cross-examination, was that she had been Hymie's lover for about a year when he asked her to come to Cleveland in February 1931. She arrived the night of February 2, stayed with Hymie at the Auditorium Hotel, checked out about 6 p.m. the next day, and left Cleveland with Hymie about 7:15 or 7:30, the exact time police had picked as the murder hour.

Martin was a good witness for himself. His unruffled calm on the stand contrasted tellingly with the prosecution's portrait of him as a vicious killer, and he probably scored points with his frank, self-effacing characterization of himself: "Who am I? I'm just a Pittsburgh punk."

Ray T. Miller pulled out all the stops in his summary argument against Hymie Martin. Arguing that Martin was a cold-blooded hit man, Miller indicted him in Biblical terms: "Motive? The motive is simple. For gold he killed Potter. The lowest that a man can sink. Judas took 30 pieces of silver and then went out and hanged himself but that man comes in here smirking and smiling and asks you to believe him."

Then, dramatically reenacting Potter's final moments, Miller donned the bloodstained hat, grabbed the murder revolver, and mimed Potter's presumed desperate struggle with his killers in the living room of Suite 4. Falling as if shot to the bloody davenport (thoughtfully brought into the courtroom), Miller turned on Hymie and shouted, "You cruelly shot that man in the back!" Then, to the jury, Miller said, "I wouldn't ask anyone to send a man to the electric chair unless he was as low as a rat—as low as a louse. And this man is that low!" Minshall did his best to counter Miller's theatrics in his final words to the jury, arguing that the witnesses against Martin—the unwholesome Redlick and Gray in particular—were far more likely candidates as the killers who ended Bill Potter's life. Minshall also noted the half score of witnesses who supported Martin's Akron alibi and stressed there wasn't a "scintilla of evidence" to connect Potter's murder with the St. Clair-Coit Road scandal, much less his client.

The jury of four housewives, a druggist, a cable splicer, a stenographer, a paint company executive, a salesman, a real estate man, a manufacturer's representative, and a carpenter went out at 2:55 p.m. on April 2. After 11 ballots and 12 hours of actual deliberation, they returned to Judge Walter McMahon's courtroom at 4:40 p.m. the next day. Reading the verdict, foreman Leander J. Hostetter announced they had found Hyman Martin guilty of first-degree murder with a recommendation of mercy.

Almost as soon as the verdict was read and Martin sentenced to a mandatory life term, the consensus on his guilt, sustained for two months on a wave of sensational newspaper headlines, collapsed. The morning after the verdict, a front-page *Plain Dealer* editorial boasted "This Is A Start"—but by the very next day its columns were whining that the questions of "Who and Why" remained unanswered. And just 10 days after that, a front-page *Press* editorial virtually repudiated Ray T. Miller's triumphant prosecution, screaming, "Nobody believes that Pittsburgh Hymie Martin alone conceived, planned and executed the murder of former Councilman William E. Potter. Nobody ever thought that." Public opinion, easily swayed by the thousands of words hurled against Martin for weeks by Cleveland's three competitive newspapers, now began to move in the other direction, no doubt a comfort to the unflappable Martin, now making shirts in the Ohio Penitentiary and reported to have lost 15 pounds.

Ten months later came news that prison guards reported just "tickled to death" the hopeful Hymie. The Third Court of Appeals in Lima, ruling on Martin's appeal, ordered a new trial. It was a complex decision with no unanimity on any one matter, but the salient points were that the state had proved neither premeditation nor a connection between Potter's murder and the city land fraud trials, and that Judge McMahon had acted improperly in advising reluctant members of the jury to bend to the superior wisdom of the majority. In his written opinion, Judge P. M. Crew further scorned Miller and Leighley: "The language of the prosecuting attorney and his eminent assistant in many particulars far transcended lawfully appropriate limits of argument, in alluding to matters highly derogatory to defendant and to defendant's defense, which were wholly unfounded by any evidence; and that the prosecuting attorney especially, persistently indulged in unwarranted, unjust, and inflammatory personal vituperation and abuse of defendant . . ."

Indeed, Crew scathingly concluded, Miller had given Martin's jury the impression that Hymie "was not even a human being."

Hymie's second trial was a lot different from the first. Betty Gray, the most damning witness against him, had mysteriously disappeared. (Rumors would persist for years that she had been "rubbed out" and dumped in a Pennsylvania swamp, but nothing concrete about her fate has ever come to light.) Before vanishing, however, she gave Martin's attorney, William E. Minshall, an affidavit repudiating her testimony in the first trial. No, she said now, it was definitely not Hymie Martin she saw at 880 Parkwood Drive on February 1, 1931—she had only sworn so because of a combination of police threats of criminal prosecution and promises that she might share in the $21,000 reward. Most importantly, she changed her testimony about the "thud or scraping noise," now recalling that it took place an hour later—the precise time Hymie Martin could prove that he was in Akron on the night of February 3. Nor was the prosecution aided by revelations, grudgingly forced from prosecution witnesses by Minshall, that Fred Laub, Margaret Laub, and Charles Stalker had received money and jobs from the police in what might be construed as exchange for their previous testimony against Martin. As Hymie had by now patched things up with his wife, "Akron Mary" Outland did not appear, but the transcript of her previous supportive testimony was read into the record. Prosecutor Frank T. Cullitan did the best he could with the changed circumstances, but it took the jury of eight women and four men only an hour and 40 minutes to find Hymie Martin not guilty on June 16, 1932. His former nemesis, then Cleveland mayor Ray T. Miller, declined comment, but Martin's reaction was a heartfelt "I'm going to my mother. How can I break the news to her so the shock won't be too great?"

That was the end of the Potter case, although echoes occasionally turned up publicly in print, usually when peripheral figures like Julius Redlick and Solly Hart (a Cleveland gangster many suspected was implicated in the Potter murder) were arrested or sentenced for unrelated crimes. Hymie himself provided a last, almost sentimental "blast from the past" when he made an unwilling return to the Forest City in December 1965. Then living in Florida, Martin was called before a federal grand jury here to answer questions related to his suspected criminal associate Shondor Birns's numbers racket. Staying in character, Hymie stoutly and repeatedly invoked his Fifth Amendment rights before returning to obscurity in Florida. And no one yet knows why Bill Potter was killed, or by whom. For all the author knows, the $21,000 reward still stands.

Chapter 19

"SHOOTIN' AND SHOOTIN' AND SHOOTIN'"

The Awful Death of Mary Kelly

Charles R. McGill was not the kind of man you take home to mother. Just 27 years old in 1877, he was already a career drunk, a belligerent barroom brawler, a spouse deserter, and a deadbeat dad. But at least give him credit for his stick-to-itiveness and his methodical approach. The sometime cabinet maker had come to the house of ill fame at 100 Cross Street (now East 9th, within the freeway access maze south of Carnegie Avenue) at noon that Sunday, December 2, 1877, with the intention of persuading his lover, Mary Kelly, to renounce her life as a soiled dove and live with him at last in legal conjugal bliss. Failing that, he intended to kill himself, reasoning "if I committed suicide in her presence that would reform her if anything would." Somehow, however, his altruistic purpose was deflected, and Charles instead pressed the muzzle of his seven-shot revolver against Mary's head and pulled the trigger. The first flash of the powder burned his face and blinded him for a few seconds. The next thing he remembered was hearing Mary cry, "Go get a priest!" and then, turning her bloody face to him, plead, "Charlie, forgive me!" It's a good guess that Charlie didn't, because he put the revolver back against Mary's head, and, in his own words, "I let her have the rest of 'em in the face and neck. I shot her and kept shootin' and shootin' and shootin' until the revolver wouldn't shoot anymore." Without a pause in his work, Charlie calmly ejected the seven empty shells, loaded up four more, and fired them as close to Mary's heart as he could. The first shot set her dress on fire, and he smothered the fire with his hand. The second set the bedsheets aflame, but he extinguished that

Charles R. McGill.   Mary Kelly.

blaze, too, before firing his last two rounds into Mary. He then went downstairs, calmly washed his hands, asked someone to get the police, and returned to the corpse of his ex-lover. Leaning down, he reverently kissed her gory face, covering his own again in her copious blood. In answer to all inquiries, he merely repeated, "I done it!" How had the star-crossed Charles and Mary come to this evil pass—a fatal entanglement that ended in the last hanging and some of the worst poetry in Cuyahoga County history?

The 1877 murder of Mary Kelly in a Cross Street bagnio (as Cleveland journalists termed houses offering commercial sex) offered much to Clevelanders of its era. To moralists, it was an object lesson in the perils of drink, the deterioration of family ties, and the foul temptations awaiting young men and women moving to burgeoning industrial cities like fast-growing Cleveland. To connoisseurs of criminal law, it provided a forum where the murky and much-disputed questions of legal insanity and capital punishment could be dramatically fleshed out in two trials involving life or death for the accused. And for the rest of Cleveland's Gilded Age citizens it provided raw entertainment, as the squalid lives, seamy sins, and violent ends of two young lovers were paraded in the columns of Cleveland's four daily newspapers for a period of almost 27 months.

Thoughtful minds might have predicted such an end for Charles McGill. Born to a perfectly respectable Athens County cabinetmaker and his wife in May 1850, Charles was a troubled youth and black sheep from his earliest years. Restless, quick-tempered, and easily roused to fight, he was a sickly child and much given to walking and talking in his sleep, or somnambulism, as it was termed in the 19th century. Charlie's father tried hard to train him in his own craft, but it was obvious that Charlie lacked the application and ambition the work required. Despairing of finding him a trade, McGill's parents sent him off to Ohio University in 1864. His two years there, however, only further confirmed his aimlessness and sloth, at the same time disclosing the first hints of those dissipated habits that would lead him to the scaffold. Returning home, Charles frittered away two more years until his father's death in 1868. Now, dropping all pretense of meeting the expectations of his eight siblings and long-suffering mother, Charlie gave himself over to "riotous living" (as a disapproving *Cleveland Press* reporter characterized it) and settled for fitful employment as a fireman on the Hocking Valley Railroad.

With any luck, Charles McGill might have remained in obscurity as a hard-drinking, ne'er-do-well, downwardly mobile, and feckless rummy. But, as is so often the case, the malignant contingencies and chances of life insured that in time he would ruin and destroy lives other than his own. In the late 1860s he met and married Miss Louisa Steelman of Columbus. At least while the joys of the honeymoon lingered, McGill seems to have resisted the lure of his erstwhile vices and settled down to bourgeois domesticity. But it didn't last long, and soon the McGill household, quickly enlarged by the arrival of a son and a daughter, was riven by emotional and physical abuse (the latter dished out exclusively by Charlie), resulting in periodic separations and reconciliations.

Charlie's renewed intervals of semi-bachelorhood did not improve his character. He was an attractive young man of handsome looks and pleasing address when sober, but his personality deteriorated as he succumbed more and more often to the lure of liquor and loose women in the dives of early-1870s Columbus. Soon becoming a figure well known to the police, he was distinguished for the brute strength and easily provoked ferocity he displayed in the many fights he instigated, often taking on and defeating multiple antagonists. He was especially celebrated in local saloon lore for pistol-whipping a drunken soldier with his own gun. Well known to gambling circles in Columbus, McGill apparently eked out his infrequent income as a hardwood finisher by working as a shill to lure the "greenies" into games with local card sharks. He was also known to Columbus cops and some anguished parents as one "in the habit of enticing young girls into forbidden paths"— some of them as young as 14. In jail on an almost weekly basis, he was familiar to Columbus vice detectives as "a low sort of gambler, a beat of the worst sort and a rowdy who never missed a fight or lost an opportunity to get in some trivial scrape." So low had he sunk by 1872, indeed, that it almost seemed like a good thing— except perhaps to Louisa McGill—when Mary Kelly now came into his life.

It is one of the unfair ironies of crime that more biographical facts are often known about murderers than about their victims, and Mary Kelly well illustrates the rule. Sexy, black-haired, and about 19 years old when she met Charlie McGill in 1872, she came from a respectable family in Columbus. But her father died when she was very young, and she was raised by an aunt and uncle. She was precociously pretty, but her teenage years were clouded by rumors that she had been seduced and abandoned at a young age. Apparently that was the work of a thug named David Lawson, who undeniably fathered a child by her and was serving a term in the Ohio Penitentiary at the time of Mary's death. (A contrary rumor was that Mary's uncle had forced her to marry the brute Lawson when she was only 15.) But whatever her faults, there must have been "something about Mary"; with all her imperfections she was vivacious and well liked, even if she supplemented her income as a seamstress and sometime domestic servant with wages earned as a streetwalker in Columbus.

It was love at first sight, especially for Charlie. One look at Mary, who was parading her personal wares on a downtown Columbus street at the time, and Charlie was a goner. Leaving his wife and children, Charlie moved in with the likewise besotted Mary, who seems to have stopped selling her body in the "first, fine, careless rapture" of her love for McGill. There was a temporary setback, when an enraged Louisa confronted Mary and successfully begged her younger rival to relinquish her hold on the father of Louisa's children. But Mary couldn't keep her promise, and by the mid-1870s, Charles and Mary seemed perfectly settled in irregular domestic felicity.

Given Charlie's habits, it couldn't last. Mary truly loved him, but she also liked middle-class comfort, and life with lazy, drunken

[McGILL'S VICTIM.]

Diagram of bullet wounds.

Charlie didn't provide that very well. Nor did Mary like the abuse Charlie visited on her when in his cups, often striking her and once tearing off her clothes in public. After nearly starving in Columbus for several years, the couple relocated to Toledo, which proved no better berth for the improvident twosome. Somewhere along the way they had a child, who was sent off to the care of a woman named Mary Murphy in Columbus and never thought of again. Then, in the spring of 1877, Charlie and Mary came to Cleveland.

Cleveland should have been the brass ring for them. It was already a bustling city on the make, with opportunities for employment expanding every day in the shipping and industrial nexus of Northeast Ohio. And it was—at least for Mary. She had no trouble finding work as a domestic in several middle-class homes, and she invariably pleased her employers with her hardworking ways and cheerful disposition. It was different, of course, for Charlie. More often drunk than not, he seems to have spent most of his time in Cleveland exploring its saloons and fleshpots, rather than seeking employment and establishing a comfortable home for his wife. Even after they started living apart for economic reasons, Mary tried hard to put up with Charlie, but the last straw came on the night of October 13, 1877, when he beat her and tore her clothes off in a house at 18 Johnson Street where they met frequently to have sex. That was it: Mary told him she was leaving him for good, and she forthwith disappeared into the anonymity made possible by big-city Cleveland.

Like Dr. John Hughes of a decade before, Charles McGill didn't understand when a woman's "No" meant "No." Frantic with rage and rejection (he later admitted that he had been on a nonstop alcoholic bender from October 13 to December 2, the day of the murder), he combed the streets of Ohio's major cities for several weeks, searching for a clue as to his quondam lover's whereabouts. (He would later boast that he spent $18,000 in this search—an unlikely but typically grandiose McGill prevarication.) But even in a drunken frenzy, McGill was not without a certain animal cunning. Sending letters to Mary, care of "general delivery," to all major Ohio cities, he surmised that she was still in Cleveland when all of them were returned except the one sent there. Returning to Cleveland, McGill composed a fake letter from an acquaintance of Mary's and mailed it. He paid an old man a dollar to watch the downtown post office, and his plan paid off on December 1, when the old man told him that Mary had picked up the letter and was in Jack Willis's saloon at 109 Broadway, near Erie Street (East 9th). She often went there to warm her feet in the winter and was a favorite of the proprietor; Jack Willis would remember her fondly when she was dead: "She may have lived in a fast house; I suppose she did. But so far as I could judge she was a perfect lady. She was certainly educated and never drank anything, never used any vulgar or profane language . . . She appeared sort of sad like almost always and never was giddy at all. She would sit in her chair there where you are sitting and look almost always into the fire."

Mary was not too happy to see Charlie when he walked into the saloon. She reiterated that it was all over between them and that she couldn't stand to be with him when he was drinking. Charlie, for his part, was relatively charming. He didn't raise his voice and made no threats, merely asking that she come back to him and be his wife. His bad old days were forever gone, he promised, and his only wish was to make her his legal wife. After a few drinks, Mary thawed somewhat, eventually giving out her new address at 100 Cross Street to McGill. Maybe it was the drink, maybe she was lonely, maybe she believed McGill—or maybe she was afraid of what he might do then and there if she didn't go along with his wishes. But it's an undeniable fact that Mary Kelly signed her death warrant when she let Charles McGill back into her life. Jack Willis would relate—too late—that as Charlie watched Mary walk out the door of the saloon he raised his fist to her back and muttered, "I'll fix you yet!"

Charles, as he had promised, came to see her that evening at her new digs. Accompanying him was a male friend with the unlikely name of Elliot Hymrod, and the two enjoyed cigars and a few bottles of beer in company with Mary, another prostitute named Mary Campbell, and the madam of the house, Laura Lane. Elliot left at about 11, but not before Charlie borrowed his coat, explaining that he wanted to make a good impression on Mary, a virtually impossible proposition in his current, threadbare garb. Elliot, an accommodating fellow, agreed and handed over the coat. The next place he would see Charlie would be in jail.

Charles spent that Saturday night in bed with Mary in her downstairs room in Laura Lane's whorehouse. Although he would later claim that he didn't know the character of the house until he entered it, it seems unlikely, given his knowledge of Mary's resume and his own profound familiarity with Cleveland vice. (Ironically, Mary had told her acquaintances the reason she went to work at Laura Lane's house was that "her fellow had found out where she was [working as a domestic on Lake Street] and she wanted to keep it away from him.") Whatever his qualms, however, they spent the night together, and Charlie departed about 9 the next morning, promising to return. Mary told her friend Mary Campbell that he cried a lot while in bed with her that night.

He was as good as his word. Journeying to Charles Stein's pawnshop on Ontario Street, Charlie pawned his friend Elliot's coat for $5. He then purchased a seven-shot revolver and a box of suitable cartridges from Stein for $2.50. Fearing that the cartridges were blanks, McGill stepped to the rear of the store and fired three test shots at objects in the basement. Satisfied, he departed with his purchases without even having them wrapped.

Charlie returned to 100 Cross Street about noon, and he and Mary asked Mary Campbell if they could use her upstairs room for a private conversation. That conversation lasted about an hour and consisted entirely of McGill pleading with Mary to leave her life of shame and become his wife. We have only McGill's version of their colloquy, but there is no reason to doubt that she refused, arguing that she had no wish to return to the starving days she had

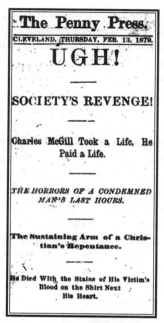

From the *Cleveland Press*,
February 13, 1879

spent with him in Columbus, Toledo, and Cleveland, and that she disbelieved his promises of future and perpetual sobriety. Charlie seems to have been particularly upset by Mary's admission that her last client, a Great Lakes sea captain, had given her $15 and a new dress. As the prim McGill would later recount at the inquest, he climaxed his pleas with an appeal to her family instincts: "For God's sake, Mary, leave this house! What would your grandma and auntie say if they knew how you are going down?" But Mary was adamant and, eventually wearying of the dispute, they both lay down on Mary Campbell's bed. Mary had her back to McGill; his arm was around her, and all seemed quiet.

McGill later claimed—as Jean Harris would a century later after her murder of a wayward lover—that he came to her dwelling with the intention of killing himself as a reproach for the way she had treated him. But that's not how it turned out. Pulling out his loaded gun, Charlie got up on the bed, put his knee on Mary's chest, and fired the first shot into her head. Firing without pause, he carefully put the next six shots into her head and neck, deliberately ruining the face that had hitherto so besotted him. After reloading the gun, he put four more shots into her chest, forgetting, as he later claimed, to save the last bullet for himself.

Charlie's activities had not gone without notice. Mary Campbell and her boss, Laura Lane, were sitting in the parlor below when some suspicious noise prompted Laura to send Mary upstairs. Opening the door, she saw Charlie pinning Mary with his knee and about to fire, with Mary "screaming and hollering." Perhaps thinking he was just trying to scare her friend, Mary Campbell said, "For God's sake, don't make so much noise on a Sunday!" Then the first cartridge exploded, and Mary screamed and ran downstairs. Laura Lane immediately sent her to get the police posthaste.

Laura needn't have been in a hurry. Charles McGill certainly wasn't: after washing his hands downstairs, he returned to kiss and hug Mary repeatedly and then discussed his awful act with all and sundry. Cheerfully admitting "I done it! Have I finished it well?" McGill even insisted on explaining the exact sequence and placement of the bullets to an astonished Dr. Norman Sackrider, who had been called to attend to the corpse. Sackrider warned him not to say anything incriminating, but the excited McGill prattled on. In due course patrolman Schnearline took him off to jail, where McGill continued his post-homicidal rant to anyone who would listen. The general tenor of his remarks is evident from such comments as "I shot the [eleven] shots and would have shot ten more if necessary," "I was determined to make a sure thing of it," and "I'd do it again if things were in the same shape." That night, a curious Elliot Hymrod asked Charlie why he hadn't changed his shirt, still encrimsoned with the gore of his afternoon's work. Genuinely puzzled by his friend's question, McGill retorted, "I would rather not. This is her blood and I love it." It is possible, of course, that McGill's nervous verbosity may have been aggravated by his consumption of cigars; he told Hymrod that he had smoked 27 of them that Sunday afternoon and evening.

McGill's trial did not disappoint scandalized chroniclers and consumers of the shabby details of his life with Mary Kelly and its violent end. He was voluble to a fault, and his incessant conversations with the voluminous tide of curious visitors who besieged his county jail cell soon convinced more than one skeptical listener that he was carefully laying the groundwork for an insanity defense. His head twitching sharply with almost every word, Charlie told reporters that he was unable to sleep, tormented by nightmares and daymares in which the dead Mary returned to beg for his love, screaming, "Charley! Charley!" Typical of the gothic anecdotes with which he edified Cleveland newspaper readers was this gem offered to a *Plain Dealer* reporter: "He dreamed that he was in a house on Johnson Street where he used to meet [Mary], that she came in, sat on his lap, threw her arms around his neck and kissed him. Then she pointed to spots on her face (where the bullet marks are) and told him they must be sores which broke out during the night."

Claiming even opiates could not stop his nightmares, Charlie committed further atrocities in the form of doggerel poetry, which, it is chronicled, he sang aloud to himself in his cell as the days of his incarceration plodded by:

> To Mary K.
> Tho' lost to sight, to memory dear
> Thou ever will remain,
> One only hope my heart can cheer,
> The hope to meet again.
> Oh, fondly on the past I dwell,
> And oft recall those hours,
> Where wandering down the shady dell
> We gathered the wild flowers.
> Yes, life then seemed one pure delight
> Tho' now each spot looks drear;
> Yet though thy smile be lost to sight,
> To memory thou art dear.

There were many more verses of like character, most of which echoed the pious thought that, although he was sorry he had riddled her with lead, fair Mary would continue to live within his heart. Whatever his gifts as a poet, most of those who witnessed McGill's melodramatic jail behavior were convinced he was faking it—a conviction lent certainty by the fact that McGill dropped his twitching mannerisms and nightmare talk as soon as his first trial was over.

The trial was by no means a mere legal formality: defense attorney Samuel E. Adams put up a terrific fight for McGill's life in the proceedings that opened on February 18, 1878, before Judge Jesse H. McMath, John Hutchins prosecuting on behalf of the state.

Avowing that McGill was mad as a hatter, Adams put McGill's aged mother, three brothers, and a dozen-odd in-laws and acquaintances on the stand to testify that Charlie had not been right in the head since birth. Subject to ungovernable rages and frequent sleepwalking from an early age, Charlie was portrayed by the defense as a love-struck swain pushed over the edge of madness by constitutional defects and the unforgivable behavior of his victim. Repeatedly referring to the dead Mary as a "brazen-faced Cyprian" (a period term for prostitute), Adams blamed Mary for the collapse of McGill's marriage and for provoking him beyond endurance by her life of mercenary shame. Not that Adams or anyone else went into the details of what that shame was—this was the 19th century, after all, and certain proprieties had to be observed. This coy unwillingness to call things by their real names led to some unintended hilarity in Adams's cross-examination of Mary's friend, Mary Campbell, on February 21:

> Adams: What is your business?
> Campbell: I don't know what you mean by that.
> Adams: Will the Court explain it to her?
> Campbell: I do everything.
> Judge McMath: This coming from a female, I suppose, Mr. Adams, you understand what that means?

Adams's portrait of McGill as a deranged man was rooted in more than childhood recollections and the anecdotes of his friends. Charlie's mother was allowed to state her belief that Charlie had been deranged by the effect of arsenic, which she had taken as a medicine when he was an infant and presumably passed on to him through her breast milk. Still more potent testimony was provided by witnesses who had been present when McGill was given a severe beating by Cleveland cops in August 1877, just four months before Mary's murder. McGill, in a drunken frenzy at a downtown beer garden, had refused to go quietly to the Central Police Station on Champlain Street and had been beaten to the ground twice by three patrolmen wielding nightsticks. Several witnesses took the stand to say that Charlie's symptoms of mental derangement had worsened in the months that followed. But the testimony about both the arsenic and the beer garden beating was nullified somewhat by the observations of prosecution witnesses who had noticed no change in Charlie's behavior during the critical months and of physicians who testified that there was nothing in Charlie's behavior before, during, or after the murder inconsistent with the effects of severe alcoholism, a chronic condition that none of McGill's defenders denied. McGill himself, perhaps, laid it on a bit thick in attempting to sway the jury by his behavior. Although he didn't take the stand in his own defense, his twitching continued apace, and he was heard several times asking his mother when Mary Kelly was going to show up in court. Seven doctors, responding to a defense questionnaire on McGill's mental condition, could not agree whether his current behavior (especially the twitching) could be faked. Dr. Proctor Thayer, who later performed a like service in Otto Lueth's 1887 trial, was of the opinion that it could not, but Judge McMath's charge to the jury expressed the cynicism of most contemporaries who saw Charles McGill in the months after his murder: "Let me say to you that you are to receive with great caution that class of testimony tending to show what has been said or done or written by the prisoner since the commission of the act . . . If, in view of all the facts, you come to the conclusion that Mary Kelly came to her death by leaden bullets shot into her head and body from a revolver in the hands of the defendant and fired by him while in sane mind, you will then inquire whether her death in this manner was caused purposely, of deliberate and premeditated malice. Does the evidence satisfy you that the shots were fired with a design to kill the deceased?"

It was probably Charlie's test-firing of the murder weapon that did him in; all the twitching in the world, even aided by his mother's courtroom tears, couldn't overcome the methodical way in which he had acquired and used the murder weapon. Or maybe it was the revolver itself, found hidden in a privy after the murder and given to the jury to contemplate during its deliberations, along with a gory photograph of the murdered girl. The 12 men good and true went out early on the afternoon of February 28, 1878, and returned with a verdict of first-degree murder at 9 a.m. on March 1. That same afternoon, Judge McMath sentenced McGill to be hung on June 26.

For better or worse, Charles McGill did not die as expeditiously as planned. Two months after his death sentence was pronounced, the Ohio Supreme Court threw out the verdict on the grounds that his jury had been improperly selected. Indeed, the record of the original trial makes it clear that both Judge McMath and Prosecutor John Hutchins had been aware of the defect—that juror Eli Stephenson of Parma had been impaneled instead of his son of the same name—but had decided to push forward with the trial, which had already been delayed by the calling and interrogation of hundreds of potential jurors. McGill's successful appeal stimulated much public cynicism, causing one Bank Street hack man to complain to a *Cleveland Press* scribe in tones of aggrieved populism: "If Mary Kelly had been one of Euclid's aristocrats or an officer of the state or county how quickly McGill would hang, and what little pains would be taken to save him. But she was a poor, unfortunate, weak Irish girl, hence the fuss made in favor of her seducer and murderer."

Apparently there were others who did not agree with Samuel Adams's characterization of Mary as the corrupting Cyprian who stalked helpless Charles McGill. Among them were 12 more jurors—culled from a pool of 500—who efficiently found McGill guilty of first-degree murder again on October 26, 1878. Oddly, the second verdict came only after 29 hours of deliberation and on the understanding that a majority of the jurors would subsequently petition Ohio governor Richard Bishop to commute McGill's death sentence. The second trial, held under Judge Darius Caldwell, saw the same parade of witnesses and experts but featured a twitchless and relatively quiet McGill. It seems by this time, perhaps fearing the worst, Charlie had got religion and was already spouting the slogans and clichés of Christian resignation that would festoon the loquacious verbiage of his final days. Oozing repentance in every public utterance, McGill pronounced himself the "happiest man in town" and talked joyfully of soon seeing Mary again. One therefore assumes Charlie was in veritable ecstasies when word came down on February 11, 1879, that Governor Bishop had refused to commute his death sentence.

Some other happy residents of Cleveland town were no doubt those lucky ones who successfully fought for the privilege of seeing McGill hung on February 13, 1879, in the Cuyahoga County jail. A little fewer than 50 in number, they watched raptly as McGill strode purposefully to the scaffold erected over an upper-floor shaft in the old county jail. Having dined "heartily" on fried oysters, ham, eggs, vegetables, and coffee, McGill was the calmest man there as the executioner tied his hands and put the black hood over his head. McGill, reputed to be mechanically inclined when sober, had already pronounced Albert Hartzell's new gallows "very nice," and he was doing his best to keep up the spirits of the Reverend Lathrop Cooley, his spiritual advisor, as he stepped to the drop. Dressed simply, McGill wore a piece of bloody cloth inside his shirt and next to his heart—a cloth encrimsoned with Mary Kelly's gore that had lain against his skin since the day he shot her. A few seconds after 12:04, McGill was heard to say to Sheriff John Wilcox, "Now, don't you make a mistake," and the next moment he shot through the nine-foot drop, instantly breaking his neck. Fifteen minutes later, his body was cut down and put in a coffin for shipment to Columbus, far from the potter's field where Mary Kelly sleeps in Woodland Cemetery. Let us hope this tragic couple found the peace envisioned in one of Charlie's last literary effusions:

> She Is Not Dead
> Although she sleeps beneath the sod,
> No headstone there to show,
> Above her quiet resting place
> The gentle zephyrs blow;
> Although the bitter, burning tears
> From 'neath my eyelids start,
> Still, still she is not dead to me,
> She lives within my heart."

Chapter 20

"STEP ASIDE, DADDY, AND I'LL FILL HIM FULL OF LEAD!"

The Insouciant Mabel Champion

We don't even know who she really was. History knows her as Mabel Champion—but that name is just a convenience for chroniclers and criminologists; how else to treat the tale of a female who changed the details of her biography and antecedents as often and capriciously as some women change their earrings? Her husband, Ausley—if he was her husband, and if his name was really Ausley Champion—sometimes called her Mabel, but also "Mary," "Inez," "Clara," "Teddy," and "May." Cleveland's newspapers called her "the Sphinx." County Prosecutor Edward Stanton called her a cold-blooded, "cunning, clever" murderess. Alternatively, Walter D. Meals, her defense attorney, called Mabel a "perfectly ladylike little girl" and pleaded that she was not only innocent of murder but had "never been guilty of any vices or even taken a drink of liquor." But call her what you will: Mabel Champion made quite an impression on Jazz Age Clevelanders by the time her personal comet had appeared, blazed, and faded before the eyes of those who followed her remarkable, daring adventures.

Mabel's improbable saga began on the night of July 26, 1922, when a flashy, late-model beige Cadillac pulled up to the curb in front of Downing's Restaurant at 1798 Euclid Avenue. It was almost midnight, and Playhouse Square was thronged with hundreds of play- and movie-goers exiting from the newly constructed and luxurious theaters across the street. Shocking to say, it was also crowded with lawbreakers—lawbreakers who flaunted their illegal acts before the indifferent eyes of blasé Cleveland policemen. After only two and a half years, Prohibition was already a dead letter in

Mabel Champion, 1922.   Ausley Champion, 1922.

the Forest City, and by all accounts Playhouse Square's sidewalks and restaurants that night were crowded with Clevelanders tossing down drinks as fast as they could be poured. And among them were the people in the Cadillac: driver Ausley Champion, his 22-year-old wife, Mabel, and their guests for the evening, Mr. and Mrs. Guy Williams.

It's a good guess that Ausley, at least, was already rather drunk when he brought the Cadillac to the curb. Pausing for a few moments, he pulled out a large bottle of hooch and shared it with the others in the car before reaching for the door handle. As he did so, he was accosted by a man named Thomas Albert O'Connell. Just minutes before, O'Connell, a 29-year-old carnival promoter known to his friends as "Eddie," had been seen drinking pure alcohol in Steiner's Cafe a few doors away. But he was still thirsty, it seems, and, spying the bottle in Ausley's hand, lurched up to the Cadillac and belligerently demanded a drink. There were some words between Ausley and O'Connell, but Ausley grudgingly handed over the bottle; O'Connell took a long pull and returned it. Ausley, Mabel, and Mr. and Mrs. Williams went into Downing's Restaurant, and that seemed the end of this sour, if minor encounter.

It wasn't. Shortly after Downing's night manager, William Conklin, seated Ausley's party, O'Connell came through the front door. Muttering "I'm going to get a drink from that man," he pushed his way through the crowded restaurant to the Champion party. Slamming his fist down on the table so hard that flatware was knocked to the floor, he confronted Ausley and demanded another drink. Ausley refused, but when O'Connell started threatening him,

Mabel told Ausley to let him have one for the sake of peace. So Ausley fished out his bottle, and O'Connell poured a stiff one and drained it down. Unsurprisingly, O'Connell now demanded yet another drink, and Ausley again refused. This time he surely meant it, but what happened next is a subject of unsettled debate. Ausley would forever after assert that the ensuing violence was triggered by O'Connell making unchivalrous slurs about women in general and Mabel in particular, shouting that the women at the table—and all women, for that matter—were "whores." Other voices, however, would later be heard to insist that the fight was the inevitable climax to a smoldering feud between Ausley and O'Connell that stretched back at least several days and through a trail of inebriated nights together in downtown Cleveland speakeasies. It's possible that both versions are true: Ausley was no ascetic pacifist, and O'Connell, although an honorable World War I veteran and a graduate of Yale University, was known for relinquishing his normally charming disposition for a more ugly, foul-mouthed persona when in his cups. As his widow put it later, "Tom was my dear, big boy—his only fault was drink."

Up to this point, the Champion party resembled most of the other groups seated in Downing's that night: two noisy couples huddled over a table spread with bottles, glasses, and mix, wearing flashy clothes and too much jewelry (Mabel herself was wearing eight large diamond rings that night). But things changed fast after Ausley reacted to O'Connell's hot words. Ausley slapped O'Connell, and then O'Connell slugged him hard, knocking him to the floor. As Ausley got to his feet, Mabel jumped up and ran toward Ausley's topcoat, which was hanging on a wall hook. Springing to his side, she pulled out an enormous .38 caliber Colt revolver and shouted at her woozy husband, "Step aside, Daddy, and I'll fill him full of lead!" At these words, O'Connell, who had been lurching forward toward the couple, staggered back, slurring, "You bitch! You're not going to shoot!"

Tom O'Connell was wrong. Maybe it was the drink, maybe it was the excitement. Maybe it was even, as Mabel later claimed, that she feared for her life as the 5'10" O'Connell loomed over 5'3" Mabel. Or maybe it was just Ausley, who helpfully encouraged Mabel by screaming, "Shoot the bastard, Mabel!" Whatever it was, shoot Mabel did, missing with her first bullet but then stunning O'Connell with a slug that stopped him in his tracks. Moaning, "Oh boy, I'm shot! Don't shoot again!" he fell to the floor. But

Mabel didn't stop. Walking up to the helpless O'Connell, she blasted him twice more at point-blank range, while her brave husband smashed the mortally wounded carnival promoter with a convenient chair. By now, the crowd in Downing's was in full panic mode, screaming and running for the exits as the patrons became aware of the lethal gunplay in the rear. Mabel and Ausley tried to flee out the door nearest to their table, only to find that it was a closet. Wheeling around, they ran toward the front door, where their Cadillac still sat at the curb. As they passed William Conklin, Mabel nonchalantly remarked, "Never mind the police, we're going now."

So was Thomas "Eddie" O'Connell, if not in the same direction. His liver, stomach, lungs, and virtually all of his other vital organs punctured, he lay bleeding heavily on the restaurant floor until Joseph Steffans, a compassionate taxi driver, took him to Huron Road Hospital. He was already in a fatal coma when he arrived there 15 minutes after the shooting, and the doctors just shook their heads. Meanwhile, Mabel and Ausley had failed to make their getaway. As Ausley struggled with his Cadillac's balky gearshift, Eyner Buhl, a Cleveland patrolman drawn from his East 17th beat by the sound of gunfire, jumped up on the running board, reached through the driver's window and pulled the ignition key from in front of the startled Ausley. Searching for the suspected gun, the persistent Buhl eventually found the still-warm weapon in its hiding place underneath Mabel's dress and between her legs. Ausley was taken off to jail, and Mabel was rushed to Huron Road Hospital.

The idea was to have the dying O'Connell identify his shooter, but his comatose condition merely precipitated a comic scene. Walking up to the unconscious O'Connell, Mabel leaned down to his face and then turned to Sergeant Charles Snyder and said, "Didn't you hear him say I didn't shoot him?" "No," replied the skeptical Snyder, "did you?" "You bet I did, old dear," riposted Mabel. "He said I didn't shoot him." Minutes later, O'Connell died without saying a word, and Mabel was removed to face the music at the county jail.

The police-beat reporters of Cleveland's three daily newspapers leaped on Mabel Champion like famished panthers on fresh meat. The year 1920 had been a great one for tabloid-style Cleveland crime stories, highlighted by the screaming headlines of the McGannon murder trials and gangster "Jiggs" Losteiner's Waterloo at the "Battle of Bedford" shootout. Nor was 1921 a disappointment when it came to sensationalism, as it featured the long-sought convictions of both Judge McGannon and Eva Kaber. But 1922 had been a bust so far, a relative journalistic drought extended by the abrupt collapse of the ephemeral "Black Widow" investigation only two months before. Mabel was manna to starving journalists, and they gave the story all the push avid readers expected from the best practitioners of the "Front Page" journalism of the age.

Cleveland News montage of crime scene, victim (misidentified as "Thomas A. Connelly"), and license plate of beige cadillac.

It didn't even matter that Mabel, at least initially, wouldn't talk to them or, for that matter, to the Cleveland police. Sizing up her stony silence, reporters immediately dubbed her "the Sphinx," and embroidered their pulpy columns with breathless conjectures about her identity and fulsome descriptions of her appearance and personality. Spitting rhetorical questions like hot lead, a *Cleveland News* writer introduced Clevelanders to Mabel and Ausley Champion this way: "Who is the prepossessing young woman held at detective headquarters on the claim of eyewitnesses that she fired the three shots that slew [Thomas A. O'Connell] in a downtown restaurant in the theater district early Wednesday? Who is the young man, possessor of a handsomely appointed new Cadillac automobile bearing a Texas license, who was with the mystery woman when the fatal shots were fired and who claims an identity that is refuted from Kansas City by a man who declares he is the individual the man in Cleveland claims to be?"

Considering the confusion deliberately wrought by Mabel and Ausley, even managing to articulate these unanswered questions was a journalistic achievement. From the beginning, Mabel and Ausley lied about themselves, their past, and their relationship to each other. At first they denied they were married; then they insisted on it, after police found a marriage license dated 1917 in their room at the downtown Hotel Huron. Addressed by Ausley as "May," "Clara," and "Mabel," Mabel coyly refused to admit to any name for weeks after she was arrested for O'Connell's murder. All she would say was that she was innocent, she had no idea who had shot O'Connell, and that she didn't care what the police thought. As she laughingly told Captain George Matowitz, "Go ahead and charge me with murder. I don't care. I've got tuberculosis and I'll be dead in a little while, anyway." Ausley, likewise, spoke little and only to the purpose of confusing the cops, insisting at first that he was "Cliff Bennett," a shoe salesman from Kansas City, an imposture that disintegrated when the real Cliff Bennett of Kansas City got in touch with Cleveland police. When confronted with the details of his past police record, Ausley eventually confirmed his identity but admitted only that he "played cards for a living" before clamming up for good. All of which left reporters with little more to do than inflate the image of Mabel-as-Sphinx and meditate at length on her personal attractions, her enigmatic smiles, her stylish wardrobe, and her soft-spoken, if laconic, charm.

For all their hard work in the weeks after O'Connell's murder, the Cleveland police had little more to go on than the glamorous myths adumbrated by the newspapers. They managed to trace Mabel and Ausley back to Texas, where they had both been arrested on divers charges—the 27-year-old Ausley had served a two-year term in the Lone Star State's penitentiary for larceny before escaping—and then to Indianapolis, where Mabel was wanted for jumping bail on a larceny charge in the spring of 1922. But who they really were, where they came from, and what their actual relationship to each other was remained unknown to all. Indicted on a first-degree murder charge by a grand jury (headed by, of all people, Raymond Moley, later famed as the kingpin of President Franklin D. Roosevelt's "Brain Trust"), Mabel was held without bail in the Cuyahoga County jail, while the luckier Ausley posted $5,000 bond on a charge of assault with attempt to kill, the result of his attentions to O'Connell with the restaurant chair. As he left Mabel at her cell door, he said, "Don't worry, I'll send you roses." And for once in his life, Ausley was as good as his word, sending elaborate nosegays of flowers and boxes of candy to Mabel every day.

Mabel worked hard to ingratiate herself with everyone as the three months before her trial plodded by. Pitching in to care for the sick girls in the county jail, she exuded kindly warmth and enticing femininity before all she encountered. Well, almost all; when confronted with O'Connell's grieving widow, she simply said,

"Don't talk to me—I don't want to talk about it." But to all others she turned on the charm, beginning with Judge Selzer on the day after her arrest. Brought in for her arraignment, a *Press* reporter noted, "she walked up to the bench, smiled at the judge, and began chatting with him as if they were old friends." When he asked her why she kept a four-inch stiletto in her handbag, Mabel batted her eyes, smiled sweetly, and demurely purred, "Oh, I peel peaches with that." Kate Carter, sob-sister writer in residence at the *Press*, captured Mabel's carefully cultivated appeal in a profile of Mabel published on August 1:

> A slip of a girl in a dark blue gingham dress, busily making a bed with the expertness of a hospital nurse. An imperturbable, smiling girl, with glossy black hair and an attractive face. Dressed with care, wearing chiffon stockings and gay satin slippers. Tucking gladiolas into a vase by her bedside, while "snappy" pictures of boats and bathing girls ornamented the walls. That may describe Mrs. Mabel Champion, "sphinx woman" . . . Mrs. Champion, who police say fired three shots into [O'Connell's] body from her husband's heavy revolver, was very polite, with an aroma of French perfume adding to the air of elusiveness which she possesses. "I really don't want to talk about it," she said, half-laughing as she picked up a box of expensive face powder. But I asked her how she passed the time in jail. "Nursing, mostly," she answered cheerfully. "Some of the girls have been ill. They seem to like to have me around. I read a little, but I don't write letters or sew anymore. I like best just sitting by myself and thinking."

Mabel's much-anticipated trial finally opened on October 23, 1922, after repeated delays caused by difficulties in securing eyewitnesses to the shooting. It was held before Judge Maurice Bernon, and Mabel was vigorously prosecuted on a first-degree murder charge by County Prosecutor Edward Stanton and Assistant Prosecutor James T. Cassidy. Mabel, attired in gowns custom-made for her trial, was defended by attorney Walter D. Meals before a courtroom packed daily with the "morbidly curious." History records that she was "clad in the latest creations of fashion in black that brought out all the attractions of her twenty-two years." The morbidly curious—mainly women and a surprising number of female teenagers—were not disappointed. Even before jury selection ended, Ausley Champion disappeared, jumping bail and leaving Mabel to fight for her life alone. Commenting on the abrupt cessation of the flood of flowers and candy to her cell, Mabel moistly lamented to reporters, "I guess I'm going to be alone. He certainly didn't do the right thing by me." Nor, as far as she was concerned, did Cuyahoga County prosecutor Edward Stanton, who proceeded to weave an airtight case against her. Practically everyone who had been in Downing's Restaurant on the fatal night took the stand, with various degrees of willingness—and offered their damning recollections of the fight between O'Connell and Ausley and how it had ended with the spectacle of Mabel blasting away with Ausley's .38 at point-blank range. Mabel's worst day came on Friday, October 27, when Joseph Shimendle took the stand. It was Shimendle who recollected Mabel's immortal assurance to Ausley ("Step aside, Daddy, and I'll fill him full of lead!"). Shimendle also unhelpfully contradicted the other eyewitnesses by remembering that Mabel had retrieved the revolver from inside her blouse, rather than from Ausley's topcoat. The state closed its case with a re-creation of the ludicrous scene at Huron Road Hospital and Mabel's

Sketch of fugitive Mabel.

farcical, if desperate, insistence that the expiring O'Connell had exonerated her. Summing up, Stanton put the state's charge against Mabel in stark, simple terms: "Cunning, clever Mabel shot O'Connell from the hip, from under her husband's coat. Mabel is from Texas, and in Texas they shoot from the hip."

Meals put up a terrific fight for his beleaguered client. His first stratagem in Mabel's defense was to blacken the character of the deceased, painting a sordid portrait of O'Connell as a brutish, drunken thug, small-time hoodlum, and "Paris Apache of the worst type." (O'Connell's actual criminal career amounted to a few arrests for assault.) Although Meals insisted that Mabel had not fired the fatal shots—he never did indicate who might have alternatively pulled the trigger—his argument was that O'Connell had brought about his own death, ingesting up to a gallon of booze that July night and digging "by his own hands the pit into which he fell." Rather than killing O'Connell, Meals pleaded, Mabel had been "playing the part of peacemaker" at

Downing's Restaurant, and her only crime had been merely "protecting herself from the lunges of a drunken, infuriated villain." "Wherever he has gone," Meals thundered against the dead O'Connell, "his respect for womanhood will be increased."

As the first week of the trial came to a close, things weren't going well for Mabel. The increasing number of tears she shed in the courtroom and the annoyed faces she made at Stanton were a good index of just how badly her case was evolving. At least six eyewitnesses had her plugging O'Connell, and a clutch of police experts testified that although O'Connell had been shot at close range, it wasn't close enough to support Mabel's claim that he was physically attacking her. So Mabel, perhaps with the advice of Meals, made two changes in her defense. One was to soften her image further by playing on public sympathy for her lonely plight, while at the same time inventing a virtuous motive for her previous stonewalling about her identity and the events of the night of July 26. Speaking to a *Press* trial reporter, she unbosomed her idealistic impulses:

> I am fighting my battle alone for only one reason. Back in the west, in a small town far enough from the big cities to prevent them from gaining access to the news of the day, are an old man and an old woman. Both are gray. Both are upright and devout. It would break their hearts if they knew that a daughter of theirs was occupying a jail cell, awaiting the decision that may mean life or death. One is my father, the other my mother . . . It is true they could give me great assistance. But in obtaining that assistance I would give them a shock that might end fatally for one or both. So I have determined to keep this situation from them.

One hopes that Mabel's parents didn't read the next day's *Cleveland Press*, for it reported the other change in her strategy, which was to admit that she shot O'Connell. She hadn't meant to do it, of course, she tearfully testified, but the big drunken lug had attacked her, and what was a poor, frail helpless girl to do? She'd only retrieved the gun from Ausley's coat to scare O'Connell, and the first shot had come as they struggled for the gun. It had gone into the restaurant floor, and her second and third shots (she denied knowledge of a fourth) were "accidental," occurring without her being conscious of pulling the trigger. And whatever the lying testimony of the crowd at Huron Road Hospital, Mabel insisted, the dying O'Connell had exonerated her in front of several policemen and doctors.

The final arguments recapitulated the highlights of the two-week trial. Stanton argued that Mabel was a brazen, deliberate murderess and demanded death for her so that Cleveland might be safe from further episodes of drunken downtown violence: "Is this Cleveland? Or is it Paris, where Apaches of the underworld shoot men down in cold blood?" And Meals reiterated his portrait of Mabel as a helpless, simpering Southern belle, citing her "ladylike" behavior in jail and in the courtroom. Mocking Stanton's argument that she might have taken the gun out of her blouse instead of Ausley's coat, Meals jeered, "The prosecution would have you believe she drew this huge gun out of her bosom. If it had been a Springfield rifle, they would have had her drawing it out of her stocking."

The case went to the jury at 3:55 on Wednesday, November 1. After 28 hours of deliberation and eight ballots, the seven women and five men returned the next evening at 7:55 with a verdict of manslaughter. When Judge Bernon asked Mabel if she had anything to say, Mabel could only sob, "No sir, I don't believe so—except I don't believe—I'm—guilty." Immediately after that, Bernon sentenced Mabel to a 20-year term in Marysville Reformatory, the minimum term for manslaughter under a recently passed Ohio law. The jury's decision made Mabel the youngest woman in Cuyahoga County history to be convicted on a murder rap. But it could have been worse: six of the seven women on the jury had voted for first-degree murder on seven out of the eight ballots.

Bernon's opinion was that Mabel's jury had been "kind and merciful," considering the evidence against her. That wasn't Mabel's reaction, as she made clear in a lachrymose statement issued the day after her verdict: "I believed I have been unfairly treated. I am a stranger here without friends, and that makes it all the harder. I don't see how any court could have permitted a prosecutor to defame a woman's character like [Stanton and Cassidy] did mine."

If Mabel was displeased, the *Plain Dealer* was ecstatic about her conviction, as it came just a year after a jury verdict that let Marion McArdle, Eva Kaber's daughter and accomplice in the murder of Eva's husband, Dan, go scot-free in 1921. Trumpeting the Champion verdict as a first fruit of the recently enacted 19th

Amendment, the editorialist crowed that Mabel's sentence "served notice that in Cuyahoga County it is no longer safe for a woman, even a young and exceptionally pretty woman, to kill a man at her own pleasure." Thanks to this kind of verdict, the editorialist continued, "neither murderously scheming wives nor gun-toting females can 'get away with it' in Cleveland." Meanwhile, the still absent Ausley was declared a fugitive from justice and forfeited his bond, while Mabel remained at the Cuyahoga County jail awaiting the outcome of her appeal.

Much to everyone's surprise, her appeal was initially successful. Ruling on April 2, 1923, the Court of Appeals ruled that Judge Bernon had committed "grave and prejudicial error" in not charging her jury to weigh carefully Mabel's self-defense plea. Mabel was ecstatic, not to mention unconvincingly pious at the news: "My prayers saved me. At the end of 20 years I would be wrinkled, gray-haired. There hasn't been a night I haven't cried as I said my prayers—the prayers my mother taught me when I was a little girl."

That was the last good news Mabel had. On September 29, 1923, word came from Los Angeles that Ausley Champion had been convicted of first-degree murder there. It seems that just three months after he fled Cleveland, Ausley had killed a man in a dice game in California. Despite the best efforts of his family—his mother perjured herself on the stand, and Mabel sold her remaining jewelry and fancy clothes to pay for his defense—Ausley went to the gallows on August 16, 1924. Mabel's explanation for her continuing fierce and unrequited loyalty was that whatever his faults ("How was I to know that he was a weakling and a drunk?"), Ausley was still her husband after all, and she had loved him since the long-ago day when he seduced her as a dewy-eyed adolescent Dallas Sunday-school student.

Mabel was already depressed enough when word came of Ausley's hanging. On January 16, 1924, the Ohio Supreme Court had upheld her original manslaughter verdict. For the benefit of reporters, Mabel, still at the county jail, waxed hysterical, raving that she couldn't survive her cruel and unfair ordeal. Blubbering to reporters, she once again put on her I'm-just-a-Texas-girlie-in-distress persona: "I cannot face this terror. I will go insane. I did what any woman would do. I shot Edward O'Connell because he insulted me. My husband was too drunk to defend me properly, so I did it for myself. Some help must come from somewhere. I am not bad. I am not a sphinx woman—which the dictionary says is a lioness with a woman's head. Why do they call me that?"

Despite her protestations, Mabel was sent to Marysville, after spending more than 20 months in the Cuyahoga County jail. Behind her fragile public image, however, lurked a colder, calculating Mabel already making plans to overcome her latest setbacks. She remarked to a fellow prisoner on route to Marysville, "A clever woman always finds a way. Twenty years? The judge may say 20 years—but Mabel won't be in Marysville 20 years from today."

How right the redoubtable Mabel was. Early on the morning of March 29, 1925, Mabel tucked a crudely fashioned dummy into her prison bed, picked up two suitcases, and walked out of Marysville Reformatory forever. Although she had been resident there only a year, it seems that she had quickly wormed her way into the confidence of her captors, winning special privileges as a "model prisoner" and gaining trusty status and access to the master keys. Dressed in civilian clothes stolen from night matron Laura Kissinger and carrying cash likewise purloined from that imprudently trusting woman, Mabel hailed a cab driven by hack man Guy Sewell and motored to Springfield, Ohio. There, after eating a "hearty meal" at the railroad diner, she boarded a train for Indianapolis . . . and disappeared off the face of the earth.

Despite a strenuous, prolonged, and nationwide manhunt, authorities never caught Mabel, although she was rumored to be headed toward Mexico, and was spotted by hysterical witnesses in Detroit, Akron, Chicago, Toledo, and Shaker Heights. It was initially thought she was Cleveland bound to revenge herself on Prosecutor Stanton, and Cleveland police chief Jacob Graul warned his men to take no chances with the diminutive gunwoman, stating, "Mabel will shoot. She is a killer. She may try to shoot her way to freedom if cornered." But Mabel never showed her face in the Forest City again. Although it's improbable, given her lifestyle and age (which today would be about 99), this writer likes to think she's still out there, laughing her low Texas belly laugh at baffled lawmen who couldn't keep this sensational Jazz Age baby tied down.

Chapter 21

"THIS IS MY LAST DAY!"

The Strange Death of Minnie Peters

All murders are not created equal. Varying circumstances of chance, style, and timing unpredictably determine that some homicides indelibly endure in the public memory while others are soon forgotten. One such inexplicable casualty of oblivion was the bizarre Peters horror of 1906—and that's a bloody shame. Although but a fortnight's sensation, its ghastly particulars comprised what still remains—after almost a century—Cleveland's best "locked room" murder mystery. It put one woman in the ground, one man in the police sweatbox, and numerous family friends and acquaintances under police suspicion and garish newspaper scrutiny. And not the least of its guilty pleasures was that it provoked a delightfully vituperative public hissy fit between respected Cuyahoga County coroner Louis E. Siegelstein and Cleveland police chief Fred Kohler.

Like most such tragedies, the Peters case was probably decades in the making—but the precipitating events with which we are concerned began exactly at 6 p.m. on Friday, November 16, 1906. For that was the moment when Albert Peters, a fortyish and mustachioed man-of-all-work, returned after a hard day of toil to find his second-floor apartment at 3805 Payne Avenue locked. Having no key and unable to arouse his wife, Minnie, by his repeated knocking, Albert repaired to the grocery downstairs. There he found the building owner, grocer Henry Soeders, and some neighbors and said, "Something is wrong and I can't get in." Accompanied by Soeders and next-door neighbor Michael McNierney, Albert led the group to his darkened three-room apartment upstairs and there, peering into the front-door keyhole, he spied the key on the inside. After discussing several options, Soeders persuaded Albert to jimmy open the pantry window (which opened onto the public hallway), and Albert crawled through it and went to the front door, which he opened to admit Soeders and McNierney. As the three men entered the front parlor, Soeders lit a candle and there in its flickering light they saw Minnie Peters lying on the floor.

She didn't look good. Lying on her left side, her hair partially concealing her face, the 45-year-old Minnie lay stone-cold dead in a large pool of congealed blood. There was blood spattered on almost everything in the room: the rug, the floor, the windows, pictures on the wall, and a mirror placed on a rocking chair close to the corpse. Even with her head partially obscured by gore and the knot of her long hair, it was obvious that Minnie's head had been beaten to a pulp with almost unbelievable ferocity. Her skirts and bathrobe were pulled up to her waist, exposing her underwear and stockings, and underneath her left side was found a large, heavy, and rather bloody machinist's hammer. Sinking to his knees by his wife's body and falling prostrate on her corpse, Albert Peters cried, "My God! My God! Didn't I tell you long ago not to kill yourself?" before lapsing into a paroxysm of broken German phrases and violent sobs. When his grief subsided, Henry Soeders sensibly said, "We must call the police."

Minnie Peters and diagram of her head wounds.

When Cleveland police detectives Lieutenant Frank Smith, Captain Schmunk, and Detective Sergeant James Doran arrived at 3805 Payne they didn't discover much more than Albert had glimpsed during his first hideous look at the murder room. Minnie had obviously been dead for some time, and the detectives were puzzled by two details. One was the fact that all of the furniture was pushed up against the walls; the other was the wall mirror sitting on the rocking chair, with a saucer of varnish next to it. With little more to go on, they did the expected thing and took Albert

Peters into custody for questioning. Seven hours later, after a vigorous interrogation during which he forcefully maintained his complete innocence, he was booked as a "suspicious person," pending further inquiry and more third-degree questioning.

Albert Peters's story was a plausible one, allowing for minor inconsistencies caused by his initial reluctance to be candid about the intimate details of his marriage to an indisputably troubled woman. Wed for about 15 years, Albert and Minnie had come to America in 1892, after leaving Minnie's two children by a previous marriage in a German orphanage. But whether in Germany or the U. S., their union had not been a happy one, continually troubled as it was by Minnie's chronic physical and mental problems. Moving restlessly around the United States in quest of surroundings congenial to the unhappy, unhealthy Minnie, they had lived in dozens of places before returning to Cleveland in April of 1906. Then, in only a short span of seven months, they lived at lodgings on Lorain Avenue, Vega Avenue, Rowley Avenue, Broadway Avenue, Pearl Court, and Willey Avenue, before finally landing at 3805 Payne at the end of October, just three weeks before. Not that any of the locations mattered much: Minnie Peters was a desperately unhappy woman wherever

Albert Peters.

she went, as evidenced by her estrangement from most of her relatives and the unhappiness she inflicted on the long-suffering Albert. Albert later characterized their life together in these sad words: "My whole life was bound up in that woman and I did not consider any sacrifice too great for her . . . When my wife first became ill I thought she was going into tuberculosis and it was I that suggested to her that we go to California. Then she began to experience those strange spells, and thence forward I suffered as much as she did."

Further disclosures by Albert Peters, corroborated by friends and relatives, revealed that in the months preceding her death, Minnie Peters's sufferings had taken a particularly morbid and ominous turn. Brooding, bedridden, and often acting in a demented, raving manner, she became convinced that an unknown enemy was pursuing her to her death, and she began to talk constantly of suicide. Once, on the train coming back from California, she had begged Albert for his knife, saying she wanted to slash her wrists before her mysterious nemesis hurled her off the train. Shortly after that, she tried to slash her throat with Albert's razor and drink carbolic acid—or so Albert said. On Sunday, November 11, just five days before her death, she had proposed a suicide pact with Albert, saying, "I don't care for my life. I have nothing to live for but you, and if we could both go together I would be happy." That night Albert heard Minnie praying that God would take them both in their sleep. Two days later, at her insistence, they both made new wills, each leaving everything to the other in case of death. On Thursday, November 15, she wrote Albert a note that read, "This is my last day. They are going to take me to Newburgh [insane asylum]." Like all of Minnie's notes to her husband, it was signed, "Your unfortunate wife." And when he left her for the last time on Friday morning at about 6, she walked with him to the public stairway and said, "This is my last day. Kiss me good-bye. Good-bye, Papa." Her subsequent autopsy show no food in her stomach, and Albert stated that she had not eaten for at least three days.

That was enough for Cleveland police chief Fred Kohler. After hearing many credible witnesses testify to Albert's unfailing solicitude and care for his difficult wife, Kohler ordered Albert's release from jail on Saturday afternoon, November 17, and immediately issued a statement that Mrs. Peters had killed herself, "beating her skull into fragments with her husband's machinist's hammer." Elaborating further to a skeptical Mayor Tom Johnson, Kohler defended his unexpected call on the Peters case: "The woman was insane. She had repeatedly threatened to take her own life. She told her husband when he left that morning he would never again see her alive." When the still-dubious Johnson asked how the frail Minnie could have so stoutly and persistently wielded the heavy hammer, Kohler had a ready answer: "The frenzy of insanity. It gives fictious [sic] strength. I have seen people who have nearly cut their own arms off in committing suicide who afterwards cut their throats."

Fred Kohler, Cleveland police chief, 1903–1913.

Kohler's decision to release Albert Peters and his comments on the case ignited a firestorm of scorn in Cleveland. Jeering at his claims that Minnie had done away with herself, the *Cleveland News* sneered that Kohler was "working apparently on the Cleveland police theory that every murder case is a suicide unless the murderer surrenders himself." Cuyahoga County coroner Louis Siegelstein, who had just finished his examination of Minnie's corpse, was even more blunt: "Anyone who says this murder is a suicide is ridiculous . . . Any one of the six wounds was a fatal one. It is out of all possibility of belief that any human being could have inflicted those injuries on himself. It could not have been done by man, woman, or beast. That is not my opinion only. It is the opinion of the two other doctors who examined the body . . ."

Siegelstein's statements were firmly supported by Assistant County Coroner J. T. Kepke, who asserted, "There is not a particle of doubt that the woman was brutally murdered." And Dr. C. L. Jaster of the Newburgh State Insane Asylum chimed in, stating that it was a "practical impossibility" for even a maniac to inflict such injuries upon herself.

Clevelanders quickly took sides in the dispute—and most of them supported Coroner Siegelstein. "How Could A Corpse Take Its Own Life?" screamed the headline in the November 19 *Cleveland Press*. As Siegelstein noted, the evidence of his autopsy made a suicide verdict almost unthinkable. Using the round end of Albert Peters's machinist hammer, Minnie's assailant had inflicted 12 severe blows on her skull, any 6 of which were sufficient to cause unconsciousness or death. Two of the blows had been forceful enough to drive broken pieces of skull into her brain. Moreover, the disarray of the parlor, the centrifugal distribution of blood, and the condition of her clothes all pointed toward a homicidal assailant. And, as all who knew Minnie agreed that she was too weak to wield such a hammer, she could not have used it to kill herself. "To assert otherwise," concluded Siegelstein to a *Cleveland Leader* reporter, "is to violate good sense."

Fred Kohler didn't shy away from fights, and he waded with gusto into the public fray with Siegelstein. Denying that the hammer blows killed Minnie, Kohler insisted that she had instead choked to death on her own blood. Noting that all the windows and the only door of the Peters flat were locked from the inside and that no one saw anyone enter it on the murder day, Kohler scoffed at the idea of an unknown intruder. Since Albert Peters's alibi checked out—Dr. Corlett swore he had been at his Euclid Avenue house all day—Minnie's death could only have been a suicide. She had long been seriously depressed, she had told Albert that Friday was her "last day," and the details of the murder scene suggested that she had carried out her self-destruction with admirable precision. In fact, according to Kohler, Minnie's modus operandi for suicide followed a script familiar to police investigations of housewife suicides:

> Police records show similar incidents. The woman prepared for death—cleaned her house from parlor to kitchen—changed her clothing from the skin out—burned her papers—placed the mirror on a chair—then took a machinist's hammer and pounded herself—the blows increasing in force as her frenzy advanced . . . She placed that looking glass on the rocking chair in such an angle that no one could see her reflection therein without standing up. This is a common practice for would-be suicides to stand before a mirror . . . the looking glasses being frequently shattered by the body striking them in the fall . . . It is not the function of Coroner Siegelstein to say how this woman came by her wounds . . . If I should declare that the woman was murdered, I would be hooted out of the office by the men under me.

Coroner Siegelstein riposted immediately. Asked why he still stuck to his suicide theory in view of Kohler's opposition, he replied: "I have only begun to stick. In the annals of surgical history there is no case of a person receiving wounds similar of those Mrs. Peters received and retaining consciousness long enough to strike the second blow."

Minnie Peters's funeral took place on Monday afternoon at the Flynn & Froelk morgue. It was attended by a crowd of "morbid persons, mostly women," and press accounts of the obsequies included the delicious rumor that a mysterious woman was seen "gloating" in triumph over the Minnie's open casket. As her coffin slid into the waiting hole at Monroe Street Cemetery, a weeping Albert was heard to mutter that it wouldn't be long before he was with her.

Anyone who thought Coroner Siegelstein's inquest would settle the acrid dispute over Minnie Peters's death must have been gravely disappointed. Opening on Monday, November 19, the inquest panel called several dozen witnesses—most of whom gave evidence supporting both the Kohler and Siegelstein hypotheses.

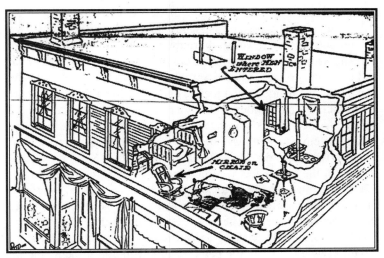

Sketch of the murder flat.

Friends and relatives of Albert Peters testified to Minnie's chronic melancholia, irrational fears of a phantom stalker, and frequent threats of suicide. Their memories of the crazed woman were amplified by the text of a note—or rather the faint impression of a note on the top sheet of a paper tablet—found by Chief Kohler himself while searching the Peters flat two days after the murder. Verified as being in her handwriting, magnified to legibility, and translated from the German by Henry Soeders's daughter, Annie, Minnie's last note seemed the final, anguished cry of a woman at the end of her psychological rope: "Schmidt, Girgen Soeders said nothing. To this I can swear. This was all that was wanted to set these people upon me. What is worse, you do not care for me. Dear friends, forgive me. If you can come as soon as possible. Your unfortunate wife."

It took some time to sort out some ambiguities in the note. "Schmidt" was Max Schmidt, a friend of the family whom police initially suspected of being Minnie's lover. But after a prolonged, uncomfortable chat with him, Kohler's men concluded his interest in the dead woman was truly platonic. Minnie's fears about people being "set upon" her turned out to be her unfounded delusion that Henry Soeders, the landlord, was about to evict them. But the core of the note clearly demonstrated Minnie's fears of an impending doom and resonated with an urgent anxiety consistent with a suicidal mood. And the police insistence that no intruder could have entered the Peters flat was supported by Annie Soeders's testimony that she had been working in the building all day as a charwoman and had seen no one in the vicinity of the Peterses' door. With the key left on the inside of that locked door, it seemed impossible that anyone could have entered the apartment during the critical 12 hours of Albert Peters's absence.

Siegelstein was having none of it—and soon a small parade of surprise witnesses dramatically challenged Chief Kohler's suicide theory. In the first place, it turned out there was no proof that the Peters apartment had been locked from the inside when Albert and his witnesses returned there on Friday evening. Henry Soeders and the others had merely accepted Albert's claim that his door was locked. No one else had actually tried to open the door before Albert crawled through the pantry window to admit them, and no one present heard or saw him actually unlock the door. A reluctant Henry Soeders concluded his testimony with these ominous words: "I want to be understood plainly in this. I do not know who killed this woman, but if what I am about to say would hang [Albert Peters] I must say it . . . It is the gospel truth that Peters never unlocked that door. He swung it right open. There was no turning of a key and no sliding of a bolt."

The greatest challenge to Kohler's suicide scenario came from Conrad Voth, a journalist for a German Baptist periodical, *Der Sendbot*, whose office was directly across the street from Albert and Minnie's Payne Avenue apartment. First contacting Kohler on Sunday, November 18, Voth claimed he had seen a mysterious old man at the window of the Peters flat at about 12:30 p.m. on Friday. Appearing for a few seconds at the second window from the southeast corner of the apartment, the man had peered down at the street and then withdrawn. After talking to Voth, Kohler and his detectives dismissed Voth's sighting as a "phantom," but Coroner Siegelstein presented Voth as his star witness at the inquest's opening session. Firmly repeating his assertions, Voth described the man he had seen as about 5'8" tall, 50 to 60 years old, well dressed in a black cloak, wearing no hat, and sporting a short, well-trimmed beard. Voth said he would probably recognize the man if he saw him again and that he resembled a previous tenant of the Peters flat, an old man named "Grover." Kohler's men did what they could to disparage Voth's statements, claiming that he had failed to identify figures at the critical window in repeated tests staged by detectives and that his eyesight was poor. But Voth stuck doggedly to his story and succeeded in embarrassing his police detractors by correctly reading distant address numbers through the window of the morgue where the inquest was held. Whatever the scoffing of Kohler's finest, Voth's serious mien and precise testimony made a lasting impression, even if he did conclude with a gratuitous speculation on the deceased woman's private life: "I would not be surprised to learn any time that a man had been found, a man whom Mrs. Peters had known, and known intimately, though without the knowledge of her husband." Interestingly, Voth's invidious conjecture was echoed the following day by Jake Mintz, Cleveland's most famous private detective. Speaking to a *Cleveland News* reporter, Mintz theorized that Minnie had been murdered by a "moral degenerate," an unknown man who "had loved her better than her husband." Dismissing Albert as an innocent simpleton, Mintz argued that it was useless to question him further: "Do not ask Peters whom he suspects, for he is a man who would never suspect anyone of anything."

Additional support for the idea of an unknown intruder, possibly even Voth's bushy-faced stranger, came on Thursday, with the dramatic testimony of Isadore Rosenthal, a neighborhood schoolboy. He told the panel that he had been standing in the Grenloch & Gensert shoe store just below the Peters flat about 4 p.m. on Friday when he heard a sound "like a body falling" above. He had mentioned the noise to the store proprietor at the time, but the latter had been too busy to pay attention. The panel then went on to consider technical and inconclusive arguments as to whether the key in the front door could have been turned from the outside by someone using a pair of burglar's "nippers."

The inquest finally petered out on Thursday, November 22, with the question of how Minnie met her death unresolved. But Kohler and Siegelstein continued their public feud, each determined to have the last word. Even before all the testimony was in, Kohler stated unequivocally, "This incident is closed," and on Friday, November 23, the day after the inquest ended, he spluttered angrily: "The coroner jumped at conclusions, which he has since come to realize were wrong, and now he is exerting every effort to vindicate himself in his prejudged verdict. I'm just vexed. It's ridiculous, preposterous, asinine. He snaps his fingers at a trained police force, trained for just such action as the solving of death mysteries, and tells us to paddle our own canoe, that he'll paddle his."

As county coroner, however, Siegelstein was entitled to the last word, which came with his official inquest verdict on December 1: "Minnie Peters came to her death from hemorrhage of the brain and a fractured skull, which were caused by said Minnie Peters having been struck a number of blows over the head with a blunt instrument by an unknown person."

And so ended, seemingly inconclusively, the Minnie Peters puzzle. Max Schmidt endured some additional, but fruitless, "sweating" as to whether his relations to the deceased were improper, and Albert eventually declared his conviction that Minnie couldn't have killed herself, saying: "She would have left a note clearing me . . . she told me many times that she would be murdered, but always promised me faithfully that she would not harm herself." Albert, who had been fired by Dr. Corlett on account of the unpleasant publicity, soon found another job and new lodgings free from disquieting bloodstains. And curious Clevelanders turned to other sensations of the day, like Mayor Johnson's protracted war for three-cent streetcar fares and ongoing public concern about industrial trusts.

But before you dismiss Cleveland police chief Fred Kohler as an utter moron, consider this: He may have been right about Minnie killing herself. Her previous behavior was consistent with such an end, and the odd circumstances of the death room—especially the mirror on the chair—closely followed the scripts for female suicides familiar to contemporary policemen. And, believe it or not, there is some evidence that Minnie Peters actually could have killed herself with her husband's hammer. Chief Kohler came in for some knowing sneers and smirks six months later, when Frank E. Woodworth of Painesville, perhaps inspired by newspaper publicity, tried to kill himself with a heavy hammer. Woodworth, despite being a heavy, muscular fellow, failed in the attempt, neither fracturing his skull nor even losing consciousness. When baited by newsman as to why the strong Woodworth failed where the weak Minnie had allegedly succeeded, Kohler replied, "Woodworth didn't have Mrs. Peters's nerve." But several other cases, relatively unpublicized, impressively bolster Kohler's hypothesis. Four years before the Peters case, on March 6, 1902, Henry L.

Dauernheim, a wealthy, 50-year-old paper merchant from St. Louis, had killed himself by beating in his skull with a heavy sledgehammer. Just 19 months after Minnie Peters's death, Rachel Goldfadoon of 2663 East 25th Street tried to kill herself with a hatchet; she did not succeed but managed to inflict seven ugly wounds on her skull. And in March 1911, businessman William Staum of Syracuse, New York, beat himself to death with a hammer in circumstances eerily reminiscent of the Peters case. Found lying in a pool of blood, the despondent Staum had locked his door and hit himself 8 to 10 times with a heavy hammer, penetrating his brain with several blows. The official coroner's verdict on Staum's death was suicide. The Minnie Peters case remains unsolved.

Chapter 22

CLEVELAND'S SADDEST CIRCUS DAY

The Ringling Brothers and Barnum & Bailey Fire

Few spectacles are harder to endure than that of a brute animal in pain. Although largely forgotten now, the 1942 Ringling Brothers and Barnum & Bailey Circus fire in Cleveland was replete with a multitude of such dreadful sights, and they remained etched in the memories of the circus folk, spectators, and Cleveland firemen who witnessed them. Even worse, lessons learned from the tragic blaze went unheeded, as the even more catastrophic Hartford, Connecticut, circus fire—in which 168 persons died—would demonstrate only two years later.

August 4, 1942, was a fine, sunny day in Cleveland. The Ringling Brothers Circus was in its second day of a four-day, eight-show stint at the circus grounds on the north side of Lakeside at East 9th. Boasting 1,009 animals and 800 performers, and specially redesigned by Norman Bel Geddes and George Balanchine, the circus brought welcome cheer to Clevelanders caught up in the toils, tears, and anxiety of World War II. It was nearing noon, and many of the circus folk were sleeping, while others prepared themselves and the animals for the 2:15 performance.

The tragedy happened at about 11:45 a.m. A pile of straw at the west end of the menagerie tent suddenly erupted in crackling flames. Quickly reaching the paraffin- and benzene- coated tent, the flames raced the length of the tent in mere seconds, fed by the straw bedding of the caged animals and the hay, straw, and feed stockpiled around the tent.

It was all over, except for the suffering, in just 15 minutes. Many

Aftermath of fire, circus grounds,
East 9th Street and Lakeside Avenue.

of the animals, such as two of the giraffes, two tigers, and a pair of lions, were simply "cooked" in their cages. Ten camels, tethered together, were trapped in place and died where they stood. A herd of zebras, many of them badly burned, fled in panic toward the railroad tracks just north of the circus grounds. When two companies of Cleveland firemen and a high-pressure unit finally got the fire out, 65 animals lay dead or dying on the Ringling lot. And it could have been worse: only a favorable wind and frantic efforts by firefighters prevented the blaze from engulfing the adjacent horse tent and its 160 horses. The only humans injured were the elephant boss, who was burned, and another employee who was accidentally clipped with an elephant hook in the afternoon's turmoil.

Most pitiful were the elephants. Four of them were terribly burned, some of the ears completely burned off, with the folds of their skin hanging in charred fragments. Highly disciplined, the elephants had refused to leave the flaming tent until Walter McClain, the elephant boss, came to lead them away.

Rosie, the pachyderm with a "bad" reputation, died first. Maddened by pain and repeatedly breaking restraining chains, she ran amok until police detective Lloyd Trunk, acting on orders of circus veterinarian J. J. Henderson, put a bullet between her eyes, and policeman D. L. Cowles emptied a submachine gun into her side. Several hours later, Ringling Rose, her pelt completely burnt off, suffered the same fate. The two remaining elephants, Trilby and Cass, were taken to the basement of Public Hall, where they and

Smoky debris from menagerie tent fire.

the other burned animals were tenderly painted with a special burn salve, "Follie," flown in from New York. Trilby died at midnight, and Cass expired early that same morning.

Ten of the victims were camels. Veterinarian Henderson tried to save another three of them—Pasha, En Route, and Tillie—but Detective Trunk finally had to end their sufferings, too, with 9 or 10 bullets apiece. Dr. Henderson remembered their deaths this way: "They lay down, staring out off into space like old men looking out of a club window, and died." The final death toll included 4 lions, 3 tigers, 2 giraffes, 12 zebras, 1 ostrich, 3 pumas, 16 monkeys, 2 black bucks, 1 sacred Indian cow, and 13 camels. The corpses of the dead animals were taken to the Stadler Products Company, a rendering plant on Denison Avenue.

William O. Walker of the *Call & Post* gave the best eyewitness account of the fire. He was close enough to see the first sheet of flame erupt, and he eloquently described the unspeakable sights he saw that day: "The most awesome aspect of the tragic spectacle was the complete silence of the animals. No agonizing screams, no anguished roars. Just silence inside the tent, with the crackle of flames outside." Later, he wrote of his anguished tour of the smoking ruins: "All about the ringed circle, where, only a few minutes before, had stood one of the finest menageries in the world, were the smoldering cages. Inside these cages were lions, leopards, and other beasts of the cat family, all burned, but not dead. In agony, they moved on feet bleeding from burns, and stared into space through eyes that no longer had vision. It was indeed a heart-rending sight . . ."

The cause of the $200,000 blaze, which was not covered by insurance, was never proven. Two days after the fire, the Allegheny

Circus employees in bucket brigade.

County, Pennsylvania, police picked up a 16-year-old drifter named Lemadris Ford, a native of Pittsburgh, who readily confessed that he and a friend named "Jeff" had set the fire in revenge for being fired from the circus just hours before the blaze. According to Ford, they had chugged a bottle of wine, returned to the menagerie tent, and thrown lighted cigarettes onto the straw. They then fled Cleveland by hopping on a convenient freight train—but only after collecting their back wages at 5 p.m. that day. Cleveland police detectives, however, found severe inconsistencies in Ford's "confession" and decided he was either seeking notoriety or suffering from hallucinations. Which left either the possibility of a carelessly thrown cigarette (by either a circus worker or spectator) or even sparks from a train on the tracks just north of the Lakeside circus grounds. Historical accounts of the tragedy list the cause of the 1942 fire as "unknown." What is definitely known is that the proper lesson was not drawn from the tragedy: two years later 168 people in an identical tent waterproofed with paraffin and benzene would die in another circus fire in Hartford, Connecticut.

The show went on again that evening and afterwards, its presenters undeterred by the catastrophe, especially as most of the animals killed had not performed in the Big Ring. But John Ringling North, the circus chief, best expressed the fire's impact when he spoke for all the circus folk that terrible day: "I can stand the loss incurred in the fire, but I just cannot stand to have the animals suffer." His sentiments were poignantly echoed by head animal handler John Sabo, who had worked with the Ringling Circus since 1915: "I would rather lose my right arm than to see something like this happen. I like them all like babies. I felt like bawling when I found out that Maggie and Mabel (the brindled gnus) had died."

Chapter 23

"IN THE NAME OF VIOLATED CHASTITY"

The Terrible Stalking of Tamsen Parsons

You could call it a "love tragedy." That's what Dr. John Hughes termed his killing of Tamsen Parsons on a pleasant summer afternoon in 1865. You could call it, after Louisa May Alcott, a "long, fatal love chase"—for Dr. Hughes's romantic obsession spelled doom for the beautiful Miss Parsons. Or you could characterize it as a 19th-century temperance melodrama: the inevitable result of the good doctor's addiction to strong drink. It was all of these things and more. It was a coming-of-age murder for Cleveland's three competitive daily newspapers—who vied for the public's favor with unprecedented paragraphs of prurience and sensation. And it was a classic feminist horror story: the terrible tale of a mature, successful male stalking a vulnerable, defenseless adolescent girl to her pitiful, violent death.

John Hughes took scrupulous pains and came a long way to die on a Cleveland scaffold. Born in 1833, Hughes was the spoiled and sole heir to landed gentry who had long resided comfortably on the Isle of Man. John's father, a Welsh physician, was a man of many talents, albeit prone to occasional drunken sprees, but his influence on John ceased with his death in 1837. Cruelly separated from his mother by his legal guardian, James Moore, John went away to boarding school. At the age of 13 he returned to his ancestral manse, only to quarrel once again with Moore, who objected to John's precocious dissipation and recklessness. An abortive attempt to run away to sea culminated in an uneasy truce with

Moore, and John was given an allowance and an independent suite of rooms on Moore's estate. Possessing, as a reproving *Cleveland Leader* scribe later put it, "any amount of money to spend and too

much time in which to spend it," Hughes dabbled with improbable careers in navigation and the ministry while he polished his vices to perfection. Freely spending the income from his father's estate, Hughes kept a race horse, frequently drank champagne to excess, smoked cigars, and was notorious for keeping company with the local harlots. Eventually tiring of this lifestyle, he enlisted in Her Majesty's 5th Dragoon Guards, just in time for the Crimean War.

Whatever his later cowardice, Hughes fought bravely in the Crimea and was badly wounded in the left leg at Balaklava.

John W. Hughes.

Returning home in 1856 in time to see his mother die, he courted a respectable lady and impressively acted the part of the retired rake. Alas!—his affections were spurned by the lady, and he revenged himself on her by immediately eloping with one of his aunt's servant girls. As is usual with such romantically spiteful gestures, the marriage soon turned sour, and tiring of Margaret Hughes, he left for prolonged medical studies at the Royal College in Edinburgh, where he took his diploma in 1857.

Apparently the combined toll of marriage and medicine was too much for John Hughes. Returning to his estate, "Hughes Bellamona," he devoted himself with renewed fervor to drinking, gambling, and wenching. His course of conduct, to no one's surprise but his own, resulted in his losing the entire estate in the space of only two years, and Hughes left in disgust for the United States.

Arriving in America in 1860, Hughes eventually gravitated to Cleveland, where there was a substantial community of fellow Manx émigrés. The next year he opened a medical practice in Warrensville Township and kept up his military skills by drilling recruits after Lincoln's call for volunteers in April 1861. Although a relative newcomer to Cleveland , Hughes quickly established renown as a hard drinker and binger and was oft observed by his medical peers performing surgery while under the influence of alcohol. (Naturally, none of his fellow physicians made any public remark about this at the time.) One of them, Dr. D. G. Streeter, later recalled encountering a drunken Hughes en route to an amputation, equipped only with a butcher knife and a mechanic's saw.

After bringing his wife and his young son, Bissett, to Cleveland in 1862, Hughes practiced medicine at an Ontario Street office (where Dillard's department store is now located) until May 1863, when he abruptly enlisted in the U. S. navy. That stint lasted only a few months, and in March 1864 he joined the U. S. army. That summer found him as Surgeon-In-Charge at the marine hospital in Vicksburg, where he once again mixed his avocation of drinking with surgery.

The fatal path that led John Hughes to Tamsen Parsons opened up in October 1864. Suddenly resigning his commission, Hughes returned to Cleveland, only to find Margaret—he later claimed—a chronic drunkard, and his home "desolate." Many witnesses would later contest Hughes's horrific tale of his domestic obliquities, but it is indisputable that after a jaunt to New York he returned to Cleveland one night in December and decided to attend a soldiers' ball at the Warrensville Hotel. As was his wont, he sampled the custom at every tavern on the way and was thoroughly inebriated by the time he got to the ball.

Hughes never did recollect exactly how the subsequent hours passed. But his next conscious memory was of awakening with a throbbing head in a bed at Thomas Parsons's Bedford home, where he had been taken by an acquaintance to sleep it off. A beautiful young woman leaned over him, lifted his aching head, and loosened his cravat. Hughes muttered blearily, "Who are you?" "Tamsen Parsons," replied the young woman, and then asked a question that has amused Hughes's chroniclers since: "Doctor, why do you drink so much?"

Avoiding a direct answer but wasting no time, Hughes glibly unfolded a tale of marital purgatory to the impressionable 17-year-old Tamsen. His marriage was a sham, he sobbed; his home life a scene from Dante's *Inferno.* According to Hughes, it was love at first sight with Tamsen. As he later recalled it—on the occasion of receiving his death sentence—"I saw in that look sympathy and pity that filled my whole soul, and I saw my feeling was reciprocated."

Reciprocated it was. Whether Tamsen actually said, "Would to

God I were your wife!" as Hughes remembered it, it is doubtless that their hearts were soon plighted. Their initial hangover colloquy was soon followed by a sleigh ride for two and, it may be assumed, further intimacies, especially after Hughes showed Tamsen an official-looking divorce degree in mid-December. Trusting Tamsen, of course, didn't know that Hughes had obtained a blank divorce form and then thoughtfully forged the necessary data and signatures, nor did Tamsen realize that Hughes's wife and son were still living in Cleveland. There were a lot of things romantic young Tamsen didn't know, and her ignorance led her into a dramatic elopement to Pittsburgh, where John and Tamsen were married on December 20, 1864.

Who were these dissimilar lovers that a star-crossed fate united on a crisp Yuletide morning? Of Tamsen we know little, as is too often the case with passion's victims. The testimony of family and friends was that she was young, beautiful, sweet, and impressionable—and that there was not a breath of scandal against her until Hughes entered her life. We have a clearer portrait of the doctor, although admittedly drawn later in the distorting light of his public notoriety:

> [Hughes] is a very good looking man, and a phrenologist or physiognomist would never spot him as an easily-made or possible murderer. He appears to be about thirty or thirty-five years of age, stands erect, a powerfully-built man of five feet ten inches in height, with a good head on his shoulders and a face that bears the mark of intelligence and resolution. His hair, which is not plentiful, is black, and he wears a becoming moustache and goatee. . . When he speaks, no matter how briefly, he impresses you as one who weighs his words well, and there is that in his every attitude, motion and speech, which suggests that he could, on occasion, be a man of courteous manners and elevated conversation.

Two other newspaper commentators amplified this pleasing profile of Hughes, one noting that Hughes "moved about with the ease and grace of a woman, while his bearing was at the same time regal. His skin was polished as marble, and his flesh firm as a granite slab." The other scribe, while admitting that Hughes's figure was like those whose shape "hint the Apollo," disclosed that his eyes could look "venomous," perhaps because "the right eye looked larger than

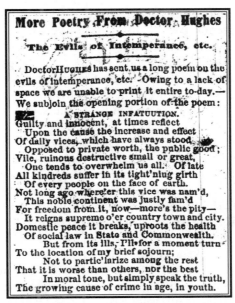

More Poetry From Doctor Hughes

The Evils of Intemperance, etc.

Doctor Hughes has sent us a long poem on the evils of intemperance, etc. Owing to a lack of space we are unable to print it entire to-day. We subjoin the opening portion of the poem:

A STRANGE INFATUATION.

Guilty and innocent, at times reflect
 Upon the cause the increase and effect
Of daily vices, which have always stood,
 Opposed to private worth, the public good;
Vile, ruinous destructive small or great,
 One tends to overwhelm us all. Of late
All kindreds suffer in its tight'ning girth
 Of every people on the face of earth.
Not long ago where'er this vice was nam'd,
 This noble continent was justly fam'd
For freedom from it, now—more's the pity—
 It reigns supreme o'er country town and city.
Domestic peace it breaks, uproots the health
 Of social law in State and Commonwealth.
 But from its ills, I'll for a moment turn
To the location of my brief sojourn;
 Not to partic'larize among the rest
That it is worse than others, nor the best
 In moral tone, but simply speak the truth,
The growing cause of crime in age, in youth.

Dr. Hughes preaches on intemperance.

the other, owing to the fact that it was once knocked so far out that it hung upon the cheek."

The Pittsburgh conjugal idyll of "Mr. and Mrs. John Hughes" was a short one. Learning of their daughter's elopement, her parents, Susanna and Thomas Parsons, sent Tamsen's brother-in-law Joseph to Pittsburgh to apprehend the errant couple, and Hughes was arrested in his bridal chamber at the St. Clair Hotel the very night of his wedding day. Although he initially breathed threats and defiance, threatening to blacken Tamsen's reputation with "unpleasant discourses," Hughes eventually calmed down and was briskly sentenced to a year in the Allegheny Penitentiary on a conviction of bigamy. No doubt Hughes's "unpleasant discourses" consisted of no more than the fact that the "marriage" had been consummated even before his sham ceremony. Or, as the *Cleveland Herald* feelingly related Tamsen's presumably indelible disgrace: "By the wiles that are known to the practiced seducer, he prevailed on this young girl, after ruining her character for all time . . ."

Alas for Tamsen, the Pennsylvania style of justice of her era proved as flexible as that of the present day. Thanks to the tearful petitions of the long-suffering Margaret Hughes, Hughes was pardoned by Governor A. G. Curtin after serving only five months. Returning to Cleveland, Hughes resumed the practice of medicine and his erstwhile drinking habits. With Tamsen in apparent seclusion at her home in Bedford, Margaret Hughes thought things were now stable enough to allow her return with their son to the Isle of Man for a visit. She left in mid-July—and it was the last time she ever saw her husband.

Only a week after his wife and son departed, Hughes appeared at the Parsons house in Bedford in the wee hours of July 24. Possibly lured there by a letter from Tamsen, Hughes was discovered by Thomas Parsons in Tamsen's bedroom at 2 a.m. Armed with a knife and gun, Hughes had broken into the house and threatened to kill Tamsen if she gave the alarm. After pleading repeatedly with Tamsen to marry him for real—"I have a home already furnished nicely and will make a lady of you"—Hughes allowed himself to be led away by friends of the Parsons family. Tamsen, whatever her behavior in encouraging Hughes's visit that night, was adamant in spurning his repeated offers to make an honest woman of her.

In retrospect, it would become clear that Hughes was in the grip of a fatal attraction that could have but one outcome. During the week that followed, while Thomas Parsons brought suit against him for breaking and entering his home, Hughes continued his drinking and uttered wild threats against Tamsen wherever he went. Claiming that Tamsen was posing as "Mrs. Hughes," John told his friend Dr. Ben F. Wray that "if that damned bitch doesn't stop, I'll shoot her." The next day, in front of three female witnesses who were acquainted with Tamsen, he said it was a pity someone "hadn't blown her brains out and saved me the trouble sometime." And that same day he told Vincent Salisbury that "he must hunt up Tamsen and kill her" if she refused to be his wife.

No one knows when John Hughes's last, fatal bender began. As he was a hardened binge drinker he may have been drinking for hours or even days before he showed up on the night of August 8, 1865, at the St. Nicholas Saloon on Bank Street. There he met Oscar S. Russell, with whom he had been living on Ontario Street since his wife's departure. After several drinks, they moved on to continue their libations at the Weddell House hotel bar and eventually, as Russell admitted, "We got intoxicated." And at some point while they were in their cups, Russell suggested that they find their friend Ori ("Bug") Carr and go in search of women.

They found Carr asleep in his cabman's rig on Superior Street, and for a $10 fee he agreed to chauffeur the two in their quest. Before leaving Cleveland, however, Hughes insisted on stopping at his Ontario office, where he snatched a pistol from a trunk. "That's a nice shooter you have," said Russell. "Yes, I guess I'll put it in my pocket," replied Hughes, and the trio jumped into Carr's rig to pursue what Hughes coyly called "a very unholy mission."

Owing to their increasing drunkenness, the trio's pursuit of loose women proved fruitless, and after prolonged drinking at several saloons, they decided to seek female flesh in the country. Hughes suggested Bedford, of all places, and they arrived at the Cataract House in Newburgh shortly after 11 p.m. After partaking of whiskey and cigars, they lurched on to Franklin House in Bedford and took a room for the night. After a breakfast that consisted mainly of more alcoholic drinks, they departed again; hotelier Vincent Salisbury would later remember that Hughes seemed "the perfect gentleman" as he left with his companions at 8 a.m.

Hughes claimed at his murder trial that his first thought that bleary morning was to return to Cleveland. But demonic spirits must have prevailed, because mid-morning found the threesome in Carr's rig, parked in front of the Parsons house just outside Bedford Village. Tamsen wasn't home, but Hughes had a pleasant conversation with her father and elicited the information from a little boy that she and her mother had gone blackberrying.

Driving to the Plank Road House for some liquid reinforcement, Hughes's party intercepted Tamsen and Susanna Parsons on the street. They began arguing publicly, and when Hughes couldn't change Tamsen's mind about returning to him, he shouted, "I have married you, and I am going to live with you, if I swing for it." Finally a neighbor intervened, and Hughes was persuaded to return to the Plank Road House with his companions.

The stage was now set for the critical act of the Parsons tragedy, and its shabby melodrama was all a temperance advocate could have wished. After some heroic drinking at the Plank Road House and a nearby grocery—Russell later testified that they consumed 25 glasses of beer and that a "Dutchman" who joined the merrymakers passed out in the middle of the revels—they jumped back into Carr's rig when word came that Thomas Parsons had gone to Bedford to have Hughes arrested. Carr's rig turned onto Columbus Street, and Hughes alighted from it when he saw Tamsen running toward the house of neighbor William Christian.

Tamsen managed to make it to the front gate but it was already too late. There were apparently some final words between the two. Hughes pleaded anew that she be his wife and she again refused, saying, "You need not follow me; I will not go." That was enough for Hughes. Pulling out his pistol, he said, "Good-bye Tamsen; we shall meet again across the big waters; half my life is gone and the rest will soon be ended when I have done the deed and paid the penalty. Good-bye, Tamsen." He then put the pistol to the back of her neck, grabbed her dress with his left hand, and fired twice. One bullet inflicted a glancing wound, the other smashed through her spine just below the base of the brain and ploughed four inches into her skull. The testimony of witnesses is that Tamsen cried, "Oh, dear!" but it is likely that she died instantly from her primary wound.

Francis Powell, a witness to the shooting, accosted Hughes first, crying, "You old villain, what have you done?" Ignoring him and other neighbors who began to congregate, Hughes walked up to Tamsen's corpse, poked his finger in the neck wound, and said, "You're a dead girl." Then, turning on his heel, he strode down the street, brushing off several men who tried to stop him. When John Price, who had heard the shots, tried to halt him, Hughes drew his pistol, muttered "No man touches me," and continued walking down the street.

Drawn from the hotel bar by the news that Hughes had shot Tamsen, Russell woozily emerged just as Hughes came down the street pursued by an angry mob. Suddenly, Ori Carr's carriage wheeled by, and Hughes jumped up next to him. Putting his pistol to Carr's head, he told him to drive fast or he would shot him dead. Russell also climbed aboard, and the chase was on.

Carr pushed his horses to the limit, but he couldn't shake the growing posse. Within minutes as they sped northward, armed men were taking shots at the rig, and several miles outside Bedford Hughes decided to take to the woods. Taking all of Russell's money, he jumped from the carriage and made for a thicket near the Cleveland & Pittsburgh railroad tracks, running in the direction of Newburgh.

Two hours later, a search party led by Bedford resident Amos Lawson discovered Hughes hiding in some bushes near the tracks. After they took his pistol and knife away, Hughes proceeded to incriminate himself to anyone who would listen. He told Lawson he had planned the murder for two weeks; he told George Cowan, who tried to incite his fellows to lynch Hughes on the spot, that he "had a right to shoot her—she was his wife." And to others he volunteered that while "some might think he was deranged, he was not; he was in his right mind."

Taken back to Cleveland, Hughes elaborated further on the motives and premeditation behind his crime and was thrown into a Cuyahoga County jail cell. But during his preliminary hearing on August 11, he began to backtrack, now claiming that the murder had been a spur of the moment act: "At the Franklin House Russell did not know that I was going to commit the murder, for I did not know it myself until Miss Parsons passed the carriage; had she not passed by within my sight, I should not have thought of her again."

No longer ranting about that "damned bitch," Hughes now warbled ingratiatingly about the "unhappy girl" he had "hurried into eternity." Indeed, within days of his arrest, he was painting himself as the actual victim of the tragedy in the columns of the *Cleveland Herald*:

> The Doctor seemed hurt at the slurs that have been cast on his professional reputation. "Liquor," he says, "always maddens him, and to the excessive indulgence in that article" he lays the commission of the murder. No one can converse with him upon the late murder, listen to his cool narration thereof, and his sad tone of voice, and witness his piteous expression of countenance, when alluding to the "poor girl" without being impressed with the fact that this is one of the most remarkable cases in the annals of crime.

The *Plain Dealer* would have none of this snuffling nonsense and consistently excoriated Hughes in the alarming contemporary context of crimes against women:

> His attempt to palliate the dreadful enormity of his crime by laying its cause to excessive drunkenness, only tends to heighten the disgust in the public mind. We have had enough women murdered in cold blood and the perpetrators released on bail of $2,000 or sent to the Penitentiary three years (such a case is still fresh in the minds of the people): enough, too, of murders such as occurred not long since on our Public Square for the committal of which a penalty, not so severe as is visited upon the thief of $50, was inflicted.

THE BEDFORD MURDER

TRIAL OF DR. JOHN W. HUGHES,

The Murderer of Miss Parsons

The Bigamy-Adultery Imbroglio.

Hughes Enters Mr.-Parsons' House at Midnight.

ACCOUNT OF THE DRUNKEN SPREE.

SECOND DAY'S PROCEEDINGS.

From the *Cleveland Leader*, December 9, 1865

Hughes was indicted for first-degree murder on November 25, 1865, and his trial began on December 6 in Courtroom No. 3 of the county courthouse on Public Square. With Judge Coffinberry presiding, Hughes was prosecuted by Charles W. Palmer and Albert T. Slade. Considering his crime and repute, Hughes enjoyed stellar legal defense in the persons of M. S. Castle, R. E. Knight, and William S. Kerruish. Thanks to massive pretrial publicity and the lurid nature of his crime, the proceedings were well attended, especially by women sympathetic to the beleaguered doctor.

Given his repeated threats to kill Tamsen and his voluble admissions of malice after the crime, it doesn't seem probable that anyone could have helped Dr. John Hughes beat the rap. For almost a week, the prosecution furnished a parade of men, women, and children, all of whom testified to Hughes's behavior and intentions before, during, and after his foul deed. But the defense got its turn on December 14, and it became immediately apparent that Hughes's lawyers were gambling on a two-pronged strategy of drunkenness and insanity. Several dozen witnesses testified to

Hughes's habitual dipsomania, although it is impossible to say whether their evidence was strengthened or weakened by numerous claims that Hughes was such a chronic sot that it was impossible to tell just how drunk he was on any occasion. And while Kerruish, Castle, and Knight leaned hard on their insanity evidence, it was pretty thin stuff. Several witnesses testified to the alleged insanity of Hughes's paternal grandmother and grandfather and various uncles, but most of the alleged crazies in the Hughes genealogy were not even identified by name. Nor did the skeptical Judge Coffinberry allow the admission of testimony that Hughes's father had been a "maniac" when in his cups.

Arguing for the state, Albert Slade opened the final plea for Hughes's death before a courtroom packed to suffocation on December 20. Emphasizing the evidence of Hughes's premeditation and citing legal precedents prejudicial to mere drunkenness as a murder defense, Slade concluded the state's case with a powerful, populist appeal to the outraged, innocent ghost of the murdered Tamsen: "The facts cannot be denied. The defendant himself boasted over the ruin he had wrought, 'that he should meet the murdered one across the great waters.' Seems to me even now and here he might see 'wandering by, a shadow like an angel, with bright hair, dabbled in blood.' Gentlemen . . . I ask you in the name of violated chastity everywhere . . . to this day mark by your verdict your estimate of the protection which shall be given to the poor man's child."

Slade's plea was a hard act to follow, but defense counsel R. E. Knight did his best. Arguing that Hughes's heredity predisposed him to suicide, Knight claimed that Tamsen's murder was actually a suicidal act on Hughes's part. He had actually done the deed as an indirect way of provoking his own death, and, given the fury of his passion—which Knight compared, presumably with a straight face, to the erotic obsessions of Mark Antony, Henry VIII, Troy's Paris, and Leander—Knight argued the aggravation of his love mania by alcoholic excess made Hughes's mad act inevitable. It only remained for fellow counsel M. S. Castle—in a tactic not unfamiliar to observers of contemporary trials—to blacken the name of the murdered girl by way of mitigating his client's crime. Tamsen, Castle argued, was no "mere child" but a "person come to responsible womanhood" who had returned Hughes's passion in full knowledge that he was married to another. Having continually encouraged his illicit addresses, she "flitted" across the path of her love- and drink-maddened adorer, and what ensued was little to be wondered at. True, Castle didn't actually call Tamsen a husband-stealing slut, but his polished rhetoric suggested as much.

Castle's slurs and Slade's excuses were all in vain. On December 22 at 3 p.m., the 12-man jury returned after only two hours of deliberation with a verdict of guilty of murder in the first degree. Permitted to speak before his December 30 sentencing, Hughes blubbered again that he had not premeditated Tamsen's murder and that he didn't even remember pulling the trigger. "It must have been a legion of devils had taken hold of me," he noted, "for it is contrary to my nature to be cruel." His real fault, he concluded, was that he "had loved her too well." It is recorded that a large number of spectators were moved to tears on the occasion by Hughes's typically shameless self-justifications.

Hughes's brazen denials and distasteful rationalizations didn't end with his sentencing. As is so often the case with condemned felons, Hughes "got religion" only days after his death verdict. Soon afterwards, speaking to a daily progression of gullible visitors to his county jail cell, Hughes issued a voluminous farrago of pious and edifying sentiments to anyone who would listen. Moreover, his speedy moral reformation in the shadow of the scaffold also sparked a personal reevaluation of the death penalty. Although he had indicated his willingness to be lynched in Bedford on the murder day and repeatedly endorsed the justice of his fate, Hughes now emerged as a public, indeed poetic, adversary of capital punishment. On January 29, 1866, the *Plain Dealer* printed his doggerel riposte to the *Cleveland Leader*'s approval of his impending hanging:

> The Leader of a class, a man to kill,
> Quotes Bible proof, swears by the "poet Will."
> Trite wisdom, man's law of God by Moses,
> 'Tis obsolete—who, to-day supposes
> Adultery, Sabbath-breaking, the breath
> Of sland'rers, each and all, be "stoned to death."
> The same for other scores—economy
> In Time compels. See Deuteronomy.
> Did Jesus say so 'mid the crowd's uproar?
> No! "Saint throw first, Go woman sin no more."

The poetic effusions of John Hughes continued in Cleveland's newspapers for several more days, but time was running out. Despite his outward bravado—he bragged in a letter to Margaret Hughes that the newspapers had called him a "man of iron"—he much feared death by the rope and tried to cheat the hangman on February 7 by taking a smuggled overdose of morphine in his cell. Alas!—the good doctor had not prescribed well for himself, and his attempted self-destruction was defeated when Sheriff Nicola and the jail physician prevented his demise by the time-honored method of keeping him awake and walking. Meanwhile, tickets to his hanging were distributed, a jail photograph of Hughes was taken, and a scaffold brought up from Summit County and erected in the north end of the jail. It had last been used in 1853 for the execution of John Parks, who murdered William Beatson of Cuyahoga Falls. Hughes was to become the third person executed in Cuyahoga County.

February 9, 1866, arrived at last, and Hughes spent his final hours with his spiritual advisor, Dr. J. A. Thome of Oberlin College, and in giving improving advice to his fellow prisoners. It is recorded that he cautioned one such lucky felon thusly: "Cleanliness is next to Godliness. Keep yourself in better trim." Even Dickens's William Dorrit could not have bettered the sanctimonious pomposity of Hughes's last actions on earth.

John Hughes died fairly game, albeit with characteristic loquacity. After asserting to a group of Manx émigrés that he had not killed Tamsen—"John W. Hughes did not fire that shot; it was the evil spirit induced by intoxication"—Hughes trudged off to the scaffold, where he addressed his final audience at 12:45 p.m. After blaming Moses ("the greatest murderer ever heard of") for inventing the death penalty, Hughes warmed to his subject and his captive auditors: "The death penalty is ridiculous, and if you consider over it you find it is wrong. One life is as good as another. What advantage is it to take my life? None! It is not an example to deter others from the crime. Did I remember pointing the pistol? No, I don't remember it to this hour."

Hughes harangued his audience for 16 minutes and, after denying the divinity of Jesus Christ, wished that his death might serve as a powerful argument against the death penalty. He then stepped to the trap and removing his collar and cravat, threw them to the crowd below. His hands were manacled and his legs pinioned. As the black cap went over his head, he declaimed, "O grave, where is thy victory, O death, where is thy sting?" Smiling as the rope went over his neck, he crashed through the 74-inch drop to forever at 1:07 p.m. Not a muscle or limb twitched, and it was assumed he died instantly from a broken neck. Twenty-six minutes later he was cut down, placed in an imitation rosewood coffin, and turned over to a committee of Manxmen for burial.

Thus ends the sordid saga of John Hughes. Being Hughes, of course, he wanted to have the last word. Just before his hanging, he withdrew his previous epitaph and furnished this alternative to the press:

> Lo, wavering hope,
> Bearing life on its fluttering wing,
> Heralds the sad note death to bring.
> In mystery grope for fraternity
> The Grave when the unseen hand
> Leads on to the Spirit land,
> With soul to elope
> Thro' Eternity.

In fairness to his innocent victim, though, let us concede the final moral of his tale to the editors of the *Cleveland Herald*. Disgusted at his glib, sanctimonious verbosity and the inappropriate sympathy lavished on him by his partisans ("But Hughes was 'so interesting,' could 'talk so beautifully,' was "so penitent,'") the *Herald* editors rendered their pitiless judgment as soon as he was cut down and taken away: "Although his deportment and general bearing has been such that no material exceptions could be taken by those who have casually called on him, or by those who have been most intimately associated with him in prison, it was evident to all who took the trouble to think for a moment that there has underlain all his motives and actions a disposition to court notoriety, and that, with all his acknowledged education and talents, there was an evident want of the finer sensibilities and a lack of the better moral perceptions. He was continually striving to make himself and his horrible surroundings as conspicuous as possible."

Chapter 24

ASSASSIN FROM NOWHERE

Christina Lipscomb's Terrible Secret

Sensational murder cases with toxic racial aspects seem to be a 20th-century American specialty. Our grandparents witnessed the lengthy tribulations of the Scottsboro boys, and those middle-aged or older recall the lynchings and homicides of the Civil Rights era. More recent years, of course, have brought the O. J. Simpson trials with their never-ending reverberations and animosities. But for sheer unpleasantness and gratuitous racial discord, it would be hard to beat several other episodes of the last decade: the Stuart case in Boston, the Smith tragedy in South Carolina, and the Tawana Brawley circus in New York. Charles Stuart, you may recall, set off a frenzied racial manhunt when he shot his pregnant wife, Carol, to death and then told police that a mysterious black man had gunned her down while the couple was sitting in their car. Susan Smith, somewhat more notoriously, triggered a similar, if briefer dragnet in South Carolina when she drowned her two sons and blamed the deaths on—you guessed it—a mysterious black killer who came out of nowhere. Not to mention the infamous Tawana Brawley, whose malicious fiction that she was assaulted and abused by white lawmen ruined both her own life and those of the accused.

Cleveland, too, has had its share of racially charged crimes during this century, from the sex- and gunfire-flecked career of John Leonard Whitfield to the bloody carnage of the 1968 Glenville shootout. But what most Clevelanders don't know is that the Forest City pioneered the bogus racial manhunt almost a century ago, back when Cleveland boasted relatively few African-Americans on whom to blame its not infrequent homicides. It is for that reason alone that the Lipscomb murder is worth remembering, not to men-

HUSBAND IS SHOT BY SIDE OF WIFE

Probably Mortally Wounded as Couple Walk Along Dark Street.

Police Place Woman and Boarder at Home Under Examination.

LIES DYING AT HOSPITAL

From the *Plain Dealer*,
February 27, 1908

tion the added attraction of Christina Lipscomb, one of the most determined and dazzling women who ever behaved badly in the Western Reserve.

The Lipscomb affair erupted on the dark winter night of Wednesday, February 26, 1908. A report came into the Cleveland police's 12th Precinct station on the far West Side that there was a badly wounded man at Schwab's saloon. The flying squad of detectives who arrived at the West 105th Street saloon at 8 p.m. found John Lipscomb, 38, covered with blood and sinking fast from three serious gun wounds. One bullet had drilled a hole through his hips, another had perforated the left side of his throat, and the third had smashed through his jawbone and almost severed his tongue. Taken to St. John's Hospital in an ambulance, Lipscomb went into emergency surgery while Cleveland police detectives scrambled to solve Cleveland's latest and most puzzling street crime.

It took a while for their investigation to get on solid ground. Christina Lipscomb, the victim's 33-year-old wife, had been with him when he was shot and had talked briefly with the police at Schwab's tavern. But the comely Christina turned up missing at the hospital, so veteran detectives James Doran and John T. Shibley went over to the Lipscomb home at 2613 East 65th Street. Unable to rouse anyone there, Doran kicked the door down and entered. He didn't find Christina inside, but he and Shibley picked her up several hours later in company with Roland ("Roly") French, a boarder who lived with the Lipscombs. After preliminary questioning, Christina and Roly were taken to the hospital bed of John Lipscomb at 2 a.m. The lawmen present there could not disguise their chagrin when the wounded man, unable to speak because of his almost-severed tongue, scrawled on a slate held up to him, "My wife didn't do it. French didn't do it. It was a white man disguised with a mask."

But was it? Christina's story, at last unfolded with copious tears and sighs, didn't exactly agree with her husband's. The preliminary details of their stories were consistent. John and Christina had left the home of her sister, Mrs. George Treat, in West Park at about 7:30 p.m. Walking east on Lorain Avenue near West 112th, they had decided to pick up the eastbound streetcar a little further east, so as to avoid an extra nickel fare. Lorain Avenue at that time was a semi-rural thoroughfare with a streetcar line down the middle, and there were no houses within 200 feet of the road. Three hundred feet behind the Lipscombs ambled a party of three men on their way to church: D. R. McGinty, Dan McGinty, and Dan's uncle, Thomas Nolan. Five hundred feet ahead trudged James Havlin, a lineman for the Cuyahoga Telephone Company. It was a calm, cold night, and the ground was covered with several inches of snow.

It happened just after 7:40. Christina's version was that John had just dropped behind her a step to allow her to pass an impeding telephone pole. As he did so, she heard him say, "What's the matter?" Turning around, she saw a black man press a revolver against her husband and shoot him three times. As she screamed, "My husband is shot; my poor husband is shot!" John fell to the muddy street, the black man fled northward through a snow-covered empty lot, and the other Lorain Avenue pedestrians began to run toward the wounded man in the street. The last thing Christina remembered was fainting beside her husband.

That was Christina's story, which she stuck to through many skeptical police interrogations. But while John's version, painfully extracted at length from the gravely wounded man, agreed in most details with Christina's, he insisted that his assailant was a white man and that he would "know him in a thousand" if he ever saw him again. The gunman, John disclosed, was about 5'9" and 175 pounds and wore an overcoat and cap. Convinced that he was going to recover, John refused to give the police any further details, vowing repeatedly that he would seek his own private vengeance when he got out of the hospital. Just in case, though, John begged the doctors to let him know if he was going to die, so he could have an opportunity to change his story.

The police were admittedly baffled by the contradiction between the couple's stories. They didn't much care for the statements of the supporting eyewitnesses, either. Tom Nolan had been the one closest to the shooter. He said he was "sure he was a Negro, for I got a good look at him." Nolan's companion, Dan McGinty, supported his vision of a lone gunman running from the scene but was unsure of the man's race. But James Havlin, the telephone lineman walking ahead of the Lipscombs, contradicted everyone, insisting that he had seen pistol flashes coming from two directions. This implied there were two gunmen, possibly one white and one black, for the police to identify and apprehend. Muddying the tangled narrative further, Havlin informed the police that when he arrived at the crime scene, Christina told him a story different from the one she gave the police: "There were two men. They jumped out at the same time. They didn't say anything but began shooting. I think one was a colored man."

Chief Fred Kohler and his detectives were very unhappy with the progress of the Lipscomb case in the days that followed the shooting. Lingering near death in his hospital bed, John Lipscomb would sometimes indicate his readiness to make a final statement, only to lapse back into stony silence when he thought he was getting better again. On the chance he might eventually make up his mind, Kohler put a round-the-clock squad of detectives in his hospital room and concentrated on his only genuine, if somewhat uncooperative, witness: Christina Lipscomb.

Fred Kohler may not have known the French expression *cherchez la femme*, but he had handled enough murder cases to know that the Lipscomb mystery reeked of domestic strife. The sleuthing of his detectives soon revealed, despite the contrary insistence of John and Christina, that the Lipscomb marriage had been a discordant one. Christina had often complained to her friends and relatives that John was a pathologically jealous man who treated her badly. The particular object of his suspicion was the Lipscomb

Principals and scenes in
the Lipscomb murder.

boarder, Roly French, and it was with undisguised satisfaction that
the investigating police discovered that Christina and Roly had
lived together in Chatham, Ontario, the previous summer. And
while Roly had an ironclad alibi for the night of February 26—he
was drinking in a Woodland Avenue saloon at the time of the shooting—the Christina-John-Roly triangle was enough to suggest a
potential murder motive. Police scrutiny of Christina intensified
after her sister-in-law, Mrs. George Lipscomb, disclosed that John
had told her only three days before the shooting that his wife had
said to him, "I'll kill you or get someone else to do it."

But if Christina was the shooter, why couldn't anyone, especially her wounded husband, identify her as the gunwoman? And
where was the revolver, for which a 20-man squad of detectives
searched vainly for hours in the sloppy winter mud of Lorain
Avenue? With both Christina and John stonewalling them, all the
police could do was wait for John to decide that he was really
dying, and to issue cryptic, if suggestive statements to the press.
"We are satisfied of the identify of the man who shot," police
inspector Rowe announced on February 29. "He was not a robber."
Chief Kohler went further in speaking to reporters that afternoon,

"POLICE MADE ME CONFESS"

Mrs. Christina Lipscomb.

Accused Woman, Pale and Haggard, Tells Story of Sweatbox Methods and Declares the Strain Broke Her Down.

Officials Refused to Allow Her to See An Attorney Before Examination, She Declares—On Grill for Nine Hours.

WHIRLED BY SHAFT; LIVES TO TELL TALE

Engineer Says He Felt No Pain After the First Great Shock —Now in Hospital.

ENGINEER J. CROWLEY, employed by Wm. Edwards & Co., W

From the *Cleveland Press*, March 25, 1908

saying, "I think it is a family affair. We are on the track of the truth. We may make an arrest within a few days." Twenty-four hours later, Kohler changed his mind, stating, "We know who did the shooting but as Lipscomb will not aid us, preferring to obtain satisfaction himself, there will probably be no arrests."

The break Kohler's men were hoping for came on Wednesday, March 18. Told by his doctors that he was about to die, John Lipscomb motioned St. John's Hospital physician Dr. J. M. O'Malley to his side. Speaking with great pain and difficulty, he managed to blurt out, "My wife did it." Two detectives and a stenographer were brought into the room, and John Lipscomb repeated his statement for the record. Early the next morning, he died after a three-week struggle with the fatal bullet, which had migrated from his throat to his lungs.

The police waited a little longer for the jaws of their trap to shut. As the inquest into John's death opened on Friday morning, March 20, Assistant County Prosecutor M. P. Mooney had Detective Shibley bring Christina in for an intensive "sweating" session immediately after John's interment in Calvary Cemetery. Mooney got right to the point: "Mrs. Lipscomb, your husband is now dead. Tell the truth. You and your husband quarreled that night. He pulled a revolver, you grabbed it, and shot him. Now if this is true, I don't believe any jury will convict you of any crime."

Still ignorant of her husband's deathbed statement, Christina merely repeated her dubious version of the shooting and said again and again, "I did not kill him. I did not kill him. I did not kill him."

The stage was set for Dr. O'Malley's dramatic disclosure at the

Monday-morning inquest session, and as soon as he finished his testimony about John's last words, Christina was taken into custody and rigorously interrogated. It was the standard police "sweating" practiced by Kohler's men at the time: a dozen detectives shouting at the suspect, no food, no water, no breaks, and absolutely no lawyers allowed as they pestered the defiant Christina for hour after hour. She held up well at first, just laughing at Kohler when he said, "Did you shoot him?" But shortly before midnight, Tuesday, March 24, Christina began to break. Going over her story for the 21st time that day, she stumbled on a detail. Minutes later, she collapsed, sobbing out her guilt and signing a confession written out by the jail stenographer. Her confession, which included the obligatory disclaimer ("It is made without promises of any kind being made, and [it] is voluntary and not under threats"), confirmed what police had suspected from the beginning. The Lipscombs had begun quarreling as soon as they left the Treat house in West Park, Christina admitted. They were arguing over Roly French's attentions to Christina, and the dispute climaxed with John striking Christina as they walked down Lorain: "I will tell you the truth now. My husband was cruel, unreasonable, and jealous from the day of our marriage. I lived in fear of him. He was jealous of every man I knew. My husband drew a revolver when we quarreled. I struggled for possession of it. It went off and the bullet struck his throat. Maddened at the charges he made against me I fired again, and the bullet lodged in his jaw. A third time I pulled the trigger and wounded him in the hip."

Concluding her statement, the exhausted widow cried, "Do what you see fit: I saw him die and he is writhing before me now!"

Within 24 hours Christina had recovered her aplomb. Shortly after her arraignment before Judge William McGannon (who 12 years later would face charges of his own, stemming from an evening murder on a Cleveland street), she angrily repudiated her confession, claiming that it had been coerced from her by threats of prison and false promises that she would not be prosecuted. Just after being indicted by the grand jury on a second-degree murder charge on Wednesday, March 24, 1908, Christina detailed the police duress that had produced her confession. Claiming that she was "sick and half-crazy," she dwelt on the pitiful image of a helpless woman beset by bullying detectives: "I was arrested at 3 p.m. Monday and from then until 12 o'clock at night I was kept going over and over that awful affair till faint and overcome, I dropped asleep on a couch at the police station. Then they all asked questions. I told them again and again what I knew. It grew late and I was so tired. Then they told me they had proof that my husband mistreated me, and that self-defense was natural."

Claiming that her "confession" was a police-dictated tissue of lies, Christina now returned with renewed fervor to her original a-black-man-from-nowhere fantasy.

Christina's stance played well in Cleveland newspapers, which gave ample publicity to her coercion claims ("Police Made Me Confess," screamed the March 24 *Cleveland Press* headline) and featured flattering sketches of the slim, black-clad widow in their pages. Both the police and the prosecutor's office were incensed at Christina's about-face, and Chief Fred Kohler spoke for Cleveland's outraged authorities the day after Christina disavowed her confession. "It's the usual sympathy plea of the man or woman who is caught," he fumed. "She is one of the shrewdest, coolest persons who ever went through the police cross-examination in Cleveland."

Christina's intensely anticipated trial probably didn't turn out the way either she or the police expected. The trial opened in Judge Simpson Ford's courtroom on Monday, May 4, and her jury was quickly selected with only one candidate dismissed. Prosecutor Mooney presented the state's expected case, arguing that Christina and John had been fighting over Roly French's attentions to her when John pulled out a gun. While they struggled for it, the gun went off, wounding John, and then Christina, fearful he would get up, shot him two more times while he was lying on the street. As Mooney presented his case, the demure, black-clad widow shook her head several times and audibly murmured, "No, no, it is not true!" several times.

Defense attorney Edmund Hitchens countered with Christina's original version of the night of February 26, claiming that a mysterious black man had cold-bloodedly fired three shots into John Lipscomb. Hitchens bolstered his mystery-gunman theory with allegations that a man, seen by two children in the house next door to George Treat's West Park home, had stalked John and Christina from the moment they left there. But Christina's improbable story, with or without the stalker embroidery, was just filler. It soon became clear that Hitchens had staked his case on keeping

Christina's March 24 confession out of the trial record. With its insistence that the police had tricked her into confessing by a combination of threats and promises, Hitchens's dogged cross-examination extracted damaging admissions from Inspector Rowe about his interrogation of Mrs. Lipscomb. Admitting that he had played the classic "good cop" foil to his menacing colleagues, Rowe repeated what he had told Christina just before she signed her confession: "Now just tell me all about it and you will be free and happy by tomorrow noon. Just say that you shot him. I know that you did what was right and I give you credit for it. Any jury in the country will say that you were justified. I know how the detectives have hounded you at the bedside of your husband. I know just how they are and I feel sorry for you."

As the next day's *Plain Dealer* put it, "On the stand, those who conducted the examination admitted they had pretended to be her friends eager to aid her." The same day the prosecution received another serious setback when Judge Ford ruled Dr. O'Malley's testimony about John's deathbed statement inadmissible. Ford had little choice in the matter; as Dr. O'Malley conscientiously testified on Monday, the dying, delirious John Lipscomb had not only accused his wife of shooting him but also his doctors, his brother, and the detectives in his hospital room.

Shortly after the afternoon session ended on May 5, the prosecution recovered some ground when Judge Ford reluctantly allowed Christina's confession into the record over the strong objections of attorney Hitchens. "I do not hold that this is a bona fide confession," ruled Ford. "I will let the jury decide whether it was obtained from her by coercion or not. They may wholly disregard it, if they see fit."

Some women sure look good in black.

But the expected struggle over the validity of Christina's confession never took place. When the next trial session opened at 9 a.m. on Wednesday, May 6, Judge Ford announced that the confession would be entered into the record. Immediately afterwards, Prosecutor Mooney rose from his seat and asked that Christina's murder indictment be nulled. Blandly admitting that the state possessed no real evidence except for the disputed confession, Mooney asserted that he had pushed the case to trial only because of Christina's unwarranted slurs on the methods of the Cleveland police and the prosecutor's office. Now that the confession had been admitted as valid evidence, the trial's purpose had been served. Justifying the unexpected outcome, Mooney said: "That confession shows that she acted in self-defense. We see no other course before us than to move that she be discharged. The killing seems plainly justifiable . . . From the first we have considered it impossible to make a case against her. The trial was for the sole purpose of bringing the facts before the public and showing that the police department and prosecutor's office did not obtain the confession by undue force and persecution of the woman . . . The case was brought to preserve the integrity of the prosecutor's office, and of the police department. Had [Christina's] charges not been made, the case would have been nulled when the trial opened . . . Had the black mark the defendant's counsel tried to give not been wiped out, police and prosecutors would have been placed under a handicap in future cases that they would have been unable to overcome."

Still dressed in grieving black, Christina Lipscomb walked out of Judge Ford's courtroom a free woman. Before disappearing into obscurity, she would only say: "I am unable to say anything. I have been sick in mind and body ever since this horrible occurrence. I am happy to be free again."

Christina Lipscomb was never prosecuted for making false statements to the police, much less for her inflammatory lies about a mysterious black gunman. It says much for the racial climate of the age that neither the newspapers nor the Cleveland police authorities even commented on her criminal, racist libel. No one but Christina was completely satisfied with the official verdict on John Lipscomb's death, especially since no one remembered him ever carrying a gun or threatening his wife. Whether Christina Lipscomb was guilty of murder remains an open question, but it is certain that she set a nasty racial precedent resounding down to the present day and, no doubt, beyond. And the Lipscomb case remains something to remember the next time someone pontificates—as in the Sheppard case—on the superior sanctity of "eyewitness" testimony.

Chapter 25

THE PHANTOM FLAPPER KILLER

The Mystery of Margaret Heldman

Although she was quiet and kept to herself, everyone noticed the girl on the outbound Canton-Waynesburg bus that cold December night. It wasn't just her striking outfit: a blue chinchilla coat cut in a masculine style; a close-fitting black felt turban hat with a brilliant pin; flesh-colored hose, oxford shoes, and gloved hands. It wasn't just her looks either: she seemed about 22 years old, about 5'4" and 120 pounds, had light brown hair, and was described by all who saw her as a "beauty." But what drew all eyes to her was the extreme pallor of her face, her brooding intensity, and the way she kept nervously putting each hand in the opposite sleeve of her coat. Here was a girl, everyone said to themselves, with something on her mind.

George Patterson, the bus driver, noticed her, too, as did W. E. McCombs, the proprietor of the Rite-of-Way Inn in the village of Waco, where the bus let her off, just several miles and about 10 minutes from Canton. Both Patterson and McCombs had seen the same woman the night before: she had gotten off at the Waco stop at 8:10, immediately taken the return bus back to Canton—and showed up again on the 9:10 bus, only to once more depart on the return bus to Canton. Both men thought she was a "spotter" for the bus company checking up on their work. This night, December 6, 1928, the young woman stepped off the bus and asked McCombs if he would turn on his light to signal the return bus to Canton; she expected to be back in several minutes and didn't want to miss it. She then turned around, shoved her hands in her sleeves, started walking up the hill toward a group of houses, and disappeared from view.

But she didn't disappear from Waco. About 100 yards away, just

Principals in the slaying.

over the crest of the hill, she turned into the driveway of Vernard Fearn. Fearn, a 35-year-old coal merchant and mine operator, lived there in a brand-new house he had built for his wife, Mary, and their nine-year-old daughter, Kathryn. Mary was making dinner in the kitchen when she heard the young woman rap at the front door. She opened it, and the woman said, "Is Mr. Fearn at home?" Mary replied, "Yes, won't you come in?" "No thank you," said the pale female, "I'll only be a moment. I'll stay right here." Mary went and told Vernard there was someone at the door for him and returned to the kitchen.

As soon as Vernard opened the front door, the young woman pulled out a .380 Colt revolver and quickly, calmly, and wordlessly pumped five steel-jacketed bullets into him. Three slugs smashed into the front of his chest, another entered his side as he spun around, and a fifth bullet went into his back as he fell to the porch. A sixth bullet grazed his neck, and then the young woman fired two more slugs into the screen door frame, as if to say, "Take that, too." She then turned around, stepped off the porch, and began walking back down the hill to the Rite-of-Way Inn. She got there just before the return bus to Canton arrived and was on it when it left 10 minutes later after refueling. About 10 minutes to seven, she got off the bus at the McKinley Hotel in downtown Canton and disappeared into a crowd of Christmas shoppers. The "Phantom Flapper Killer" sensation had begun.

The Stark County police had no idea as to the identity of the mysterious, vanished killer. The search for the shooter, immediately dubbed the "Phantom Flapper" by newspaper writers, focused on the meager clues provided by those who had seen the attractive, quiet gun girl during her bus trips to Waco on December 6 and the previous night. But other than her physical appearance and demeanor, they had nothing to go on in this seemingly inexplicable murder. Within hours, it was rumored in the newspapers that the "Phantom Flapper" killing would never be solved.

Mary Fearn wasn't much help to Stark County sheriff Edward Gibson and his investigative team. Although she and her daughter Kathryn had gotten a good look at the gun girl as she finished firing, the newspapers reported that both of them said she wasn't anyone they had seen before, although Mary allowed as there was something "familiar" about the assassin. Drawn to the porch by the sound of the gun, Mary had tried to help her husband as he staggered, bleeding heavily, to the kitchen. Cradling the dying man in her arms, she said, "Who did this to you?" "I don't know. I . . . never . . . saw . . . her . . . before," groaned Vernard before expiring a few moments later. Mary also remembered that she had heard Vernard say to his killer as he was falling, "Why are you doing this? What did I ever do to you?"

Inevitably, the focus of the investigation turned to Vernard Fearn's private life. With no apparent motive, such as robbery or a feud with a known enemy, Sheriff Gibson's men concluded that Fearn's killing had to have been an act of private vengeance, triggered by unknown aspects of his lifestyle. And although Mary Fearn and his friends fervently described the late Vernard as a paragon of uxorious behavior and manly virtues, Stark County lawmen soon began to think otherwise. A local boy, Vernard was remembered pleasantly by Canton-area folk as a promising semi-pro baseball player, a brave veteran of World War I, and a hard worker and entrepreneur who paid his debts and was active in community affairs. But the Vernard Fearn who worked so hard also played pretty hard, Gibson's men discovered, and they began to search among the many area dance halls that he had passionately frequented in the months before his death and interview their female habitués. They didn't come up with a definite suspect immediately, but they did find that Fearn had often flirted heavily with female strangers at the all-night dances and marathon contests he had attended. Moreover, he had asked some of these women out on "dates," although the police couldn't unearth any proof that he had kept any of them. Six days went by without any apparent progress on the case, although Sheriff Gibson and Stark County prosecutor Henry Harter Jr. kept promising that they were on the verge of arresting a suspect. Wild theories began to circulate to fill the vacuum created by the absence of substantial clues. One story was that Fearn had merely been lured to his front porch by the attractive chinchilla-clad stranger, while another, unknown man had ambushed him, shooting from a hidden spot on the front lawn. Another idea was that the phantom gun girl was a professional "hit man" from Canton's underworld, the downtown "Jungle," whence she had been recruited for the job by unknown persons. Still another theory had her acting as the outraged champion of a younger sister—presumably a soiled dove whose soiling had been the work of Vernard Fearn—while a still-wilder rumor had it that Vernard had been assassinated by a man disguised as a woman. Meanwhile, Sheriff Gibson and Prosecutor Harter fed the rumor mill by taking flying trips to small towns in Ohio and Pennsylvania to run down tips on supposed sightings of the gun girl.

Actually, Gibson and his men had quite a bit of information about the killer, if not her actual identity. With nothing amiss in Vernard Fearn's business dealings, it was obvious, whatever Mary Fearn said about her husband's saintliness, that his killer had acted out of strong personal motives. Moreover, it was clear that she hadn't cared about getting caught after she pulled the trigger eight times. She had made no fewer than three trips to Fearn's house, taking two bus trips to Waco on December 5, only to find that he was not at home that night. She had made her final journey on December 6, still wearing the same clothes she had worn the night before. It was also obvious that she was not a person of means, as the police had never known a killer who would take the bus in lieu of an available automobile. So, when not taking side trips to check out fugitive clues, Gibson and Harder kept hammering away at Mary Fearn, hoping that she would eventually reveal the sordid wrinkle in Vernard's life that had led to his violent death. In the meantime, public interest—and greed—was stoked by the announcement that the Stark County commissioners were offering a $1,000 reward for the apprehension of the phantom flapper. Within days, wary policemen and alert citizens were harassing every good-looking woman wearing a chinchilla coat or a black felt turban. On December 12, three young men in New Philadelphia were charged with assault and battery against a young woman whom they tried to capture for the reward money.

Unexpectedly, the "Phantom Flapper" mystery ended with the same surprising and sudden violence with which it began. On Thursday, December 13, at 6 p.m.—exactly one week to the hour after Fearn was murdered—a car screeched to a halt in front of Sheriff Gibson's office in downtown Canton and began honking frantically. Gibson ran out to find Wilbur Heldman, 27, a furnace salesman, sitting in his car. In the passenger seat next to him was Margaret Heldman, the "Phantom Flapper Killer," bleeding and near death from a bullet through her heart. Jumping on the running board, Gibson directed Wilbur to Canton's Mercy Hospital, where Margaret Heldman died at 7:30 p.m. Before expiring, she tried to speak but she could not, and she never really regained consciousness.

The story Wilbur Heldman told lawmen and reporters seemed to put an end to the week-long mystery. It was a sad tale. Like Vernard Fearn, Wilbur was a product of the Canton area and had worked there selling furnaces for some years before he met Margaret in August 1927. Fresh out of DuBois, Pennsylvania, the impressionable Margaret Horner, just graduated from high school, was working as a ribbon clerk at a Canton department store when she was smitten by the older, seemingly worldly Wilbur, and they were married only three weeks later after a whirlwind courtship. Their mutual infatuation, alas, did not last, and their subsequent months of married life

Sketch of the
Phantom Flapper Killer.

Husband and wife–and gun.

were marked by frequent quarrels, separations, in-law squabbles, and fleeting reconciliations. By Wilbur's account, at least, Margaret was a cold, morose person and a psychopathic liar, and even his best efforts failed to satisfy his unhappy, restless wife. A child, Emmett Heldman, born in September 1928, failed to cement their precarious union, and in November of that year they moved to Lorain. Wilbur's initial story to the police was that they had gone there to make a fresh start—but Margaret's in-laws and Wilbur's acquaintances said it was so Wilbur could establish a 30-day residency in Lorain as a legal prelude to divorcing Margaret. At the same time they moved to Lorain, they placed their infant son, whom Wilbur claimed was neglected by his mother, in foster care in Canton.

How much Wilbur Heldman knew about his wife and when he knew it would become the crux of the ensuing investigation and the nub of unanswered questions that resound to this day. Wilbur told police that his first inkling that there was something going on between Margaret and Vernard Fearn had come in early November. Casually perusing some letters that she had written to her mother and sisters, Wilbur discovered that Margaret was telling them that

Wilbur was about to divorce her because of a man named Fearn. Margaret went on in these letters to disclose that she had met Fearn at a dance and that she had later agreed to go for a "ride and x x x" with the married coal merchant. That was enough for Wilbur: he confronted Margaret with the evidence of her adultery and insisted that they relocate to Lorain and start all over again.

Margaret had left Wilbur on Monday, December 2, telling him that she was going to visit her sister, Mrs. Laura Pierce, in Canton. When she returned home on Friday, the day after Fearn was shot, Wilbur asked her how her trip had been and she replied, "Just fine." Wilbur's suspicions, however, became aroused over the weekend. While reading the *Cleveland News*, he became aware that Vernard Fearn—not exactly an unknown name in Wilbur's house—had been shot with an unusual weapon, a .380 Colt that, police said, was a difficult gun for which to find cartridges. As it happened, Wilbur possessed just such a rare gun, and he looked up from his paper and said to Margaret, "You know, I believe you killed this man Fearn." "Don't be foolish," replied Margaret calmly, "why would I want to do a thing like that?" Wilbur—or so he told the cops—let the matter drop.

After all, it didn't seem probable that mousy little Margaret could have done such a thing, even though the clothes of the sought-for gun girl—the blue chinchilla coat and black felt hat with pin—matched Margaret's only complete outfit of clothes perfectly.

Three days went by. Wilbur tried to ignore his growing suspicions, but he couldn't put them off anymore after finding a crumpled note in some trash he was about to burn in the furnace. Dated December 2, the day she left to "visit her sister" in Canton, it read: "I am leaving out of your life forever and I truly am sorry for all the trouble I have caused you, and rather than try to go through the rest of my life under a lie I am taking this means to tell you the truth. I can't face you and tell you this, so I am leaving this to explain the thing you don't know. He has made my life a hell on earth. He came to my house . . . he threatened to expose me if I didn't do as he wanted me to . . . I can't stand the worry any longer and to be away from my baby. So I do hope you can forgive me and give our baby a good home. Love him even if you don't me for I do surely love you. (Signed) Margaret. Please do not tell my mother."

That was enough, even for slow-on-the-uptake Wilbur. Confronting Margaret, he said, "Get your coat on, we're going to see Sheriff Gibson. If you've done this, you'll have to pay for it." According to Wilbur, Margaret didn't even try to deny her guilt. She simply stalled for time, begging Wilbur to wait until the morning. But Wilbur, for once, was firm, and they left for Canton late on the afternoon of December 13.

It must have been a tense two-hour drive to Canton. While Wilbur drove, he later told police, Margaret haltingly confessed the terrible sequence of events that had brought her to this fateful journey. She had met Vernard Fearn at a dance hall, she said, sometime before she married Wilbur. As Wilbur didn't dance, the lonely Margaret soon found opportunities—perhaps during her periodic estrangements from Wilbur—to dance with Fearn at the all-night hops that went on until Sunday morning in Canton. Sometime in 1927, Fearn picked her up in his coal truck while she was hitchhiking home from the Canton library. Instead of taking her home, however, he drove her to a remote spot in the country and raped her. She was too ashamed to tell her new husband about her outrage, and in the months that followed, Fearn forced his physical attentions upon her repeatedly, threatening to tell Wilbur and to ruin her public reputation if she resisted his vile desires. She had taken all she could take by the fall of 1928, and she decided to kill Fearn with Wilbur's gun, which was kept in the house and which she knew well how to use. She had made two futile trips to Waco on the night of December 5 and returned the next night to find and kill Fearn. Although she had expected to be caught immediately— hence the discarded "suicide" note to Wilbur—she had managed to make it back to Canton safely and then taken a bus to Akron, where she spent the night at the Bond Hotel before returning to Wilbur on Friday morning.

Just before they entered the outskirts of Canton, near Mallet Creek and the Red Raven gas station, Margaret turned to her husband and said, "What do you think they'll do to me? You don't think they'll be brutal to me?" "Well," replied the maddened Wilbur, "if you don't get the electric chair, I'll miss my guess." There was a moment of silence and then Margaret said, "Be sure to take good care of baby." Wilbur riposted, "Better than you ever did," and then, as the "Welcome to Canton" sign on Route 57 came into sight, he sighed, "Thank God. It won't be long now." A moment later, without a word, Margaret reached into her blouse, hauled out Wilbur's .380 Colt, and shot herself in the chest. The bullet entered her lungs, penetrated the apex of her heart, smashed through her back, and embedded itself in the metal frame of the front-seat upholstery. Screaming, "Margaret, don't die!" and side-swiping other cars in his haste, Wilbur sped to Sheriff Gibson's office and thence to Mercy Hospital.

That seemed to wrap it up, at least to the satisfaction of Wilbur, Sheriff Gibson, and the avid newspapermen thronging the Canton area. But just as abruptly as the case was resolved, it began to dissolve anew. Margaret Heldman's mother and sisters were outraged at Sheriff Gibson's ready acceptance of Wilbur Heldman's story, and they demanded—and got—a second autopsy of Margaret's body, conducted by physicians in DuBois, Pennsylvania, where she was taken for burial the following week. Although that post-mortem confirmed the conclusion of Stark County coroner T. C. McQuate that Margaret had died from a single bullet in the heart, Margaret's relatives refused to believe Wilbur's version of their last day together. Margaret would never have committed suicide, they insisted, and her so-called "suicide note," like her November letters confessing adultery to her family, had either been forged or written under Wilbur's dictation and duress.

Public opinion, which had initially rallied around Wilbur, began to sour toward him in the days that followed Margaret's dramatic demise. Much of the rationale for Margaret's shooting of Fearn depended on an uncritical acceptance of what Wilbur—with no corroborating witnesses—claimed that Margaret had allegedly told him on their last ride together. But there were conflicts in Wilbur's varying stories as to how Margaret had procured the cartridges for his gun and just how much he had previously known about her affair with Fearn. The letters written to her sisters and mother implied that she had committed voluntary adultery with the straying coal merchant. But at the same time, the dates on the letters, their postmarks, and internal evidence suggested that Wilbur had enjoyed full knowledge of their contents well before they were posted and that he might have even forced her to write them. The Stark County authorities and the public wondered what kind of man would: 1) insist on taking his wife to the police before getting her a lawyer or even checking her story out; and 2) continue the journey to Sheriff Gibson's office—instead of the hospital—after Margaret had critically wounded herself. Within a week of her death the Stark County police—together with much of the public—were beginning to believe that Wilbur Heldman was at the very least an insensitive, inhuman creep, if not a lying murderer who had pulled the trigger on Margaret himself. Two days after her death, Wilbur was arrested by Sheriff Gibson and held as a witness for the judicial hearing into the deaths of Vernard Fearn and Margaret Heldman.

Mrs. Heldman's Suicide Letter

HERE IS NOTE MARGARET'S HUSBAND FOUND IN BASKET

From the *Cleveland News*, December 15, 1928

That hearing, which opened before Justice of the Peace Donald Smyth on December 31, further sullied the reputations of the two dead principals. Despite their previous public statements, it turned out that both Sheriff Gibson and Mary Fearn had suspected Margaret Heldman was the phantom flapper pretty much from the start. So had Margaret's family, and the hitherto unknown appearance of Margaret's father in Canton during the post-murder week suggested that there had been some clandestine communication and negotiation between Margaret's family, the authorities, and Mary Fearn. Such suspected behind-the-scenes collusion would also account for the fact that Sheriff Gibson had apparently been waiting for the Heldmans when Wilbur's car pulled up at his office. At the hearing the exposure of Margaret's letters frankly confessing her adultery to her kin further undermined the rationale for Wilbur Heldman's story about an avenged rape. The hearing ended with his being booked on a charge of "moral murder" and bound over to the next session of the grand jury. Wilbur Heldman, Stark County Prosecutor Harder charged, had either shot his wife himself during their last car ride or had deliberately frightened her—with his brutal talk of the electric chair awaiting her—into pulling the trigger herself. Wilbur's behavior, Harder continued, was all the more callous, as no jury in Ohio would have convicted Margaret Heldman after hearing the story she never got to tell anyone except Wilbur.

No one believed at the time of his arrest that Wilbur could be convicted on the existing evidence—and they were right. As the *Cleveland News* forthrightly put it, the murder hearing before Smyth established only that Heldman had been "mighty frank about his domestic affairs," not that he had killed Margaret or forced her to kill herself.

Moreover, Prosecutor Harder never produced a pair of witnesses who, he claimed in late December, would disprove Wilbur's claim that Margaret had shot herself at the location he identified on Route 57. And so the weeks went by, the story disappeared from the newspapers, and finally, on April 11, 1929, after he had spent four months in jail, the Stark County grand jury refused to vote a true bill on Wilbur Heldman, and he walked out of court a free man.

It is a maddening fact that no one will ever know the whole story behind the murder of Vernard Fearn. The evidence of Margaret's November notes and the grudging later admissions of Wilbur Heldman and Mary Fearn support the conclusion that Margaret and Fearn slipped freely into an adulterous relationship sometime in 1927. Whether he initially raped her or subsequently forced his attentions on her is unprovable, but his truck was frequently seen parked outside Margaret's home while Wilbur was away during the next 16 months. How much her husband knew about this affair is also unknown, although both he and Mary Fearn knew or suspected a lot more than they initially told police in the wake of Vernard's murder. But exactly what caused Margaret to kill Fearn is a secret that died with her. Did she fabricate or fantasize some or all of the terrible story she allegedly told her husband about Vernard's predatory behavior? Did she kill Vernard because he forced her to continue their relationship—or because he wanted to break it off? Did Wilbur Heldman make her write those self-incriminating letters to her family? Did he force her to write her final "suicide" note, or did he forge it himself? Did she really murder herself as the car passed the Red Raven gas station on Route 57? Or did Wilbur either shoot her himself—his continual lack of knowledge concerning the whereabouts of his gun remains a puzzlement—or, did he, as lawmen charged, deliberately terrorize her into doing the deed herself? All we can really be sure of is that Margaret Heldman, the "Phantom Flapper Killer," took all of these secrets to her grave with her. Let us bid farewell to this unhappy, mysterious woman with the verses of a poem which was found in her handbag after her death:

A house to clean and a man to scold
And a warm little sleeping babe to hold.
What does a woman want but this,
A house and a man and a child to kiss?
A cake to bake and a floor to sweep
And a tired little child to sing to sleep.
And a man to welcome when work is past—
These are the things whose lure will last!
A vote and a job? Oh, I suppose
That there are women who yearn for those.
Who'd rather be footloose, gay and free
But—a house and a child and a man for me.
For a house I'll choose this house to keep
To scrub and dust and paint and sweep;
For the child our own Elizabeth Ann:
And silent: awkward for you the man!

PHOTO CREDITS

For all newspaper reprints, the date of the featured headline is listed under the image.

Auth—Author's collection
CPL—Cleveland Public Library Photograph Collection
CSU—Cleveland Press Collection, Cleveland State University Archives.
CPHS—Cleveland Police Historical Society
WRHS—Western Reserve Historical Society
PD—*The Plain Dealer*
Press—*The Cleveland Press*
News—*The Cleveland News*
Leader—*The Cleveland Leader*
World—*The Cleveland World*
Gazette—*Medina County Gazette*

Cover	left—CSU; middle—CSU; right—CSU
Chapter 1	p. 16, Press; p. 17, Press; p. 20, Press
Chapter 2	p. 30 left, PD; p. 30 right, Press; p. 30, Press; p. 33, Press
Chapter 3	p. 44, Press; p. 45, Press; p. 46, Press; p. 49, Press
Chapter 4	p. 52, World; p. 53, Press; p. 56, Press; p. 59, World
Chapter 5	p. 62, Auth; p. 65, PD; p. 68, WRHS
Chapter 6	p. 72, PD; p. 74, Press; p. 75, CPHS; p. 77, Press
Chapter 7	p. 84, Gazette; p. 85, PD; p. 90, PD
Chapter 8	p. 94, CPHS; p. 97, CSU; p. 98, Press; p. 103, Press
Chapter 9	p. 106, PD; p. 107, Press; p. 109 left, PD; p. 109 right, News
Chapter 10	p. 118 left, CSU; p.118 right, News; p. 119, News; p. 123, Press
Chapter 11	p. 132, World; p. 133, PD; p. 134, PD; p. 137, PD
Chapter 12	p. 140, Press; p. 143, News; p. 146, News
Chapter 13	p. 150, Press; p. 154, Press; p. 155, Press; p. 158, PD
Chapter 14	p. 164, Press; p. 165, Press; p. 168, News; p. 171, Press
Chapter 15	p. 176, News; p. 177, Press; p. 178, Press; p. 181, Press
Chapter 16	p. 188, News; p. 191, News; p. 194, Press
Chapter 17	p. 198, PD; p. 203, Press; p. 206, CPHS; p. 207, CPHS
Chapter 18	p. 214, CSU; p. 215, CSU; p. 216, CSU; p. 221, CSU
Chapter 19	p. 226, PD; p. 229, Press; p. 232, Press
Chapter 20	p. 240 left, CSU; p. 240 right, CPHS; p. 243, News; p. 246, Press
Chapter 21	p. 252, Press; p. 253, Press; p. 254, CPHS; p. 257, Press
Chapter 22	p. 264, CPHS; p. 265, CSU; p. 266, CSU
Chapter 23	p. 268, WRHS; p. 271, PD; p. 276, Leader
Chapter 24	p. 282, PD; p. 285, News; p. 286, Press; p. 289, Press
Chapter 25	p. 292, PD; p. 295, News; p. 296, PD; p. 300, News